PROCEEDINGS

OF THE

SEMI-CENTENNIAL CELEBRATION

OF THE

Rensselaer Polytechnic Institute,

TROY, N. Y.,

HELD JUNE 14-18, 1874,

WITH

CATALOGUE OF OFFICERS AND STUDENTS,

1824-1874.

TROY, N. Y.:
WM. H. YOUNG, 8 & 9 FIRST STREET.
1875.

SEMI-CENTENNIAL CELEBRATION

OF THE

Rensselaer Polytechnic Institute.

RESOLUTION.

At a meeting of the Association of Graduates of the Rensselaer Polytechnic Institute, held June 26th, 1872, the following resolution was adopted, viz :

WHEREAS, It is deemed expedient to take suitable notice of the close of the first fifty years' work of the Institute.

RESOLVED, That Prof. Charles Drowne, Prof. H. B. Nason, Charles F. Winslow, Rev. J. H. Brodt and W. H. Doughty, be a committee to make all necessary arrangements for a semi-centennial celebration.

At a meeting of the Association, held June 18th, 1873, it was resolved that the services of the above committee be continued, in connection with the Directors, for the ensuing year.

At a meeting of the graduates, former students and friends of the Institute, residing in Troy, held at the Board of Trade Rooms, April 23d, 1874, Dr. R. B. Bontecou in the Chair, A. J. Swift, Secretary, the following local sub-committees were appointed :

LOCAL SUB-COMMITTEES.

On Reception.—Hon. Wm. Gurley, G. H. Starbuck, G. B. Wallace, B. C. Gowing, H. M. Geer, D. M. Greene, I. F. Bosworth.

On Finance.—E. Thompson Gale, J. Hobart Warren, J. W. Fuller, T. A. Tillinghast, J. M. Landon, Dr. R. B. Bontecou, Wm. H. Young.

On Entertainment.—J. H. Quackenbush, E. W. Arms, W. A. Peck, H. B. Dauchy, P. H. Baermann, T. C. Walbridge, Dascom Greene.

On Excursion.—Hon. Uri Gilbert, W. A. Shepard, H. B. Nason.

On Alumni Dinner.—H. B. Nason, E. G. Gilbert, R. H. Thompson, W. T. Kellogg, A. J. Swift.

FIRST CIRCULAR.

On the 1st of May, the following circular was sent to all persons who have attended the Institute, whose residence could be ascertained :

The Sixth Annual Meeting of the Association of Graduates of the Rensselaer Polytechnic Institute, will be held June 16th, 1874, at 2:30 o'clock P. M., in the Institute Hall.

The exercises of the Semi-Centennial Celebration will commence Sunday, June 14th, and close Thursday, June 18th. Besides the usual reading of theses, and conferring of degrees, arrangements are being made for addresses, receptions, an alumni dinner, one or more excursions, and a grand reunion on Thursday Evening.

A cordial invitation is extended not only to graduates, but to all who have ever been connected with the Institute and to their families, to be present and participate in these exercises.

Special arrangements will be made with the proprietors of the several hotels for the accommodation of visitors at reduced rates, and many citizens have signified their desire to extend hospitality.

In order that all may be provided for without confusion or delay, it is requested that persons intending to be present at the meeting notify this fact to the Secretary before the 1st of June when practicable, and also when possible state the day they will arrive, so that the Committee may engage rooms at the hotels or in private families, as they may desire. On receipt of such communication a second circular will be forwarded immediately.

Copies of this circular will be supplied to any who may desire them, and all are earnestly requested to make the above known as far as possible.

H. B. NASON, *Secretary.*

OFFICERS OF ALUMNI ASSOCIATION FOR 1874.

President.—Strickland Kneass.

Vice-Presidents.—A. C. Boller, A. J. Cassatt, Frederic Grinnell.

Treasurer.—David M. Greene,

Secretary.—H. B. Nason.

Directors.—William Gurley, E. Thompson Gale, G. H. Starbuck, Henry Burden, Jr., Dascom Greene.

SECOND CIRCULAR.

TROY, N. Y., June 1st, 1874.

The special object of this circular is to afford information in regard to the time and order of the various exercises of Commencement week, and to give some directions for the convenience of those who may attend.

The Committee on Reception will be in waiting at the Union Railroad Depot in Troy, on the arrival of trains, to direct visitors to the office of the Local Committee at the store of Messrs. Gurley, near the north end of the depot, where after recording their names, information will be furnished in regard to lodgings in hotels, private families, &c.

In order that all may be provided for without confusion or delay, it is requested that persons intending to be present at the meeting notify this fact to the Secretary before the 10th of June when practicable, and also when possible state the day when they will arrive, so that the Committee may engage rooms at the hotels or in private families, as they may desire.

(Here followed Programme, for which see page 7.)

A cordial invitation is given to all who have ever been connected with the Institute, and to their families to be present and participate in the above exercises.

Copies of this circular will be supplied to any who may desire them, and all are earnestly requested to make the above known as far as possible.

H. B. NASON, *Secretary.*

P. S.—A large number of graduates and others have already signified their intention to be present, and everything now promises a very large and interesting meeting.

PROGRAMME.

SUNDAY, JUNE 14.

10:30 A. M. Sermon by Rev. G. N. Webber, D. D. First Presbyterian Church.

MONDAY, JUNE 15.

10:00 A. M. Reading of Theses by members of Graduating Class. Institute Hall.

4:00 P. M. Single Scull and Tub Races. Laureate Course.

8:00 P. M. Concert by Institute Glee Club, for the benefit of the R. P. I. Rowing Association. Rand's Hall.

TUESDAY, JUNE 16.

10:00 A. M. Reading of Theses by members of Graduating Class. Institute Hall.

2:30 P. M. Meeting of Alumni. Institute Hall. Address by Alfred P. Boller, C. E., Presiding Officer. Reports of Committees. Information concerning Graduates and former Students of the Institute. Miscellaneous Business.

4:30 P. M. Dedication of the Eaton Monument. Oakwood Cemetery. Prayer by Rev. H. N. Brinsmade, D. D., of Newark, N. J. Addresses by Prof. James Hall, LL. D., Albany; Hon. Martin I. Townsend, LL. D., Troy, and Prof. H. B. Nason, R. P. I.

A special train of cars will leave Union Depot for Oakwood at 4:00 o'clock, P. M., and returning, leave Oakwood at 5:45 P. M.

7:30 P. M. Address of Welcome by President James Forsyth. Addresses by Prof. E. N. Horsford, of Cambridge, Mass.,—Subject, " America at the Vienna Exposition "; and Henry Sedley, Esq., of New York,—Subject, "The Engineer in Eldorado." Rand's Hall. Music by Doring's Orchestra.

Reception by His Honor, William Kemp, Mayor of Troy, to the Alumni of the Institute.

WEDNESDAY, JUNE 17.

10:30 A. M. Alumni meeting. Address by Prof. James Hall, of Albany, N. Y. Notice of Memorial Windows by Prof. H. B. Nason. Address by Norman Stratton, Esq., of New York. Institute Hall.

2:00 P. M. Alumni dinner. Poem by Dr. J. G. Ambler, of New York. Harmony Hall. Music by Doring's Orchestra.

8:00 P. M. Graduating Exercises, and Address by the President of the Institute, Hon. James Forsyth. Rand's Hall.

THURSDAY, JUNE 18.

9:00 A. M. Excursion to Saratoga. 1:00 P. M. Dinner at Grand Union Hotel, Saratoga.

8:00 P. M. Closing Exercises, and Promenade Concert. Harmony Hall.

SUNDAY, JUNE 14.

SERMON,

BY

REV. GEORGE N. WEBBER, D. D.

PASTOR OF FIRST PRESBYTERIAN CHURCH.

During a long and somewhat eventful history, the First Presbyterian Church has been frequently thrown open for gatherings of great local interest and importance. Many will recall the varied objects for which these gatherings were held, and the crowds which attended them. In all its history the old, yet new edifice, never contained an audience more remarkable than that which assembled on this occasion. The middle portion of the Church was occupied by the trustees, faculty, students and alumni, and the remainder was filled to overflowing by friends of the Institute.

A large number of chairs were placed in the aisles, but still many went away unable to procure seats.

The pulpit and immediate vicinity were profusely decorated with flowers.

The services began at 8 o'clock, with a short voluntary upon the organ by the organist, S. B. Saxton, Esq. The Anthem "Cantate Domino in C," by Dudley Buck, was rendered by the Choir, and the congregation joined in singing the hymn "All hail the power of Jesus' name."

Before commencing his discourse, the speaker congratulated all connected with the Institute upon their celebration of its fiftieth anniversary, and then alluded to the Rev. Dr. Beman, who for forty years filled the pulpit of this Church and was also during some of those years President of the Institute, and lecturer in one of its departments, and who, were he living, would have entered most heartily into the exercises and festivities of the occasion, and gladly welcomed them to this place. Although a stranger to most, the speaker added, so large a portion of his public life has been spent in institutions of learning that he could thoroughly sympathize with those present in their pursuits.

THE MORAL INFLUENCE OF TRUE SCIENCE.

"Knowledge puffeth up, but Charity edifieth. And if any man think he knoweth anything he knoweth nothing yet as he ought to know."—I *Cor.* viii, 1, 2.

Too profound a thinker was the Apostle Paul to accept, save for convenience of naming, the distinction so often made of knowledge, secular and divine. All knowledge is of God, as all being is of Him, and through Him, and for Him. Nature is the manifestation of the unseen thought and will which originated it, and acts in it all. He who learns the structure and organization of a plant or animal; the elements of bodies, and their modes of combination; the laws of force and motion; the features of the earth's crust, and where is the place of gold and the vein of silver; the conditions that regulate the currents of air and vapor; the balancing of the clouds, the fall of the dew, the track of the storm, and "the way of the lightning of the thunder"; the place of the sea and the courses of the rivers; the laws that "bind the sweet influences of Pleiades" and "guide Arcturus with his sons," the order of human history and the operations of the heart and mind of man; he who learns any of these truths that belong to the several sciences, reads in every one of them a thought and volition of God!

The nineteenth Psalm, beginning with a rapturous description of the glory of God which "the Heaven's declare," passes abruptly to mention "the law of the Lord that is perfect, converting the soul," binding thus the two books Nature and Revelation into one volume, showing the writer's insight of the oneness of natural and spiritual truth. The Bible expresses the *direct* relation of man to God, as science does the indirect, through the media of Nature. Let us not forget it. We live in an awful divine world, blazing everywhere with the forth-beamings of a spiritual presence and power. Search for *truth*, no matter where, is search for God, "who is not far from every one of us." The only real distinction in knowledge is not *what*, but what manner of spirit.

To this the text fastens attention. "If any man think he knoweth anything he knoweth nothing *as he ought to know*." The last words are the point of the sentence. There is an *ethics* of science; a right and a wrong way to know anything, be it Bible or nature, arithmetic or the catechism. There is a knowledge that puffeth up, and there is a knowledge that edifieth, and the difference is not in the *department*, but in the spirit and purpose which the student carries into his pursuit. Here is the distinction between *true* science and science "falsely so called." And this brings me the topic whereof I have a mind to speak at this time.

THE MORAL USES OF TRUE SCIENCE.

By *moral*, I mean the influence on the character of the student. Here is found the highest use and worth of knowledge. As a means of enriching the material conditions of man, science has a value. I do not mean to underrate this fruit of the tree of knowledge. Mind, through the body, feeds on the juices of the plant as does the tree, converting them into its own substance. Diogenes of Apolonia was not all astray when he accounted for the superior intelligence of man, to that of the prone and earth-bowed beasts, from the purer air he breathed and the drier nature of his food. Whatever helps production and multiplies wealth, aids the growth of mind. Here is the worth of science in the *economic* point of view. It may unearth the hid treasures in nature's field, harness her obedient forces to our service, span the Continent with railways and telegraphs, fertilize soils, set the streams to work, till the land hums with factories, and rivers groan under the burdens of commerce, and the graneries are bursting with the finest of wheat; but unless this material product can be coined into character—this material force transmuted in mental force, and men and women grew big and fair on this augmented nutriment, it is all as cheap as the dirt out of which it grew.

I say these things "in limine" because so many in our times think chiefly of the material gain that experimental science has given to man. Once men said knowledge is *power*—that was selfishness. Now men say of knowledge, *there is money in it*, that is meaner still; as if nature were a pocket to be rifled and not a spectacle to be studied and adored! I say to you, gentlemen, knowledge is character. Its fruit is manhood. By this alone, its real worth is to be estimated. We will omit then from our thought "the bread and butter view" of science and ask ourselves what qualities of soul knowledge must beget in the student; what purpose must inspire him who knows anything "*as he ought to know.*"

I. *The first fruit of true knowledge is humility.* Sound science is modest. Men deepest in the secret of nature, mind, God, have usually been humble. Socrates was pronounced by the Delphian oracle to be the wisest of men, because he did not seem to himself to be wise: did not think he knew anything. There was truth as well as wit in that repartee of one, who, when an angry disputant said to him, "You are a fool and you know it," replied: "In that case I am wiser than you, for you are a fool and don't know it." The sciolist is puffed up. A little learning is a dangerous thing, for it makes a man swell.

"The sciences," says Pascal, "have two extremities that touch each other. The one is that native ignorance in which we are born; the other the point to which the greatest minds attain, who, having gone the whole round of possible knowledge, find that they know nothing, and that they end in the same ignorance in which they began. But then this last is an *intelligent* ignorance which knows itself. Out of the many, however, who come forth from their *native* ignorance there are some who never reach this other extreme. These are strongly tinged with scientific conceit and set up the claim to be learned." In the same strain Hamilton: "There are two ignorances. We start from one, we repose in the other, and the pursuit of knowledge is but a course between the two, as human life is a traveling from grave to grave. The highest reach of human science is a scientific recognition of ignorance and its first fruit is humility."

Authorities aside, I appeal to experience. Somewhat of the middle of things we know, but the beginning and the end of anything who can understand either? Astronomy, pushing her research into trackless voids, never plants her foot on the outposts of space; nor has the chemist in his subtlest analysis caught the simple atom. The smallest thing is a universe

"Where suns and systems inconspicuous float."

A cloud hangs over either end of the narrow span along which the toiling intellect travels back and forth, weaving its web of thought. We are like men climbing up winding stairs to the summit of some high tower; below are stairs along which we have come, above are more that go out of sight; the bottom and the top are alike invisible. "We know in part," never the whole; even the *part*, we never know, but *in part*. We cognize nothing as it is in itself; not even the commonest thing of the senses. Our knowledge is *relative:* of things as they *appear*, in the shaping coloring lenses of our kaleidoscope faculty of representation. "Instead of receiving the ideas of things as they are, we tinge, with the qualities of our compound being, all the simple things that we perceive." Our own *minds* we know, not as they are in themselves—in their essence—but only as they *seem* in the deflecting, refracting mirror of consciousness. Both body and mind are apprehended by us only as the unknown causes, which, impinging one upon the other, evolve that luminous play of sensations, thoughts, feelings, volitions, which make up the varied conscious experience we call *ourselves*. Push the inquiry one step back and we find we are in the profoundest ignorance respecting our own being. How much more, of the Infinite Mind, we name God! We must humble ourselves with Job of old and consent that by no searching can we find him out. Even Revelation makes him known to us, divested of the fullness of his attributes and reduced to the limit of our finite mode of comprehension. Above, below, on the right hand and on the left, darkness compasses us about. Sufficient indeed for our practical need is the knowledge we may gain of this middle sphere in which our lot is cast; but as Pascal puts it, "extreme things are not ours, any more than if they were not. We were not made for them. Either they escape us or we them. We burn with the desire to sound the utmost depth and to raise a fabric that shall reach infinity. But all we build crumbles, and the earth opens in fathomless abysses beneath our deepest foundations." Surely then he knows nothing as he ought to know, who in the highest reaches of intelligence is not humbled at the thought, how like nothing is all we know, to what we do not know.

I have dwelt long and repetitiously on this point in order to expose the perversity of that conceit of over-much knowing, which has been, and is, the bane of learning. Ambition, on the part of burning intellects, to transcend the limit of our faculties is the temptation that has beset the path of thought ever since man in Eden, aspiring to be as Gods, fell from his high estate. This makes of most difficult attainment, that which some philosopher said was the greatest wisdom, "*Quaedam aequo animo nescire velle.*" The intellect is restive in its ignorance and struggles against the limit set to its march like a caged bird against the wires that confine its flight. Every one familiar with the history of human thought, knows how this ambition to understand all mysteries has perverted religious inquiry from the right way, crowding the tomes of theology with endless subtilties and refinements and debates, darkening "counsels with words without knowledge." Says Hegel, in his introduction to the History of Philosophy: "Courage for the truth, faith in the might of the intellect, is the condition of philosophy. Man, because he is intellect, may and should reckon himself worthy of the Highest. He can never think enough of the greatness and power of his reason; and with this confidence, nothing is so concealed, that it will not open to his call. The veiled and secret essence of the universe has no power to withstand his search. It must unbar itself to his approach and lay its riches and its mysteries before his raptured gaze." In a spirit like this, the aspiring philosophers of Germany went daft in the attempt to penetrate the secret of existence and establish the "science of man on an identity with the omniscience of God." This windy conceit swept the land, assailing established moral ideas and religious faiths, until the institutions of Church and State trembled like a forest in the march of a whirlwind. Like scenes, (only more terrific), from the same cause, were acted over in the vine-clad regions of France. To-day this "vain deceit" of knowledge is invading the field of physical science, imperiling all its highest interests, by leading it away from the modest and safe path of experiment, in which it has made such solid and brilliant achievements, into the fog-banks of *a priori* speculation. Instead of studying phenomena and orders of sequence, setting down what they find, some of the more ambitious savans are about writing a new book of Genesis. Postulating matter and force and a necessary law of evolution, they construct a theory, deductively, of the way the world emerged from a homogeneous, nebulous stuff, next to nothing, into what it now is, with plants and animals and finally man at the summit of the grand procession. Reading the writings of such thinkers as Herbert Spencer, one cannot fail to see how far they have wandered from that simple experimental study of nature which characterized the inquiries of Newton, Cuvier and Franklin, and to which we owe those solid discoveries that have so ennobled and enriched our modern world. For one, I glory in science as the grand inheritance of our age. But I say to all young students, beware of that false science that is puffed up with the ambition to know everything: that is not content to know "in part"—demanding in the boastful language of Hegel, above quoted, that the whole universe shall give itself into its hand. For "if any man, (in this way), think he knoweth anything he knoweth nothing yet as he ought to know."

II. I pass to a second use of science. *It encourages a religious spirit.* This sentence may sound strange to some ears. It is more or less the fashion of these times to denounce science as the enemy of religion. I do not say that all men of science are religious. It is sadly otherwise. What I say is, the natural tendency of the pursuit of knowledge is to beget a disposition not hostile but favorable to religion. If true science fosters intellectual humility, it cannot fail to be a preparation for that higher spiritual knowledge revealed, not to the "wise and prudent" but "unto babes." The proposition, "ignorance is the mother of devotion," is a true one, if we mean that ignorance in which all knowledge *ends*; that consciousness of the limit of our faculty, of which all are aware, who know anything "as they ought to know."

Reverence is the native sentiment, out of which religion springs, and on which it is built. Religion, in general, may be defined—adoring love of the Infinite. All worship requires faith in somewhat beyond our apprehension. That which we know, as far as we know it, is on our level. We lift ourselves up to that which we fully comprehend and veneration ceases. The object I can see all round and through no longer fills me with awe. Hence the saying of St. Bernard, I think, "A God known is no God at all." The truth that lifts us to admiration, is not the truth exactly defined and compassed with a clean circumference, but that which looms up vaguely out of mists and hints at more than it reveals. It is not those luminous points that we see twinkling on the face of night, but that infinite expanse which they suggest, and along which the imagination wings its way, that makes us bow our heads in awe of the starry heavens. Here may we not see the final cause of that limitation, on our knowing faculty imposed, of which I have been speaking? We know "in part," that we may believe more, and adore that mystery of being we cannot know. In the words of an unknown poet:

> "Full many a secret, in her sacred veil,
> Hath nature folded. She vouchsafes to knowledge
> Not every mystery, reserving much
> For human veneration, not research.
> Let us not therefore seek what God conceals.
> For even the things, which lie within our hands,
> These knowings, we know not, so far from us,
> In doubtful dimness, gleams the star of truth."

First knowledge, then a sense of ignorance, then faith, then worship; such is the succession of mental states that conduct us to religion and to God. What can better inspire adoration than the study of nature? Not a fact discovered but opens a territory of limitless mystery to reverent faith. For every question which science answers, a hundred others start up which it cannot put to rest. Take this flower—Botany has classified and named it. It can explain something of its structure and the vital circulations by which it grows. But tell me, if you please, why these leaves, unfolding from the same bud on the same stalk, are so differentiated that one is crimson, its neighbor purple, or perhaps green in the center edged round with white. A painter being asked how he mixed his paint, replied, "with brains, sir." What brain mixed these paints; what artist's pencil spread these colors and tints in such exquisite arrangements over the petals of the flower? Science stares helpless in the presence of this miracle of life, this potency behind the germ that builds it into being, and may well bow down before the mystery of the simplest flower.

There is not the slightest tendency in the *progress* of knowledge to diminish faith and reverence. We watch the process and order of nature, and correct and enlarge our conceptions, and resolve some things that before were not understood, but we never penetrate the secret of existence,

"Which, dive we, soar we, baffles still and lures."

The more our comprehension of phenomena enlarges, the more does the inscrutable Reality, of which all sense perception is only the sign, deepen and widen on the mind, humbling while it exalts; inspiring with awe and worship the contemplative soul. This is the fruit and highest end of science—to teach man worthily to *adore*.

How perverse then, and blind, is that unbelieving, irreverent spirit that marks much of the so-called learning of our times. It boasts of being free from superstition and slavish credulity. It would banish God and miracles from nature, and faith and awe of the Unknown from the reasonable mind. Compte affirmed that theology belonged only to primeval ignorance, and that, passing first into metaphysics, it was destined to vanish under the clearer light of the positive philosophy. In nature he found no God; no supernatural presence and providence; nothing but phenomena, and their laws. Of course, if he did not find these, they could not be there; for what secret could escape the eye of such a Demi-God of intelligence as Augustus Compte. So Deity is read out of the list of entities, man no more immortal, the spiritual world a fiction, religion a bug-bear of tyrannical priest-craft, and worship of the Deity a sentiment without an object. And this is what men call science, and trumpet abroad as a new Gospel; the emancipation and upbuilding of the race. It is not *science* but the knowledge that puffeth up; wasting the moral energies, dwarfing the majesties of manhood and turning this grand temple of nature, built for the worship of the eternal into a curiosity shop or a house of merchandise. Hang science if it have nothing better to teach us than this! I would rather, as Bacon says, "believe all the fables of legend and Talmud and Alcoran, than that this universal form is without mind." Shall we, for whom this age has made such wondrous discoveries in the fields of matter and mind; who are taught to explore the world without and the world within; to regulate the moving spheres, and tell how the planets swing, to solve the elements and divide the beams of light, and cage the lightning in a jar and send it forth a messenger of tidings round the world, shall we gain from all this enlarged intelligence less of reverent impulse and inspiration, to exalt and expand the soul, than did the ignorant pagans of old? Because science has corrected and enlarged our conception of nature, and many things once referred to supernatural agents have been explained, and their mode of coming to pass understood; because the divinities are now banished from Acadian groves, and Eolus no longer in his mountain cave chains or lets loose the winds, and Neptune has abandoned the empire of the sea; because human life is no longer implicated with the courses of the stars, and a comet is not dreaded as a messenger of wrath, and plague and famine are known effects of natural causes, stayed by drainage, not by prayer; and miracles are unlooked for in the territories of sense, is there, for this reason, nothing to be believed and adored? Because astronomy, with its glass, has

> * * Thrust far-off
> " The heaven, so neighborly with man of old,
> To voids, spare-sown with alienated stars,"

does it any the less declare the glory of God to us, than to the Chaldean shepherds and the nightly visions of the Hebrew poet-king? Because geology patiently spelling out the unwritten record on the rock-ribbed earth has brought into discredit the Mosaic cosmogny, with its days and dates, and pushed the beginning into a period indeterminately remote, and shown us its building—not the work of a week, but of incomputable ages, is the origin and constitution then any less wonderful and in need of an infinite Creator? If Darwin were to establish on satisfactory evidence—which seems to me as yet all too slender to support such conclusion, —man's descent from some lower form of animal, and all animal from the plant, and all plants from an original germ, are we then in the presence of any less a mystery than has confronted the thought of all ages? That original cell, in which is deposited the possibilities of the vast kingdoms of vegetable and animal life, now spread over the surface of the earth, that original cell, I say, in whose infinitessimal compass is packed a universe of mortal and possibly immortal beings, is no object of ready comprehension for us, to be thought of with careless irreverence as a familiar thing. The existence of such a world-teeming seed, requires a cause of power and wisdom equal to that of building a universe outright. Let us understand this. The growth of intellect will never supersede faith, or quench devotion, but the more it penetrates the secrets of nature and the laws of its evolution and ongoings, the more grand and adorable will appear that inscrutable Reality of which the whole visible universe is but the manifestation. True science, not only by teaching us the limit of our faculties and inspiring a humble spirit, but by banishing from the mind the idols of superstition, can never fail to be the handmaid of religion. As knowledge increases, nature becomes more and more an illuminated temple in which faith converses with and worships the Invisible.

III. A third use of true science is *to create a sense of the need of, and faith in, divine revelation.* Some will think, doubtless, that the exact opposite of this statement is the truth. Grant that science begets humility and reverence, and so makes men religious in a way, it certainly has no tendency to prepare the mind to accept revealed religion. Is not science in open war with the scriptures? Has there not ever been, and is there not now, an irreconcilable antagonism between the belief of the Bible and the reception of scientific ideas? I have no time to enter on a full discussion of this most vital question of the times—the relation of Science to Revelation. A few words on this point, however, I will venture to utter. It is not with the Bible, but with a false *theory* of the Bible, that science can ever be at war. If it be claimed, as it once was, and now is by many, that the Bible is, in all parts, of co-equal authority, its every statement absolute truth; if belief in the Bible means belief in the correctness of all its statements and theories of the origin and phenomena of the material world, and the way man came into existence upon the planet; then surely the mind, trained in scientific knowledge, cannot believe it; for such a mind knows some of these representations concerning natural things are not true, and may have reason to expect that further investigation will prove others not to be. When the sacred writers had occasion to speak of the outward world, they adopted the language and conceptions of nature current in their day. Many of these conceptions were erroneous, and, as science progresses, must be discredited and discharged. These are not the real subject matter of revelation; they are merely its frame work and setting. The infallibility of the Bible pertains only to that matter which constitutes its essence and the end for which it was given; to instruct mankind in moral and religious truth; to tell us how to live and do the will of God; in a word, to make man "wise unto salvation." If faith in the Holy Scriptures, as the word of God, means that God inspired men to declare to the successive generations moral and spiritual truth, and to make statements respecting his purposes, ways and acts in respect to man—which things are the *real* revelation, and all the Bible stands for—in a word, that the scriptures of the Old and New Testament are an infallible guide in religious faith and practice—then I think the study of science is calculated to encourage such devout belief. For, in the first place, there is nothing in the knowledge of phenomena and their laws which can *disprove* the existence of a God such as the Bible sets forth. There *may* be such a God. Indeed the attributes ascribed to the Deity in the Bible are such as a thorough study of nature would incline the scientist to assign to that First Cause which, in all of his investigations he assumes. And, in the second place, the true scientific spirit, which evermore forbids to fill up the chasms of its ignorance with conjectures and imaginations, but requires that men stop where the evidence stops, and beyond that neither affirm or deny anything, is sure to develop in the mind a sense of need of a supernatural enlightenment to answer those "obstinate questionings" concerning the Unknowable which advancing knowledge of the cosmos perpetually conjures into consciousness, but can never answer; and in case it has any reason to believe such revelation has been given in the Bible, it disposes such a mind to study its pages with the docility of a little child and to render to Faith the things that are Faith's.

The flippant and superficial wit of Voltaire found matter of derision in the fact that the author of the Principia, had written a commentary on a book of the Scriptures. To his conceit of reason, it seemed an amusing instance of the union of intelligence and credulity in the same mind. But that sober, cautious, profound thinker, to whose reflective mind the mystery of revolving worlds was opened, and the track and speed of the sunbeam on its journey to kiss the violet, was too conscious of his ignorance to dare construct a theory of the universe *a priori*; too thoroughly scientific in his method of thought to affirm or deny anything of that invisible realm which transcends the reach of finite faculty. Without some authentic tidings of that infinite world which eye hath not seen, and of which the visible gives only far-off intimations to our listening faith, he knew we could know nothing of it. But finding something in his inmost consciousness that linked him in mysterious union to the Being above all being ; something that physical science could not explain, and which the Bible did explain, (answering all those intimations of an origin and destiny of wider scope than sense, putting to rest those " obstinate questionings " and " unstilled desires " of the immortal nature,) how reasonable, how philosophical, in this masterly genius, to seek in the Bible light to relieve the darkness of natural knowledge. No better proof than this example is needed to show that the truly scientific spirit affiliates with the religious, and a study of nature creates a sense of the need of, and encourages a faith in, a divine revelation.

It is true that some brilliant discoverers in the realm of nature are inclined to deny and scout the very idea of a book revelation of God. But the skepticism of science must not be overstated. Have we not Boyle and Oersted, Davy and Faraday, Herschel and Newton, Hitchcock and Hugh Miller, names second to none among the lights of science, to say nothing of many others living, who are devout believers in the written Word, as witnesses to the truth that there is no necessity, or even strong tendency, in true scientific culture to prejudice the mind against belief in the religion of the Bible?

IV. The last moral fruit of true science I can mention, is *charity*. If science teach men humility and the fear of God, it must also bear the fruit of benevolence. It was a vain and atheistic culture that uttered this selfish sentiment of Lucretius, "'T is a pleasant thing, from the shore to behold the dangers of another upon the ocean * * from which you yourself are free; 't is a pleasant thing to behold the contest of warfare arrayed on the plains, without a share in the danger; but nothing is there more delightful than to occupy the elevated temples of the wise, well fortified by tranquil learning, whence you may look down upon others, and see them straying in every direction, and wandering in search of the path of life." It is a grand perversion of mental culture when it exalts a man, in the conceit of his own wisdom, above his fellows, retires him from sympathy with the toiling, ignorant masses of mankind, makes him indifferent to their woes and errors, and content to enjoy his own light, and nurse in solitude his delicious loves and dainty tastes. Too much of this high-minded, exclusive culture there is, I know. But unless learning makes a man compassionate of the ignorance of others, and prompt to spread his knowledge, and go down into the plain where the toiling millions are struggling, and teach them how to live, and help them to bear their burdens, he surely knows nothing as he ought to know.

Gentlemen—I have pointed out the moral uses of true science. Its legitimate fruits are humility, religion, benevolence. As knowledge is means to these high ends of character, they are superior to it, and give to intellectual culture all its permanent worth. The understanding is rightly employed, when it gathers nutriment to feed the will and the affections, to quicken and refine the moral sense, to inspire the sentiment of worship, and build our souls upward towards God, and outward in all generous loves to men. Science, though not religion, as some seem to think, may and should be the fore-court and vestibule of its temple; in its highest elevations, a shining summit like the Delectable mountains, "in the sight of the city, and on the borders of heaven." He who knows any truth has light to guide him in doing the will of God, and attaining a divine manhood, which is the one business of life. Science is thus an ally of faith. The student's calling is a consecrated one. His mission is to stand for truth, and duty, and God, against all shams and expediencies, and mammon-worship, and every false thing that exalts itself against the purities and dignities of life. Such men the times are in urgent request of; men who are ready to stand for ideas, for principles; men who, raised above the consideration of mere material well-being, and all narrow utilitarianism, are ready to consecrate their lives to the service of the True, the Beautiful, and the Good. Next in inconsistency to the selfish and worldly-minded saint, I set down the time-serving, mercenary, undevout scholar.

MONDAY, JUNE 15.

READING OF THESES

BY THE

GRADUATING CLASS OF 1874,

AT THE INSTITUTE HALL.

1. Review of the Wrought Iron Girder Bridge, over the Hudson River, at Troy, N. Y. Harry D. Pattison, Troy, N. Y.

2. Review of a Jonval Turbine, at the Ogden Mill, Cohoes, N. Y. William J. Fabian, Lake Forest, Ill.

3. Review of the Verrugas Wrought Iron Viaduct, on the Lima and Oroya Railroad. Enrique C. Zegarra, Piura, Peru.

4. Review of the Collective System of the Brooklyn Water Works. William P. Mason, New York City.

5. Review of the Locomotive Engine, "No. 59," of the Union Pacific Railroad Co. George W. Carnrick, Troy, N. Y.

THE INSTITUTE REGATTA.

At 4:00 P. M., the annual Tub and Shell Races for the championship of the Institute, took place on the Laureate Course, Hudson River, above the dam. A large number of the friends of the students gathered on the banks of the river, and in the various boat houses.

The following gentlemen took part in the

TUB RACE:

W. L. Fox, Class of '75, J. Bushnell, Jr., Walter F. Crosby, H. B. Duane, H. N. Elmer, H. R. Griffin, Charles G. Griffith, G. E. Ingersoll, W. A. Nicholson, H. Stutzer, C. G. Williams, A. Underwood, F. A. Yeager, of the Class of '77.

The distance rowed was from the shore to a boat anchored out in the river about seventy-five feet, and return. A start was made punctually on time, and for a half hour the spectators were greatly amused by the ineffectual attempts of the contestants to reach the boat. Some who reached this point were unable to turn around, but Mr. Bushnell finally succeeded in this and in returning. He was declared winner of the race, and was awarded the prize.

THE SHELL RACE.

There were three entries for this race, viz: J. A. Hutchinson, Jr., Class of '75, A. G. Baker, Class of '76, and B. B. Newton, Class of '77. The course was three miles with one turn. The Judges were A. J. Swift, graduate of '73, and J. Bushnell, Jr., Class of '77. Charles Nash, Esq., President of the Laureate Club, acted as Referee.

Time made was as follows: Hutchinson, 25:49; Newton, 26:30; Baker, 27:20.

The water, although in tolerable condition, was too rough for fast time.

R. P. I. SEMI-CENTENNIAL CONCERT.

BY THE INSTITUTE GLEE CLUB.

RAND'S HALL, JUNE 15, 1874. 8 O'CLOCK, P. M.

PROGRAMME. PART FIRST.

1. My Home by the Sea.................................CHORUS
2. Peter Gray..............................MR. ZEGARRA AND GLEE CLUB
3. Piano Duett...........................MESSRS. BREESE AND LAY
4. SOLO—Parting..MR. FORD
5. Butcher's Dog.......................MR. HOUSE AND GLEE CLUB
6. Quartette...........MESSRS. ZEGARRA, HOUSE, DAVIS, MCLEAN
7. Medley..CHORUS

PART SECOND.

1. Rig-a-Jig-Jig [new version]...........................CHORUS
2. Quartette.............MESSRS. KAY, ALDRICH, FOX AND CHAPIN
3. Sweet and Low...CHORUS
4. DUETT—Larboard Watch...........MESSRS. FORD AND ALDRICH
5. Noah's Ark..CHORUS
6. Evening Bells...CHORUS
7. DUETT—Violin and Flute..........MESSRS. HIRST AND GEUDER
8. Seven Crows..

The following notice of the Club accompanied this programme:

The want of an organization on a good basis for the improvement and systematizing of what musical talent could be found in our institution, had been felt for many years. Quartettes and small Choruses were formed among intimate friends, which, from the lack of system, soon died out. On the 25th of October, 1873, a meeting of a few students was held and the foundation of our present Glee Club was laid. For some time we studied a few pieces for our own amusement, and the improvement of what talent we possessed; and not until the following March was a thought entertained of our giving a public entertainment. Our Boat Club had labored for some time under serious embarrassment, and had tried every means in their power to keep their heads above water. To keep out of debt was as much as they found it possible to do. The Glee Club embraced many members of the Boat Club, and as we grew to have confidence in ourselves, faint murmurs were now and then heard regarding our competency to give a concert to help the Boat Club along. The members of the Boat Club encouraged us by repeated assurance that we would find a lenient public, and probably an enthusiastic audience, consisting as it most probably would of students and their friends. A concert was decided on, to take place about the first of May, but as arrangements for the programme of the Semi-Centennial Celebration were being made and we were invited to take part in it (thus adding a new and pleasant feature for the old graduates, who, under the influence of familiar College songs, will revive old memories of happy days passed at Alma Mater), the time of the concert was changed to June 15th.

Since commencing the sale of our tickets, we have found many outside taking an interest in our concert, and are thankful to them for thus subscribing to an enterprise of whose merits they knew comparatively nothing. Our repertoire embraces no really scientific music, and indeed we have had no time to study and practice music of a very high order; but we aim to please in what we have selected, common though it may seem, trusting to the kind indulgence of our friends, who, we think, will not regret having assisted us in a worthy undertaking.

I. G. CLUB.

TUESDAY, JUNE 16.

READING OF THESES

BY THE

GRADUATING CLASS OF 1874,

AT THE INSTITUTE HALL.

6. Review of the Wrought Iron Girder Bridge, over the Schuylkill River, on Girard Ave., Philadelphia, Pa. George S. Griffen, Phœnixville, Pa.

7. Review of the Lake Tunnel of the Cleveland Water Works. Frank L. Ford, East Cleveland, O.

8. Review of a "Standard Passenger Locomotive Engine," Constructed at the Grant Locomotive Works, Paterson, N. J. William H. Powless, Norwood, N. J.

9. Discussion of the Principal Methods of Constructing Foundations in Water. Lyman E. Cooley, Canandaigua, N. Y.

10. Review of a Floating Derrick, Department of Docks, New York City. Alexander P. Gest, Philadelphia, Pa.

A large number of visitors were present at the Reading of the Theses, and among them Chancellor J. V. L. Pruyn, Secretary Woolworth, and Hon. Martin I. Townsend, of the State Board of University Regents.

The drawings made during this past term by members of various classes were on exhibition, and consisted of topographical and bridge drawings, maps of railroad, hydrographical and compass surveys. The collections of plants which the members of the class in botany are required to make, were also exhibited.

RECEPTION.

Hon. and Mrs. J. M. Warren gave a reception to the graduating class, their friends and the alumni, at their residence on Eighth Street, at 1 o'clock, P. M. The attendance was large, but the ample provision generous hospitality had made within doors, together with the beautiful grounds and charming views without, left nothing wanting for the enjoyment of those present.

PROCEEDINGS

OF THE SIXTH ANNUAL MEETING OF THE

ASSOCIATION OF GRADUATES,

And Semi-Centennial Celebration of the Institute.

The meeting was regularly organized in Institute Hall, at 2:30 P. M., on Tuesday, June 16th.

In the absence of President Kneass, Vice-President Boller took the Chair, and after calling the meeting to order, addressed the Association as follows:

Gentlemen of the Alumni Association:

In the absence of the President of our Association, it becomes my duty to call this meeting to order and to welcome the Alumni of the Rensselaer Polytechnic Institute, to the scenes of earlier days. The pleasure of any meeting of this character, is tinged with a shade of sadness, as the quickened memory spreads out in panoramic view, the events of the years gone by. The pictures are of varying length, according to our years, but they are all blurred more or less with anxiety and care, disappointments and deferred hopes. Neglected opportunities and unfulfilled resolutions flit by in a ghostly procession, and almost seem for a time to chill the sunnier aspects of the picture.

The story of our undergraduate life comes back to us with almost startling vividness. Our classmates, in eager, hopeful and good natured rivalry, we recall with the alphabetical precision of the Catalogue. How ambitious we all were, and how important we felt. Armed with the degree of Alma Mater, the climax of our Institute life, we felt that we were engineers indeed, with the whole world waiting for our advent. We went forth to conquer, little dreaming that the world judged us by other standards than our own. It no doubt took a longer time with some than with others, to be brought to a realizing sense of the fact that we were barely on the threshold of professional life, when we received the coveted parchment from the hands of the dignified "President of the Board of Trustees." Sooner or later we learned that the only road to success was the old, old one, of commencing life at the beginning, to take the bitter with the sweet, and learn to labor and to wait. So closely linked with our student life, that to speak of one recalls the other, are the Professors, whose dignity it was often our pleasure to ruffle, and whom student fancy christened with names not to be found in the Catalogue. The responsibilty of their office looked differently to us then, and a painstaking discharge of duty on their part was too often regarded as imposing unnecessary restrictions upon us. Such of us who formed intimacies with members of the faculty, had privileges we did not then appreciate, and which now in after years form one of the most delightful pages of our reminiscences.

According to the circular of invitation, you will notice that this is the Semi-Centennial Anniversary of the Institute's life! A half century of work has been accomplished, and to what good purpose, let the speaking pages of the records bear witness. Limited, comparatively speaking, as has been the number of its graduates, hardly a State in the Union but has felt their influence. Few public works of any magnitude now in progress are without Institute representation, and it has a remarkable share in contributing to the material development of the country. Standing alone for years this pioneer school of science has struggled and lived through discouragements of no ordinary character. It has not only had to educate scientific students, but it has also had to educate the public, so far as it could reach, to the idea that theory and practice were not antagonistic, but supplementary to each other. The last duty has been far the more difficult. The past decade has witnessed the culmination of a struggle between the scholastic systems two centuries old, and the new demands of modern times. While the enthusiasm of the "new education" idea has modified the popular estimation of the value and importance of scientific knowledge, there is more work to be accomplished. It is one thing to recognize this importance of science,be it ever so grudgingly given, but it is quite another to fasten its position in the world of knowledge. What are called the "learned professions," do *not* embrace that of the scientific man, and whatever distinction of superiority that may have existed in times past, exists no longer, if utilitarian considerations are entitled to any weight. It is true that the heretofore sacred ties of learned professions, like old wine, have had the flavor of age to commend them, and appealing as they do with traditional force to the comprehension of the mass of society, and intimately associated with the whole network of social life, society has acted but a natural part in elevating to a pre-eminence what it best could understand. But the times have changed, and men have learned that there is very little nutriment in the polite mustiness of antiquity, and that it should be administered in the new era of education in homœopathic doses.

The last half century has seen science raised in all its vast ramifications to a distinct profession, and among its devotees may be found as much intellectual wealth, sound learning and untiring industry, as can be found in any other calling. If bettering the material condition of society, if increasing its comforts, if developing its sources and avenues of wealth, if teaching it how to live, is any criterion of learning, then I say that science should have the highest seat in men's estimation. If nobility of work is asked for, for admission to the coveted eminence, then I ask can man be engaged in a more ennobling work than the study and application of the laws and forces of nature; to wring from nature her secrets, and divert them to the benefit and elevation of the human race. Science is more felt than heard; it dwells upon deeds rather than words. Its subtle influence pervades civilization, and its privileges are enjoyed day after day, without a thought given to "whence it comes or whither it goes." The labor of years develops a necessity which becomes part of our daily lives. Who, for instance, realizes the study, labor and research, that has brought our railways into existence, and has been perfecting them ever since?

England thought Stevenson worthy of a tomb in Westminister Abbey, and she has knighted her prominent men of science, recognizing them as benefactors to the race. Some such recognition we must strive for in this country, in our own American way. While we do not bestow orders on the men that rise above the mass of their fellows, we have been conferring honorary degrees upon men of letters, the law, and clergy. Why not upon men of *science?* Our colleges have been so profuse in hastening to recognize this expression of pre-eminence in a scholastic direction, that the number of complimentary degrees given out at every annual commencement, is legion. They have cheapened their honors, until the whole intent and purpose has been virtually lost. Honorary degrees of this character cease to be a compliment, and I only refer to them in this place to emphasize the idea previously expressed, regarding work yet to be done, and indicating one method for science to assist itself. While men's estimate of themselves or their calling, does not always accord with the judgment of their fellows, it is as certainly true, that unless they assist themselves, others will not do it for them. Scientific schools, in this country at least, do not give special or complimentary degrees, and it well becomes the Rensselaer Institute, the oldest and best known institution of its class, to initiate the system. If the honor was used sparingly and critically, it would be a coveted prize for the deserving, and a mark of accomplishment that would still further elevate the profession of the scientific man in the estimation of society. It is high time for science to assert itself in every legitimate direction, and demand a seat on the Olympian Height, so long occupied by law, medicine, and theology. I would further present for your consideration, the matter of incorporating the Alumni element in the governance of this institution. This seems to me worthy of discussion, for many reasons, and has been found of value in such colleges as have adopted the principle. No one knows, better than the graduate of practical experience, the shortcomings of our Alma Mater, and it is eminently proper that he should be consulted in matters of systems and policy. In an age of such wondrous activity as the one we are passing through, to stand still is to be left behind, and to be left behind is a lingering death. Competition is a tireless rider, forever spurring on all who enter for the race. Striving for perfection, unattainable though it be, is characteristic of the age, whether toward things good or towards things bad. Radicalism and conservatism are the two great conflicting social forces, each one tempering the other, yielding a resultant of real progress. Separate them and we have communism on the one hand, and mediævalism on the other. The Rensselaer Institute stands alone, as a purely scientific school, no longer. The demands of the "new education" have created, I must say, almost beyond present requirements, technical and scientific schools in almost every important State in the Union, either on their own basis, or as adjuncts to established institutions of learning. These schools are for the most part well endowed, and present inducements that this Institute cannot hold out. Thus far, despite all these aspirants for popular favor, the R. P. I. has held its ground, if the number of students may be taken as an index of prosperity. Even with its limited facilities, and higher tuition fees than any other similar school, there are more names now upon its register than ever before. This is easily accounted for from the fact that its age has given it a reputation through its graduates, not yet reached by its young and vigorous competitors, and its reputation is further advanced by a knowledge of the rigidity of its graduating requirements. This disparity must lessen year by year, until the newer schools occupy the same vantage ground, having in addition thereto, the attractions growing out of material prosperity. The position of the

Rensselaer Polytechnic Institute is to-day largely due to the comprehensive mind of B. Franklin Greene, former Director, as I think will be generally admitted. His report, made in 1850, to the Board of Trustees, and adopted by them at that time, as the basis of the Institute system, showed an appreciation of the subject far in advance of the time. The Institute then, as it does now, needed a large endowment, and the prospects then were about as good as they are now—possibly better. The interval of twenty years has done nothing for us, and we must make up for a slender purse, as was done by Director Greene, by still furthering its educational usefulness. The Alumni comparatively have nothing to give; they are too few in number, and as a rule their riches are not in excess of what usually falls to the lot of scientific men. But if they can not give of worldly possessions, they can counsel through ripened experience and sympathy. The professors are more or less "book men," and hard-working and painstaking though they be, they cannot always estimate truly the value of their systems, as to the effect upon the after life of the student. It was evidently some such feeling that prompted the Board of Trustees to appoint a peculiarly able committee in the Spring of 1870, to investigate the educational system of the Institute. That committee made a careful investigation and report, so complete and encyclopædic in its information, as to claim for it a high position in the literature of technical education. It was expected at the time by many of the Alumni that steps would be taken to adopt its recommendations, in part at least, and that the time had come when the Rensselaer Polytechnic Institute would make another stride forward. So far as I can learn, and from causes that do not appear, this document has exerted no influence as yet upon the Institute system. Giving full credit to the dead weight of impecuniosity, the *bête noir* that springs up at every turn, the Institute can do more than she is now doing, at least so it appears to many of its graduates. Far be it from me to cast reflection on any one of its faculty, for a harder-working or more painstaking body of men it would be difficult to find. Year by year they have raised the standard of scholarship, and their courses have been filled out and extended. There is no human institution under the sun that does not run in a groove unless carefully watched, and the pruning knife is essential to a healthy advance. The work of the Institute being to prepare young men for certain professional duties, it certainly seems reasonable that those young men in after years should have a voice as to the kind of preparation those coming after should receive. While this Association of Graduates has no competence to pass any measures affecting the character of the Institute system, or the mode of its government, it certainly has the right of petition, and could exercise that right in no better way than requesting an alumni representation among the Board of Trustees.

Another matter occurs to me as one in which the influence of the Alumni Association can be wholesomely exerted, and that is, in discountenancing the tendency of the undergraduates to affect the class names of distinctive collegiate institutions. It must sound strange to an old graduate, on visiting the scenes of his youth, to hear Division A spoken of as the "Senior Class," or Division D as "Freshman." The divisional names were given originally to make a marked distinction that the present race of students do not appear to understand. The Rensselaer Polytechnic Institute pretends to no parallel with the American colleges, but theoretically stands on a higher plane, to enjoy the full benefits of which a preparatory college course is necessary, and it is falsifying its true position before the public, in attaching to it the college nomenclature. Inasmuch as the Institute is a special school, to train its students for special work in life, its educational position is alongside of other professional schools, such as Law, or Medicine. General literature, or miscellaneous cultivation, forms no part of the system of special schools, while it is the whole aim of the college course, and it would be much better for the special schools, if it were possible, to insist upon a previous college training. High aims alone produce high results, and it is certainly to be hoped that the present and future students of the Rensselaer Polytechnic Institute will look upon it as an embryo professional duty to keep the line distinctly marked between general and special education.

I must apologize for thus trespassing upon your time, and deem it proper to offer as my excuse a desire to see the alumni of the Rensselaer Polytechnic Institute perform, if possible, some effective work for their alma mater, and interest themselves in seeing the Institute keep the proud position that it has so long held. I have indicated certain directions for effort, that seem to me eminently practical, and now yield them to the winnowing process of many minds, trusting that the seed will be found worthy of the sowing.

The minutes of the last meeting of the Association of Graduates, (1873,) were then read by the Secretary, Prof. H. B. Nason, and approved.

The chairman of the committee on subscriptions to, and for procuring a monument to Prof. Eaton, reported that the money had nearly all been obtained, and that a monument had been placed in the Oakwood Cemetery, costing $525; also a memorial window of stained glass had been placed in the Institute Hall, costing $365.

The small deficiency ($85,) in funds for these memorials, was immediately made up by the Alumni present.

Prof. Nason, on behalf of the committee for the Semi-Centennial Celebration, reported the programme as already given in the second circular. (See page 7.)

The following were appointed a committee to nominate officers for the ensuing three years: James P. Wallace, class of '37; D. M. Greene, class of '51; A. J. Swift, class of '72; W. H. Morton, class of '56; Prof. Dascom Greene, class of '53.

Remarks were then made by Dr. G. F. Horton, late President of the Pennsylvania State Medical Society, of the class of 1827; also, by Dr. S. E. Arms, of Elizabeth, N. J., a member of the first graduating class, 1826.

Upon invitation, the Alumni present then signed the register.

At four o'clock the meeting adjourned to the Troy Union R. R. Depot, and from there proceeded to the Oakwood Cemetery in a special train of four cars drawn by the locomotive "Gen. Wool," provided by the Troy & Boston R. R. The officers of the association, speakers, and a number of guests, were provided with carriages.

The exercises commenced at 4:45. Hon. James Forsyth, President of the Institute, introduced Rev. H. N. Brinsmade, D. D., of Newark, N. J., brother of the late Dr. T. C. Brinsmade, a former President of the Institute, by whom prayer was offered, concluding with the Lord's prayer, in which all present joined.

Hon. Albert R. Fox, of Sandlake, then spoke briefly of the late Prof. Amos Eaton, of the desire of his pupils to erect a monument to his memory, of the method which had been used to obtain necessary funds, and the interest which all had manifested in the matter. The speaker closed his remarks with a touching tribute to the memory of the departed.

Hon. Martin I. Townsend, LL. D., was then introduced and spoke as follows:

Friends of Prof. Eaton:

The eminent citizen, in whose honor we have assembled to-day, was a man of no common mould. Nature had endowed him with intellectual powers far above those conferred upon ordinary men, and a life of tireless labor placed him in the front rank with the first minds which the world has produced in any age or country. Prof. Eaton entered upon the study of the natural sciences at a period when those sciences were very little developed. He was a pioneer in those paths which his labors and the labors of his contemporaries have served to make smooth for coming generations.

For more than thirty centuries, the records engraved upon Egyptian monuments in hieroglyphic characters were a sealed book to the whole race of mankind. In our day Champollion and his co-laborers have broken the seals of the book, so long closed, and read to the wondering world the legends of Egyptian story.

So the records which God himself had written on every rock, had concealed in every bank of sand, had impressed upon every mass of plastic clay, from the centre of the earth to the top of the highest mountain peak that raises its snow-clad head towards mid-heaven, had been closed for a hundred centuries. Even man, the representative of the Divinity, had stumbled blindly over these records until such men as Eaton discovered the key to their interpretation, and taught us to read from them the story of the world's history, in letters written in ineffaceable characters by the pen of the Divine Author of all. Nor is this all which our age has learned from such men as Eaton and his associates. They have shown us that in our walk upon the earth we are treading amidst a vast extended grave yard, where the bodies of the animal dead have in successive generations been buried and stored away as in vast museums for millions of ages—yea, for millions of ages before the primeval man was fashioned by the hand of the Creator, and they have opened up to us the exhaustless storehouses in which the early animal dead have so long rested in fossil forms. They are now all ranged before us, from the huge forms of iguanodons and megatheriums and the saurian monsters of the early world, to the glittering scales of the tiny fish that sported in the primeval seas. What tongue can adequately describe the world of wonder that naturalists have opened up to us?

I have only alluded thus far to the wonders of geological and zoological history developed in our day, and in whose development Prof. Eaton aided so efficiently. But his services and those of his associates have developed wonders in the science of Botany, no less amazing, and no less useful to the world of mankind. They have not only taught us the character of the flora of the new-born world, the conditions of vegetable life when the coal was formed, which was for such untold ages buried in the bowels of the earth, but they have ranged in order, and taught us the nature and uses of the living flora that now cover the earth with beauty and fertility, and not only minister to man's comfort and elegant enjoyment, but which are necessary to render even his physical existence possible. In all these works, in all these fields of inquiry, Prof. Eaton was a most efficient pioneer.

But it is most appropriate to speak of Prof. Eaton to-day as the founder of the Rensselaer Polytechnic Institute. His far-seeing mind fully appreciated the importance of establishing in this wide, though youthful land, a school where young men, by a thorough training in the natural and exact sciences, should become prepared to lead in developing and utilizing our varied and exhaustless resources. Our country was young, and our people to a great degree, destitute of accumulated wealth. But his was an enthusiasm that was discouraged by no denial, that brooked no defeat. Through his exertions the Rensselaer Institute was chartered and started upon its course. At the outset the patronage was small, and the facilities meagre, as compared with those enjoyed in this and similar institutions at the present day. But the work has gone steadily forward from that day to this. The methods of instruction have, from time to time, been adapted to the advancement in human knowledge which has electrified the world during the last fifty years. The buildings, the chemical laboratory and the apparatus of the institution, although not in every respect as extensive as we hope to see them, as the institution advances in usefulness and public favor, are yet such as would have warmed the heart of the old sage to have even dreamed of, as likely to be enjoyed at some future day by his beloved Polytechnic. The graduates of the institution have gone out into the world and vindicated its power to prepare its scholars to compete

6

successfully with the graduates of any similar institution on the continent. In the war of the late rebellion, in whose conduct and successful termination science bore so great a part, the graduates of the Rensselaer Polytechnic stood side by side with the graduates of the nation's military school at West Point, and in everything except mere technical military engineering, fully vindicated their claim to equality of rank with them. Nay, I am disposed to go still further, and to say that this institution gives to its students as complete and perfect an education as civil engineers as can be acquired in any institution in Europe or America. The nation is becoming aware of this fact, and the large attendance upon its course of instruction shows that others concur with me in the conclusion which I have announced.

When, a few evenings since, I saw one hundred and seventy-five stalwart young men of the institution, in the prime of their manhood, with their arms entwined and shoulder set against shoulder, marching through our streets in the shimmer of the moonlight, and thought of the power that these young men were to exert upon the prosperity of the country, I felt that the Rensselaer Polytechnic was indeed a power in the land.

The success of Prof. Eaton in his scheme to benefit mankind is but another instance, vindicating the sacred text when it tells us that, "They that go forth weeping, *bearing precious seed*, shall doubtless come again with joy bringing their sheaves with them."

Prof. James Hall, of Albany, Class of '32, being introduced, said:

Friends: I could not refuse to say a few words on such an occasion as this. When we assemble here voluntarily to pay our tribute to Prof. Eaton thirty-two years after his death, it is certain that the man has a hold upon us not that of a common man. It was my happiness to know Prof. Eaton as a teacher, adviser and friend. One word we ought to say. At a time when no schools of natural or applied science existed he became a pioneer in founding the Rensselaer school. He lectured in Williams College and at New Haven. It has been my good fortune to meet two men who were his pupils before the founding of the Institute. One of them is Hon. Elias Leavenworth of Syracuse, who, as a legislator, has always appreciated science. The other is Judge Parker of Albany, always interested in scientific men. Mr. L. considers his effort to advance science one of the brightest ornaments in his escutcheon.

To establish a school of science the Professor had the enthusiasm, but not the means, and in that respect was like nearly all men of science. Stephen Van Rensselaer had, and with a wise provision he established this school. Taking a small number of students, it gave special instruction, and the students were required to tell to others, in groups of five or six, what they knew. To young men intending to teach, this was important. In the lectures of Prof. Eaton at Utica came the teachings which resulted in the scientific interest of Prof. Dana, and Prof. Gray, and Prof. Torrey, our greatest botanist. In the progress of civilization, it is not the slow, uniform motion of the great masses that helps it forward, but the few men who come out from them and strike a new key. Prof. Eaton taught us the manipulations in science with the simplest materials, so that a student could go into the forest and construct a pneumatic trough, or a balance, and perform there his experiments in chemistry or physics. To his memory we owe much. His name has been neglected before the public, but cherished in the bosoms of those who knew him, a man capable of interesting young men, having a brain one-fourth larger than the mass of mankind, and that brain devoted to the service of science. If we with great means do what he did with small, we shall deserve well of coming generations.

Prof. H. B. Nason then spoke as follows, concerning the moral and religious character of Prof. Eaton:

The death of Prof. Eaton occurred on the 6th of May, 1842. Nearly the last words that fell from his lips were: "I submit to my Heavenly Father's will"—words uttered without doubt in the greatest sincerity, and words expressive of that calm, peaceful, loving, child-like submission which have so often been uttered by those who have had a firm, unswerving faith in the forgiving, tender mercy of an ever indulgent Heavenly Father. The same sentiment has been expressed by the high and the low, in the palace, in the hovel, before the glitter of the executioner's axe, surrounded by blazing fagots, as well as when life has gently closed like a summer's day. "Thy will be done!" "Father, I trust in Thee!" "Into Thy hands I commit my spirit!" "It is well!" Each dying sentence breathes the same trusting faith. Sir Humphrey Davy, whom science has always been pleased to honor, once said: "I envy no quality of the mind or intellect in others; not genius, power, wit or fancy; but if I could choose what would be most delightful and I believe most useful to me, I should prefer a *firm religious belief* to every other blessing." From what I have been able to learn from those who knew him best, Prof. Eaton was a firm believer in the Christian religion, and was sustained and comforted by its truths amid trials and afflictions which seldom fall to the lot of man. Being called away very frequently from home, he was in the habit of writing often and with great frankness concerning his thoughts and views of religious subjects. In one of these letters, written to his wife after some deep affliction, he says: "I feel that these trials are but the chastisement of a Father, which, though seemingly severe, are designed to eventuate in my more substantial good. My faith in Divine revelation and in the immediate agency of an all-seeing God is greatly strengthened."

Again he writes: "I think He who formed all hearts has pierced mine with a true conviction of my lost and sinful state. My little office has become to me a house of prayer. I can close my work by strenuous exertion so as to gain two or three hours each day for reading of the Scriptures, contemplation and prayer, vigorously struggling to be relieved from my heavy burden of sin." "At last," he adds, in speaking of his conversion, "I seemed to consent to all the terms of the Gospel, and to throw myself wholly upon

Divine mercy without reserve. I called aloud upon the Redeemer as an elder brother in the flesh, who had influence with our Heavenly Father, to present me as a candidate for mercy. I have faith to believe that he heard my prayer, and gave my soul its first moments of real peace for eighteen years. I could not refrain from solemnly committing my wife and children to the hands of the God who gave them, and dedicating them to the service of the Father of Mercies."

Again, when absent from home, he says: "I rarely neglect to address the Throne of Grace for my family and myself morning and evening." Years afterwards, in referring to the period of his conversion to religion, he says: "Though I have daily good reason to reproach myself for want of zeal in so important a cause as religion, I hope I have never lost sight of the great duty of man, for any considerable period of time."

In all his religious writings he seems to show a feeling of deep dependence upon divine strength and wisdom, and a sincere repentance for his shortcomings and failures. A desire to know and perform his whole duty, at whatever cost or sacrifice, was often expressed. In making application for admission to one of our churches, after stating his views, he writes: "I wish to be directed on the ground of duty alone. I beg of you to view it both with regard to my individual duty and the general interest of the great cause of religion. I can readily bring my feelings to cordial acquiescence in whatever duty commands. But I cannot consent to be viewed by you as an enemy of religion."

There are those present to-day who can tell you from personal experience of the many qualities of mind and heart which made Prof. Eaton one of the best and truest of friends. Although perhaps at times somewhat rough in his appearance and manner, yet whenever occasion required, the big generous heart within prompted deeds and actions which can never be forgotten. Perhaps nowhere were these traits better seen and appreciated than in his own family.

One of his children who has honored the memory of her father by a zealous devotion to the cause of the education of her own sex and who honors us and this occasion with her presence to-day, says in a recent letter, "I was blessed by the genial, loving Prof. Amos Eaton's tenderest care and influence." One who often visited in his family told me that nowhere was there ever seen a better exhibition of true parental care and affection, and no one ever mourned with deeper sorrow the loss of those near and dear to him of his own family.

There seems to be a principle in the human heart which leads us ever to speak kindly of the dead, and with them to bury anything of wrong that may have existed in their lives or their character. And to-day as we recount the many virtues of the truly great man whose remains repose beneath us, let us draw the mantle of charity over any weakness of nature, and trust that the record of an earnest life is inscribed against his name, and not only the tear of the recording angel, but the all-saving blood of a forgiving Saviour purified that soul from the dross of earth and made it a fit inhabitant of heaven.

As in ancient times the brows of bloodless victors were crowned with a myrtle wreath, so to-day as we dedicate this block of granite to the memory of Amos Eaton we place upon it the wreath of myrtle. True it will soon wither and die, but the good deeds, the noble actions and words of the teacher will live on in the hearts of those he instructed, and their influence shall be felt when this massive block of granite shall have crumbled to dust; yea, till time shall be no more.

The exercises then closed with the benediction, pronounced by Rev. Dr. Brinsmade.

Miss Sara Cady Eaton, for many years Principal of the Rochester Female Seminary, and Mrs. S. L. Marsden, of New Haven, Conn., daughters of Prof. Eaton, also a grandson, S. Arthur Marsden of New Haven, were present at the dedication.

The monument is a cubical block of light gray Granite, measuring four feet six inches, by five feet, and bears the simple inscription, "Prof. Amos Eaton, born May 17th, 1776, died May 10th, 1842." The stone was taken from the quarry of George Marks on Clark's Island, coast of Maine, and weighs eleven tons. It was cut by Messrs. W. H. & L. L. Dyer, of Troy.

The remark was made by one of the oldest graduates, that he could not conceive of a monument more appropriate to Prof. Eaton, for like the man, it was simple, massive and substantial.

RAND'S HALL, 8 O'CLOCK, P. M.

The meeting of the Alumni was called to order by the acting President, Alfred P. Boller.

Hon. James Forsyth, President of the Institute, was introduced and delivered the following address :

Gentlemen of the Alumni :

The fiftieth anniversary of the foundation of the Rensselaer Polytechnic Institute has so many features of interest to all who have been connected with it, as well as to those who have witnessed its rise and progress in this city, and present success as a scientific and professional school, that they have felt it to be not inappropriate to mark this year in its history with more than usual ceremony.

You have assembled for that purpose. Be assured of the interest and hearty sympathy of all our citizens in your exercises at this time, and of their cheerful co-operation in making them worthy of the occasion.

On behalf of our citizens, and especially the Trustees of the Institute, who desire to make your visit to this school, at this time, happy and profitable, and on behalf of the chief magistrate of the city, who, this evening opens the doors of his hospitable mansion for your reception, I welcome you, one and all, to the Institute, to our city, and its hospitalities.

Prof. E. N. Horsford, of Cambridge, Mass., Class of 1838, late U. S. Commissioner to the Vienna Exposition, then delivered the following address:

ADDRESS BY PROF. E. N. HORSFORD,

CLASS OF 1838.

Gentlemen of the Alumni of the Rensselaer Polytechnic Institute :

I might, as a loyal son of our Alma Mater, try to pay the tribute of my respect to the Institution which has grown from comparatively small beginnings to its present commanding position. I might speak of the genius of its founder; of his discovery of the system of object teaching, and of the then new method of training young men to become teachers; of his great services of other kinds to the cause of education; of his vast acquisitions and perfect command of them at all times. I might glance at the career of the graduates I have known. I might recall to your memory the names of some of the friends of the Institute in the days of my membership—of some who still live; of more that have gone—but at the best, I should indifferently fulfill the task. It will be performed by others better fitted, by sons more familiar with the record. I will not add, by sons who remember, with a warmer gratitude than I, the privileges that were secured to us here.

It was a source of pride and satisfaction to me when, some years after my graduation, it was my fortune to enter Leibig's Laboratory as a pupil, to find that the methods pursued under the guidance of that great Teacher, were in many respects the methods I had been familiar with in the Rensselaer Institute; carried out with the ampler facilities furnished by Government, but essentially the same in conception, in fitness, in certainty of result.

In a recent visit to Europe it was refreshing to see in the Polytechnic Education of Austria, which now unquestion-

7

ably has no superior in the world, the methods of the Rensselaer School of fifty years ago. It will not do to say that the methods were copied from ours, but it is proper to say that the inspiration that gave them to the eastern world moved the mind of Prof. Eaton at a period as early as it did that of Pestalozzi, and Fellenberg, and Leibig, and under circumstances much less favorable for development. The mention of the Old World, as we are accustomed to call it, suggests to me a theme.

I can think of nothing with which I can better occupy the few moments allotted to me, than in presenting a picture of the life that showed itself last summer to an American Commissioner, at the grandest show of the products of polytechnic industry that has ever been gathered for the study and entertainment of the world. We do not meet here solely to be enlightened. We meet to revive cherished memories—to lay the foundation of new ones. I confess I should like of all things to listen to the personal history of the classmates with whom I used to wander in search of plants, and minerals, and birds; with whom I used to conduct wonderful triangulations of the Hudson Valley, and extemporaneous surveys of impossible railways in the direction of the Hoosac Mountain. About the time I was ready to leave the Rensselaer School some thirty-six years ago, there came to town for the purpose of delivering a lecture, Col. William L. Stone, for many years the editor of the *New York Commercial Advertiser*, better known to this generation as the author of the "Life of Red Jacket, the Seneca Chief." He commenced his lecture by answering the question whether he had come to Troy supposing he could enlighten its citizens, by relating the anecdote of a man found digging a hole in a cellar. On being asked its object, he answered by saying that "it was to let the dark out." My object is humbler than Col. Stone's was. I propose only to try to entertain you.

In crossing the old city of Vienna, by the way of the Kaenrtner street, from the neighborhood of the Burg to that of the Hotel Metropol, you pass not far from the St. Stephens Cathedral an apothecary's shop. Over the door is the unique sign "*Apotheker zum heiligen Geist.*" When I first read it, I was startled with what seemed to me an unworthy appropriation of language associated in all our minds with some of our most sacred thoughts. "Apothecary to the Holy Ghost." Could this quaint sign cover up some mediæval legend? Vienna is full of very unique usages connected with the Catholic Church. Some of them—such for example as the procession on Corpus Christi day, in which the Imperial family, the Ministers of State, the Dignitaries of the Church, the Capuchines, the Benedictines, and Franciscans, the societies and the soldiery take part,—in oriental magnificence of costume is something marvelous to behold, and is scarcely to be elsewhere seen. One must not decide too hastily. The sign always challenged my attention when I crossed the city "*Apotheker zum heiligen Geist.*" At another point a little inn has the sign, "*Zur Auge Gottes,*" To the eye of God. Perhaps this is a form of inviting and promising fair dealing. It is undoubtedly free from the charge of being purposely irreverent. But what does the Apothecary to the Holy Ghost mean? One day it flashed upon me. This *Heiligen Geist* does not mean the Holy Ghost. *Heiligen* means healing. It is the Apothecary to the *healing spirit.* This was interesting. It was quite satisfactory. We have made a special appropriation of the word as applied to spirit, but in its compound of holiday we maintain the use of the Germans. The holidays are healing days. Days when the torn or tired spirit may rest and be healed, and restored. The holy days too are healing days. The Holy Spirit is a healing spirit. I confess that this little line of reflection helped me much to understand a great deal that I saw in my recent visit to Vienna. There were numerous healing days in Austria. Let us have a healing hour.

In passing from England to the Continent and especially to Austria, you go from a country of rare beauty, and towns in general of sombre look, to a country of less beauty, perhaps, but to towns that impress you at once with their bright cheerful sunny aspect. Liverpool and London are dark.

They bear the stain of the Mersey and the Thames. Dwellings and shops and public buildings seem draped, in London. Vienna looks as if departing sunlight had been caught and ingrained in the walls. This remark applies to Paris, Brussels, Berlin, Frankfort, Wiesbaden, Liepsic, to Linz, to Munich, to Pesth, Innsbruck, to Kolin and Wittingan—as well as to Vienna. Paris owes possibly much of her architectural splendor to the proximity of quarries, whose blocks, easily wrought under the chisel, acquire hardness with years. This softness of the building stone has developed a race of sculptors. Vienna owes much to her command of an abundant light drab cement, which in its plastic condition invites the art of the modeller, and when the form has gained its proportions, time hardens it to very stone.

The old city of Vienna owed its location to the junction with the Danube, of a small and now insignificant stream called the Wien. The city sprang up at the angle. The Danube is a vagabond sort of river like the Mississippi, wandering about the great plains of Austria and Hungary, cutting its way through an easily yielding soil, and forming new channels with every season of high water. The Imperial government in recent times has spent vast sums of money in carrying out plans for narrowing and confining the Danube so as to maintain its navigability. A few years ago there was the city of Vienna surrounded by a wall and ditch, and glacis, and entered through gates, while around it were numerous suburban villages. These villages have enlarged and grown together up to the glacis, and ten years ago the walls were thrown down and the ditches filled up, and a part of the glacis appropriated to buildings, and a broad avenue and parks. Now from the Danube on one side around the old city to the Danube on the other, the site of the ancient wall and ditch is occupied by a magnificent street or boulevard, some 250 feet wide, skirted throughout most of its length by long, lofty palatial blocks, often spoken of as a succession of palaces. Indeed many of them much exceed in splendor and majesty of external appearance most of the imperial residences of Austria. As you pass into the old city you enter upon narrow streets, with here and there little open squares or markets too picturesque to yield to description. Come with me into the square of the Neuer Markt, on one side of which is the old church of the Capuchines. In the crypts of this ancient edifice, which is not at all imposing in appearance, rest the remains of the imperial family of the Hapsburgs, in massive bronze sarcophagi of most elaborate workmanship. Grandest among them all is the tomb of the great Empress Maria Theresa, who was to Austria almost as much as Washington was to our country. On one side, among the most recently brought, there was the sarcophagus in which rest the remains of the poor unfortunate Maximilian, the last Emperor of Mexico, and the husband of the beautiful and devoted Carlotta. It was touching to see the fresh wreath of flowers with which pious hands daily testify to the affection in which the memory of this Imperial Princc is held. There were a great many others which might be described in dimensions and weight, of Emperors and Empresses, of Princes and Princesses, and Royal Dukes and Generals and Admirals, but what impressed me most was the absolutely free entrance to the last resting place of the imperial, illustrious dead.

It was a type of the general arrangements that prevail in Vienna. One of the chief entrances to the old city leads through the great palace, the residence of the Emperor. Everybody drove or walked there to whom it offered a shorter way. The gardens at Schœnbrunn were accessible, with all their wealth of beauty, the walks and groves, the botanic garden and the zoological gardens, on the same terms. So you might be conducted through the palace at Luxembourg and see the family portraits and the apartments which have *echoed* to so many *welcomes* to the august crowned heads of the old world, and which, last of all, were occupied by the Shah of Persia. The imperial household seems to be so *near* the people. In one of the porches, or rather long corridors, I noticed that the swallows had the common right of free entrance with the additional privilege of permanent and undisturbed residence with their households. Their social twitter in the midst of the gardens of the imperial palace reminded me of one of George Robbins' famous advertisements of a private residence near London, which he was about to sell at auction. There was much to be said, he remarked, of the beauty of the situation, the extent of the landscape, and the picturesqueness of the surroundings, but he must not conceal two drawbacks—the songs of the nightingales and the litter of the rose leaves. Cross over the street from the Church of the Capuchines to the hotel of the Monck, 500 years old, and lunch in the dining room. You reach it by descending some thirty feet from the level of the sidewalk. What massive columns support the groined arches above you! You are in a place safe in time of seige. How many have shared this protection in the wars of Austria! How many hearts have been wrung with the intelligence brought from the front to mothers and sisters and children in these retreats! Here all day long you find ladies and gentlemen breakfasting, lunching or dining, in a quiet easily imagined. Come around to a narrow street a short distance towards the Danube, to another more famous cellar, and quite as old as the dining hall of the Monck. It is the Esterhazy cellar. I will tell you a story about it. I was one day invited by a party of four gentlemen from North Germany whose acquaintance I had made on my way to Vienna, to visit the Esterhazy cellar. What it was I did not then know, but I thought it must be some famous old restaurant, like Auerbach's cellar in Leipsic, or the White Horse in London, and accepted the invitation. I afterwards learned that it was one of the famous places of Vienna; a cellar founded 500 years ago by one of the Esterhazy Princes as a charity, where it was provided for at all time to come, that any man on Sunday between twelve and one at noon should be able to obtain at cost a glass of some one of the best varieties of Hungarian wine.

I did not find time to go with my friends, but one day while sitting at lunch at the hotel of the Wildman, as old as the Esterhazy cellar, three of my four friends came in, and not observing me, took their seats at a table about five yards distant, and were soon in the midst of their soup. They said nothing to each other, but occasionally their faces were wreathed in smiles, and from time to time they indulged, as I imagined, in an undercurrent of satisfied chuckle that may have indicated their judgment of the wine they had taken. A few moments later, the fourth of the party came in, and looking about in vain to find a familiar face, seated himself at a table about as far from his three friends as I was—that is about five yards—and ordered his lunch. A moment later I crossed to the table where my three friends were sitting. They gave me a very cordial reception, but each added in turn that they had been to the Esterhazy cellar, but had somehow lost their friend and could not imagine what had become of him. Parting with them, I went to the table where the fourth gentleman was sitting. He received me also with great cordiality, and added that he and his friends had been to the Esterhazy cellar, but that he had somehow lost them and could not imagine what had become of them. I resumed my seat to see the party of three pay their reckoning and leave, without seeing or being seen by the fourth of their group;—from which it may be inferred that under certain circumstances, even in Austria, the capacities of the auditory and optic nerves are not effective beyond a distance of fifteen feet.

I might tell you of the great Cathedral of St. Stephen, and of the beautiful votive church, erected by a former Emperor in fulfillment of a vow made in severe illness, and of others of rare design, and of the Protestant Church kept alive by the Americans during the Exposition in an edifice in which it was next to impossible to hear a sentence the preacher uttered. So I might speak of the public institutions, or such as I had the fortune to see. But let me first turn to what was of *special* interest in Vienna this last summer, the great World's Fair, the International Exposition.

When I reached Vienna, there were on exhibiton two cases of pistols and fire arms, and a crayon wall picture illustrating the pork slaughtering and packing of Cincinnati, which perhaps I may say was prepared in Cincinnati at my solicitation to illustrate one of our great industries. The remaining articles of American contribution were in piles of boxes in the great building, in cars on the tracks near the doors, on the way, or on side tracks, everywhere between Vienna their destination and Trieste, Paris, Bremen and Hamburgh, the ports through which they had been sent. Mr. Shultz entered on his duties as chief commissioner the day but one after my arrival, May 16th. On the 10th of June the American department was formally opened, the barriers at the entrance being removed and a little procession with the American Minister, Mr. Jay, and Mr. Shultz at its head, passing through the principal avenues. Looking at it as it was and thinking what it might have been made, there was a feeling of regret, but the American exhibition was nevertheless creditable to us. It surpassed any former one that we have made at the International Expositions of Europe, and was certainly more numerously visited than any other department of the Exposition. The juries awarded us a larger percentage of prizes than was received by any other nation.

I could give an account of the organization of the juries, of their numbers and their weight as men, judged either by their rank, including princes, dukes, earls, ambassadors, officers of the navy and army, physicians, artists, manufacturers and professors, or by their great experience in International exhibitions, or by their grand culture. It may be enough to say that I never before looked upon a body of seven hundred men who have, as it seemed to me, such and so much influence upon the great interests of civilization. The work of the juries was arduous. I usually took my coffee and roll at the Exposition, two miles from my lodgings at eight o'clock, and with the interruption of an hour, or an hour and a half, for the lunch at twelve, I remained till five or six, for a period of about six weeks, when the labors of the juries were brought to a close.

There were about 70,000 exhibitors. In the single department of textiles there were over 6,000. Of exhibitors of wines and liquors I do not know the number. But of the samples gathered for examination by the sub-sections of the food jury at one cellar in Vienna, there were 30,000, and these did not include the French or Italian wines. The total number of varieties could not be less than 15,000. The language in constant use in the juries was of course German, but most of the jurors spoke French, and in the meetings of the juries when all the sections were assembled, the president put every question both in German and French. Without German, the juror was illy qualified. With French, but little better; with neither, he was unfortunate, as was the country he represented.

The International jury, the designation of the whole body was as a general thing elected by the exhibitors from each country, from the commissioners sent by the government of that country. Ten exhibitors in a class were entitled to a juror, over one hundred entitled a country to two jurors, over two hundred to three, and so on. The deficiencies in the American department shut us out from representatives on the juries in several classes, and in but two were we entitled to two jurors each. In not one, to more than two. The juries in each class resolved themselves into sections, and those sections into sub-sections. My own jury, that of food as a product of industry, numbered about seventy, of which there were five sections, covering grains, wines, sugar and conserves, canned meats and fruits, and tobacco. Under grains, there were two sub-sections, one of flour, and everything connected with milling; and another including everything connected with bread baking, and the preparation of macaroni, sago, and so forth.

The independence, fairness, earnestness and thorough fitness and accomplishment of the jurors were conspicuous. It so happened that I was placed on the food jury by the voice of the American exhibitors; and on the jury of commerce, on that of the history of prices, and that of waste products, by the Imperial direction; mainly doubtless, because I happened to be the only American who was at the same time a commissioner, had served as a juror, and had some command of the language. The duties on the last three juries were especially pleasant. Among the exhibits was for example, a collection from England of a sample of each and every kind of article imported into England in 1870. A collection accompanied by elaborate statistical tables, all prepared by Prof. Archer, of Edinburg. There was a sample of every article imported into Austria through the port of Trieste, and of every kind of export from Austria.

The greatest interest was taken in the types of graphic delineation of the commercial statistics of different countries. Some of them were most ingenious. These had been printed, some of them, indeed most of those from Hungary, at an enormous expense for this exposition. We had brought to us a collection of statistical tables prepared by the Japanese, exhibiting their commerce for the last ten years. Its appearance greatly interested the jury, as showing the progress of this people, and it received the highest award of the imperial direction. The different methods of delineation were all interesting and some very original. We are accustomed to the exhibition of statistics on scales of ordinates yielding profiles, as in showing the line of level of a railway, or the amount of rain-fall or variations of temperature or barometric pressure, but we had at the exposition a great variety of devices. From Russia, industries were represented in sectors of circles. The area of the total circle representing the collective production in a given district, and the areas of the sectors variously colored, the relative production of the different industries. The tea trade was exhibited in uniform blue stripes going out from China to all the world, and the narrower red stripes showing in their width the relative amount of redistribution to other countries from particular ports, as London for example. Switzerland gave the topography of her industries, showing where the wood carving, the watches, and bijouterie, the silks, woolens, iron ware, &c., were produced, and in an atlas of charts their development for the last hundred years or more.

In other atlases the extension of their foreign trade and its different kinds, and the kinds and amounts sent to each country were graphically displayed.

I was desirous that there should be some recognition of the great cartoons from Cincinnati illustrating the pork slaughtering and packing. When I brought the picture to the attention of the food jury, they discussed the subject at length, but decided that as they could not eat pictures, the cartoons did not belong in their class. I succeeded in the commerce jury on the ground that the picture was a graphic delineation of an industry, partly I think, as a graceful compliment to our country.

The New York Historical Society gained the medal of progress on the ground of the vast amount of statistical material contained in its selection of volumes of reports from the several States, though they were not by graphic delineations.

It would be an idle task to attempt to describe the exposition, which was five times as large as that of Paris in 1867, and stamped as it was especially by the influence of its vicinity to the Orient. The spaces were ample, the ornamentation something which it was sad to think was to last for only half a year. Every country had its school house, its restaurant, and characteristic preparation of food and beverages, its peasant house, and many sovereigns had their miniature palaces in the grounds of the exposition. That of the Khedive of Egypt was a wonder of oriental show.

Of the 70,000 exhibitors over 20,000 received prizes of one grade or another.

The labors of the jurors were lightened by excursions to various points of interest. These were upon a grand scale. The agricultural and food jurors were more fortunate than some others. On one occasion these two juries were taken one hundred and twenty miles into Bohemia, to visit the great estate of Ritter Horsky, of Horskysfeld, in a special train traveling by night. We passed a marvelously beautiful day in the latter part of June, in looking over an estate of 5,000 acres, one-half under cultivation, the rest in forest, employing steam appliances of every approved form, and a vast variety of implements of original device, and the labor of 1,500 men and women. The noblemen and gentlemen for thirty miles around sent their carriages to conduct the party of about four hundred all over the estate. Here was thorough under-drainage, here were trout preserves, and mills, a brewery and vineyard. Every farm road was bordered in fruit trees. Here were two thousand acres of beets in cultivation at the same time in various stages of progress, to suit the delivery of roots to the capacity of the sugar mills. At evening there was a grand dinner, after which there were speeches in Russian, Swedish, Czeckisch, (the language of Bohemia), German, Hungarian, French, Italian, Spanish, Portuguese, Latin and English. The jury returned at night to Vienna to resume their work after an interval of two nights and a day.

Another excursion was made to Wittingan, the centre of the great estates of Prince Schwarzenberg in Bohemia, which was in some respects more interesting than the excursion to Ritter Horsky's. Here were fish ponds where fish have been bred for sale for five hundred years, where the dykes, thirty feet high, are overgrown with oaks three feet through, and where 250,000 florins worth of fish are produced and sent to market annually. Here were separate dairies, having vast numbers of beautiful cows in stalls, so gentle and warm, and sleepy and clean. The most interesting feature of the excursion, next to the charming entertainment of the elder and younger Prince, and the wife of the latter, was perhaps, the performance of the minstrel at dinner, where for an hour and a half he improvised in verse. Among other things he gave was an account of our visit, and he rehearsed some legends of the family, accompanied by his own violin and the refrain, supported by a clarionet and bagpipe. All seemed to afford infinite amusement to those who understood Czeckisch. One story was of the Prince who transgressed his own law that no one should shoot a doe on the estate. On a hunt one day by accident or oversight he shot a doe. The grief and consternation among his people were boundless—that their own beloved prince should do so cruel a thing and break his own law; but in the midst of their amazement the prince fell into the water and came near being drowned. Whereupon the crowd of peasants plunged in to his rescue. This plunge, and the successful restoration of the prince to dry land, arrested, with their gratitude for his deliverance, their current of upbraiding, and they were all made happy and contented. This relation in Czeckisch, translated by the prince to two American ladies to whom he had given the honor of seats on either side, enabled those who did not understand Czeckisch to share the infinite amusement of the crowd of Bohemian guests at the table. A gentleman at my side told me there were not less than two thousand people's songs in the Czeckisch language. The princess of Schwarzenberg did us the honor to take a seat in our compartment on an excursion to see one of the great fish ponds. She called her daughters to present them and spoke with pride of her nine children—two of whom, lads on horseback, came down to wave their adieus on the departure of the train. She told us of the occupation of her people through the long winter, their little festivities, their employment in making baskets, bowls and wooden pails, their poverty. She spoke of the anxiety at the palace when they learned that the elder prince had invited two American ladies to join the excursion, as to how they should be entertained. She supposed they would desire to hunt on horseback through the fields and forests, and I am half inclined to think she rather regretted that she had not an opportunity to show with what skill she could guide the movements of a thorough-bred over the plains of Bohemia. It would be ungracious were I not to say that I do not remember ever before to have seen so much of loveliness, grace and simplicity, hearty goodness and sympathy, combined with such perfect physical health and such grand beauty as I saw in the young princess of Schwarzenberg.

Of the vast extent of these estates in Wittingan you may form some idea, when I enumerate some of the manufacturing establishments which minister to the wants of the eighty thousand people on the prince's domain in Bohemia. There are twenty-three breweries, as many saw mills, only one distillery, and that not for producing whiskey, seven iron forges, one Bessemer steel works, one steam bakery, one oil factory, forty-six tile and brick kilns.

Still another excursion by special invitation was given by the imperial direction, over the Sœmmering Pass into Ober-Steyermark, upper Styria. The grandeur of this Alpine pass, the first, I think, overcome by railroad, is familiar to travelers by this route to Trieste. While at dinner a few miles south of the summit of Mürzzuschlag, we were entertained of course with speeches, and a regimental band, and in addition, a band of Tyrolese or Styrian singers. The occasion was every way enchanting. By invitation we stopped over Sunday on our return at Glognitz, to dine with a gentleman who had greatly to do with our comfort at the exposition, Dr. Arenstein, the vice-president of the imperial direction. He had been educated as a Capuchin. He took interest from an early period in the industrial development of Austria. On one occasion of an annual agricultural show, he was elected as delegate. His superior gave him permission for the day to lay aside his gown. The experience of the day led him to decline ever again to resume his gown or his priestly functions. He is now married to a protestant lady, and occupies a superb chateau near an extensive paper manufactory of which he is the chief proprietor. He takes the warmest interest in everything connected with the now astonishing advance of Austria. He particularly desired me to send him any publications, throwing light on methods of interesting the artizan and operattive class of our citizens, in the way of lectures. When a millionaire of Austria, hitherto desired to do the public a great service, he opened a park or a bathing home, or a music hall. Perhaps hereafter he may find pleasure in following in the path of Lowell, Lawrence, Peabody, or Cornell.

When I spoke on one occasion of the munificent but fatal

gift to our dear Agassiz of Penakese, and for the support of a zoological museum, my auditor, a gentleman of high rank in the government of Austria, said, "It is America only that produces Peabodys."

There was a memorable excursion made at the close of the labors of the jury. All the jurors who had not left Vienna, and their ladies, numbering in all about five hundred, were invited by the authorities of Pesth to visit that ancient and royal city. Two steamboats were chartered to take us one hundred and sixty miles down the Danube. We left at seven on the beautiful morning of the 26th of July. It is quite impossible to describe the scene, where all nationalities were gathered on the decks of these steamers, listening alternately to the weird music of gypsy bands on board, salutes of artillery from the towns on the banks, from old Presburg, frowning Comoran, and greetings from Waizen, and from a hundred other towns and villages gay with brilliant flags of welcome. A few miles above Pesth we were met by a steamer crowded with gaily dressed people, and shrouded in banners, who came to convey us to our landing. The whole city seemed to be on the wharfs. The Hungarian magnates in their incomparably picturesque costumes received us, and we were conducted to the several hotels to which we had been assigned, but not to rest. In half an hour the guests were to be present at the great Redouten hall to sup and to dance, and for three days we were driven and feasted and overwhelmed with attention impossible to picture. The palace, the zoological gardens, the hot baths and swimming school, the imperial library, the picture gallery, the academy of sciences, the launching of a ship, the abattoir, the visit to the Margarethin Insel, the Margaret island, where the royal duke has built a bathing house, and constructed cascades and fountains, and a restaurant, and laid out avenues at an expense of 7,000,000 florins, all a gift to the people,—were made to minister to our entertainment. And all this and much more at an expense of forty-thousand florins to Pesth, but not a farthing to the guests. We returned by rail to Vienna.

I made still other excursions, but I am afraid if I relate them I shall compromise my character as a commissioner, whose duty it was to look after the interests of our exhibitors. Without these excursions we should have broken down. They gave opportunity for the representatives of the different nationalities to know each other,—opportunities for mutual courtesies,—for social intercourse. I must however, refer to the last long excursion I made. It was made after the jury work was over. It was first to visit an old classmate under Leibig, now a professor in the University at Gratz, a noted city on the line of railway over the Sœmmering to Trieste. It is a University town, where, because of the relative cheapness of living, and its picturesqueness and seclusion, numerous old army officers and persons of earlier prominence but of decayed fortunes, have taken up their residence. Here a retired army officer had busied himself in translating one of the beautiful volumes of Prof. Longfellow. You are shown the house in which some of the Buonapartes have lived in exile, where the late Queen of Spain found temporary repose. One of the most prominent hotels in the city is called the Hotel zum Elephanten—the Elephant Hotel, from the circumstance that two hundred years ago the first elephant that ever visited Europe was entertained and exhibited there. The fact is commemorated by a huge highly colored picture of an elephant on the wall of the court. In the midst of the city rises an Acropolis some three hundred and sixty feet, crowned with the remains of an old fortress which the Turks often beseiged—so the history runs—but never captured. On the same eminence is now the tower with its bells and cannon ready to alarm the city in case of fire.

While wandering around the streets I came into a quarter where all over the pavement and sidewalks, under booths and outside of them, were all imaginable household relics on sale or for exchange. It was a market day of odds and ends. Even old primers, buttons, cast-off clothing were not wanting. Two or three of the articles proved more than I could resist. One was a wooden water bottle of

Hungary, another a hunting bag ornamented with the skins of young chamois, and a third was the sword of an official of a period about eighty years gone by. You see what an easy victim you may be to circumstances. When Mr. Bergh dies he will be canonized, if nowhere else, certainly in the city of Gratz. In this old town are numerous charities providing for the feeding of birds through the winter.

On my return I stopped to visit a somewhat renowned land's poet Father Schmelzer, whose acquaintance I had made when the excursion given by the imperial direction brought us over the Soemmering, to Mürzzuschlag. He lived at the old castle of Ober-Kindberg, and was the agent of his cousin, a Count Lombody, now residing at Gratz. I had provided a large box of our canned meats and fruits from the American department of the exposition, and these comprising some twelve varieties were made the basis of a dinner given to our friend and his family at the little inn, the Wolfbauer in Kindberg. It was interesting to observe the party of four ladies and as many gentlemen, beside the American party testing the clams, succotash, green corn, peas, beans, lobster, preserved pears, peaches, and so forth, in this little old inn in an open garden, from eight to eleven o'clock of a summer's evening, followed up as it was with numerous kindly toasts and speeches, and at a later hour with a Styrian serenade. I regret to add that I learned the next morning that our excellent friends who loyally ate of every dish, were not wholly of the conviction that such a miscellaneous collection of food was suited to all times and places. The next day, after a visit to the collections and grounds of the castle, and a foot excursion to the summit of a neighboring mountain commanding most beautiful views up and down the valley of the Meir, we returned to a dinner given by our friends, of wholly Steyermark dishes, including a bit of vension, which with a chamois had been shot the day before. Those of you who have read that most healthy and charming of novels "Quits," will remember the schmarn which Nora's cousin Jack relished so keenly. This was one of the dishes. It seemed to me to be a kind of previously boiled hominy, thoroughly roasted and served with an adequate measure of butter, but what it really was I did not learn. The dinner was closed with songs, coffee and cigars, in all of which our lady friends from Ober Kindberg took part; employing the cigar holders brought down by one of the Ober Kindberg party, an under officer of the war department at Vienna, who told us they were made by himself of the paper and quills paid for from the Imperial exchequer. The songs had several of them been composed as well as the music, by our old friend Father Schmelzer, who is the Hans Sachs of Ober Steyermark, a man of great goodness and gentleness, to whom the respect and deference shown by the people of the town, were something beautiful to see. When we parted late at night he did me the honor to kiss me repeatedly, after the style of the country, and to give us his benediction. From this unique and altogether charming experience, we went to Castle Nikilz, near Oedenburg, Hungary, one of the country seats of Earl Zichy, who was the president of my jury on food at the Exposition.

Here we were introduced to a chapter in medieval life, surpassing in interest almost everything we had seen before. Here was a family that for centuries had been one of the leading families of Hungary. Since the execution of Cassimer Zichy, the brother of the Earl, in the Kossuth times of '48, our host had eschewed politics and was devoted to education, to railways and to agriculture. Here was the little old Catholic chapel in which were services every morning for the inmates of the castle. Here was a dining hall hung round with swords and guns, and pikes and spears, and hundreds of antlers, all the latter, trophies of the Earl's individual share in the chase. Here were quantities of rare objects of art of great antiquity, portraits of the members of the family that had intermarried with the Esterhazy's, the Liechtensteins, and other princely and renowned families in Austria, Hungary, and Bohemia. Here was an organized household, as it was centuries ago, except that the serfs had quietly and gracefully and in perfect harmony of relationship passed over to become freemen. One morning the Countess took us to see her dairy, where she superintended the cheese and butter, and her collection of preserves. She took us to see where the bees were housed, that their honey could be easily removed without danger, and where the hens and turkeys, peacocks and guinea hens were cared for. Each setting hen sat in a little basket cradle with a sort of chaise-top hood from which she looked out with becoming dignity and satisfaction over quite an area of covered promenade. She took us to her stables, where were carriages, horses and harnesses, riding horses and saddles, and hunting horses and costumes. We drove to a hunting lodge several miles away, starting up deer in the woods as we passed, and learning of a curious fact that there seemed to be a murrain among these graceful creatures, as frequently of late, the bodies of deer that had evidently died of sickness were found scattered about the forest. The village near the castle was a village of Croats—not a Hungarian among them, every house the copy of every other. Two or three miles away was a village exclusively Hungarian, each house distinct in arrangement from the Croatian, and all among themselves of a common pattern. As far in an another direction was a village exclusively German, not a Hungarian or Croat among them, and their houses again unique. The young men and maidens of each community marry among their own people, but never in either of the other communities. Each community preserves its national language. Outside of one of the villages we encountered an encampment of gypsies, some of whom like deer for swiftness and wildness of look, pursued us till they won a gratuity from the carriage. When we were ready to leave, and the trunks, which were of the kind furnished with india rubber knobs at the corners, were brought out, the Earl called the family together, as he said, to see how Americans traveled. These Hungarian people are in many respects quite by themselves. You see a land of proprietors and of laborers, in which the proprietors are as a general rule devoted to the best interests of the laborers, and in which the laborers have as much pride and self-respect and as well defined privileges as the nobleman whose estates they work.

But I must stop. I cannot tell you of an Imperial reception at Schönbrunn and the Burg in Vienna, or the delightful weekly receptions on behalf of the Emperor, at the residence of Baron von Zagern, or the visit to Klosterneuburg, or to Vöslau, Baden, Mödling and the Brühl.

After this sketch of an experience somewhat unusual, you will naturally ask what impression was left upon me as to the relative place held by these people in the best civilization. We were enchanted with Hungary. The fascination of the hospitable, cordial, enthusiastic, handsome people, was something rare to experience. The transition from serfdom to freedom has been so wisely conducted that you may see all the grace and charm of feudal times, mingling in perfect harmony with the new order of things. The Austrian court is recognized as the most refined in the world. Doubtless each people has characteristics that favorably distinguish it from all others, and possibly an American might be unable to give absolute precedence over all to any one people. I asked the question one day of one of my colleagues from Berlin, as to which European state stood first in general culture. His reply surprised me. It was, "Bohemia, beyond all question." On the whole, from the little I saw, I think I should acquiesce in this judgment. It was in Bohemia that Baron Horsky's estates are situated, which probably present the finest farming in the world—finest as an exhibition of the application of science to the various branches of the art of agriculture, and most satisfactory as an exhibition of financial success. One is a little blinded on such excursions as were made by the jurors, and probably no trustworthy opinion can be formed at such times. Baron Horsky was an excellent illustration of the advantages of a thorough technical education applied to farming. He had indeed nothing for the foundation of his career and fortune, except the training of a Bohemian boy. Most of us know little about Bohemia, except that in elegant and fancy glass-ware it has from our earliest recollection maintained its ascendancy over the rest of the world. We might presume that in a country whose claims to such high position are conceded by neighboring states at the outset, that we should find deference to age, ready recognition of worth, respect for steady industry, high average of general health, and organization of labor in all its departments. These you do find.

An American lady, who had been passing the summer in a Bohemian village, returned in the same steamer with myself. In conversing about the characteristics of the people, which she enumerated with great particularity, and expressing herself surprised at the contrast they presented to the characteristics of the Anglo-Saxons on either side of the Atlantic, she closed with the remark, "And we talk of sending missionaries to Bohemia.

As for myself, I can speak best of their illustrations for object teaching which were seen in the department of Education at the World's Exposition. The Bohemian geological and topographical work took precedence over all others, in originality of design, in elegance and finish. It occurred to me that there must have been completed for Bohemia what the Ordnance survey has commenced for England, —with this difference in favor of Bohemia, as I gathered, that for the individual schools in each district there are models and collections marvelously detailed, which could only have been perfected by the pupils of the whole schools uniting in the work. It was as if one class in the Rensselaer Institute should devote its Saturdays and its vacations, for the years of its undergraduate life, to producing a model of the trough of the Hudson, embracing the region of Cohoes on the North, and extending to and including the Wynantskill on the south. The model should display the rocks below and above, the soils, the forest trees, the swamps, the ponds, lakes, springs, streams and water power, roads, bridges, and sites of factories. What a model might be made! Another class might take the botany, and another the zoology; another the manufacturing industries.

Besides this, individuals might take specialties, being careful to make the field sufficiently narrow to accomplish something. For example, one might devote his whole labor to the habits of a particular enemy of the apple, and present actual specimens of the insect in all stages of its development, and then larger models for use in teaching. But I had almost forgotten that this was the very plan encouraged by Prof. Eaton, our early master. It was in following a kindred suggestion that the schools of some of the States of the old world have, I suppose, without large grants of governmental aid, placed their schools in the foremost rank. It was by the evolution of this system, the germs of which were planted by Prof. Eaton, that there has grown the stately Institute which is our pride and glory to-day. May it not be by prosecuting the same original plan, that you may not only maintain your present ascendancy, but continue to keep the lead in your particular field, in the Western world.

ADDRESS BY HENRY SEDLEY, ESQ.,

OF NEW YORK.

CLASS OF 1848.

When Lord Macauley spoke in favor of removing the civil disabilities of the Jews, he reminded the house of commons of a certain saying of Sir James Mackintosh. This saying was uttered in the same chamber, and was to the effect that the strength of the case of the Jews was a serious inconvenience to their advocate; since it was hardly possible to make a speech for them without wearying the audience by repeating truths which were universally admitted. It is much the same, I think, with the case of the Rensselaer Polytechnic Institute. Its good wine needs no bush of flowering advertisements or of complimentary rhetoric. Fifty years of use have proved its quality and tested its effects. Through the length and breadth of the land its name is "great in mouths of wisest censure;" and, least of all, in the beautiful city which for half a century has honored the Institute, and been honored by it, are needed words thus manifestly shown to be of superfluous eulogy. Still, just as on festal occasions, ornaments are permissible that would be in bad taste for everyday wear, the garlands and trappings of praise may be forgiven perhaps, on an occasion like this; an occasion that must always be memorable in the history of the Institute; an occasion that marks the rounding of a systematical epoch in the record of her usefulness and in her fame. And, if the children of a cherished mother may thus be indulged, for once, in decking her austere front in holiday attire, the egotism of personal reminiscence may be pardoned, he trusts, in one of those children, illustrating as it does, the material teachings and example wherewith he was sent forth to buffet with the world.

I ask leave, then, to narrate to you some cursory personal adventures of a young graduate immediately on leaving the Institute many years ago, and which happened to be cast in that romantic land of gold, which has since filled so large a space in the eyes of our own country, and indeed of the whole world. Few here need to be told that in those days the course of study at the Institute was much less extended than it now is. I do not believe that, so far as it went, it was less thorough. But it was completed in less time, and youths were admitted at an earlier age; so that occasionally, as in my own case, the course was finished and the diploma gained before it could legally be bestowed. Thus it happened that I first saw the Golden Gate at an age when most lads are pursuing their studies; a circumstance that has interest only as showing that in spite of a liberal allowance of the crudeness, presumption and experience of boyhood, I was able, thanks to what the Institute had done for me, not only to fight my way, but to turn a very pretty penny in a short time by the operation.

And this exemplifies the point to which I venture especially to direct attention, which is, the exceptionally practical character of the Institute's training. In doing so, I must be allowed to disregard both the obvious imputation and the natural promptings of vanity, and say at once that my mental qualities as an engineer, were certainly no more than mediocre, while I had positive physical disqualifications. Barring some share of resolution and industry, then the little I achieved was entirely due to the Institute. Thrown absolutely upon my own resources, without guardian or responsible adviser, being I should add without capital, save my moderate fund of knowledge and a few engineering instruments, my case, fresh from the Institute as I was, afforded a pretty good, and certainly, tolerably severe test of its merits.

Well, facts and figures are now greatly in vogue, and I am going to tell you exactly what I did. In my first four months in California, I cleared by professional work, over and above expenses, about one thousand dollars a month. This was in gold, and it is fair to remember that the worker was barely eighteen years of age. I am quite convinced that, but for what he learned at the Institute, he would not have gained a tenth of the sum named. Circumstances were undoubtedly favorable. There were then but few on the Pacific coast who could perform the simplest operations of engineering. A good share of city work was attainable, including the location of some of the minor streets and wharves; and there was suburban surveying and miscellaneous labor which, added to the rest, had the young graduate possessed the steadiness or continuity of purpose which not even the Institute could teach him, might easily have brought him fortune five times over. The force of the intended illustration is not nevertheless, weakened by this. I do not think there was any member of my class who, in the same circumstances, would not have done as well as I did; and am sure there were some who would have done better; so that I trust a substantial demonstration has been furnished of the practical advantages of the Institute and a right established to inscribe after it "*Quod erat demonstrandum.*"

San Francisco in those days, was a bewildering, not to say a distracting city. Its most striking characteristic was its strangeness. You felt that, to every one you met in the streets, it was as strange as to you. There was nothing like it, had never *been* anything like it. Each new comer might fitly say—

"Then felt I like some watcher of the skies
When a new planet swims into his ken;
Or like stout Cortez when with eagle eyes
He stared at the Pacific, and his men
Looked at each other with a mild surmise,
Silent upon a peak in Darien."

There was, to be sure, no silence and little contemplation in the golden city; but every one seemed in as chronic a state of amazement as the Spanish freebooter; and, as with him, there mingled with the astonishment the insatiate thirst for gain. In the rush for it almost everybody was engaged in some unwonted and anomalous employment. There were clergymen doing the work of porters, and a college professor was waiter in a restaurant. Ladies by birth and culture took in washing, and young gentlemen of social distinction at home, peddled cigars and matches. These constant incongruities gave rise to a perversive air of burlesque or masquerade, which heightened the novelty of the situation. Vast saloons, open to the street, in which public gambling was going on day and night, the perpetual music of bands, the brisk chatter of a dozen different tongues, the diverse costumes of as many nationalities, lent to the scene wonderful vivacity and bustle; while blending with dapper new comers by ocean steamers, people who often possessed nothing but the clothes they stood in, came figures fresh from the mines, red-shirted, booted and hirsute, heavy laden with bowie knives and revolvers, with fierce faces shaded by Spanish hats, fit in a word to be painted by Salvator or Murrillo, and frequently owning gold to the value of tens of thousands, "dug from the bowels of the harmless earth," on the Sacramento or Tuolumne.

Within six weeks of our arrival the "confusion" was rendered "worse confounded." There came what proved at once San Francisco's greatest curse and greatest blessing—a prodigious fire. A day or two before we got in, there had been another. Nearly the whole place had gone down before the fiery tempest, and as we sailed up the bay our eager eyes—weary with the one hundred and sixty-five days of our passage round Cape Horn—fell on hundreds of tents whereof the burned out people had improvised habitations.

Six weeks, however, had been ample time to build the prostrate city up again; and this time, albeit somewhat of the ginger-bread order, there was no little attempt at architectural display. The facades of some of the gambling hells and tippling shops were quite gorgeous—as became such profitable establishments—and there were other edifices of almost equal pomp and splendor. Nearly all the structures however were of the flimsiest description—lathe and plaster, chiefly, although there were here and there buildings of the native *adobe*, or sun-dried brick, and a very few eastern brick warehouses, in one of which I slept on the morning of the fire.

On the whole, the city looked quite imposing; and remembering its aspect on the day of our arrival, there was something marvellously suggestive of Aladdin's palace in the change. The swiftness, however, with which the new city went up, was nothing to the magical rapidity with which it came down. To many the catastrophe was ruin, and to me it seemed scarcely less, since it involved the loss of a transit. Not, I need scarcely say, the transit of Venus. To me, at that time, it was one of much more importance. It came from Troy, too, and was made by Phelps & Gurley. It was just daylight on a hot morning in June, and a dozen of us were sleeping on the third floor of a brick warehouse just erected by a relative of mine for business purposes. This gentleman—who accepted misfortune, either for himself or neighbor with a sportive equanimity wondrous to behold—happened to be first stirring. I think I was next awake, for I remember my attention being attracted to the fact that my relative was busy at a box of mine, and that in truth he was arraying himself in a suit of my garments which happened to strike his fancy. Presently he went to a window and looked out, and, after a moment's deliberate consideration, observed affably, that if we wanted to get out alive, we might wisely bestir ourselves to that end without delay; since the street above us was in a light blaze and the flames would be upon us in a very few moments. No second hint was required it may well be believed. Quicker time was probably made by that company in dressing than any member of it had ever made before. In the safe, below, there was a large sum—a great many thousands—in gold dust and coin, besides valuable papers. To get the safe out of the building was the most important, and to this task all present vigorously devoted themselves. It was done, but by the time the heavy iron box was rolled into the street, burning fragments were falling all over us, and the warehouse was one vast sheet of flame. Only then did some one remember that a huge pipe stood close by the door filled with canisters of gunpowder. This dangerous neighbor was canted over and rolled into the bay.

Probably among the many narrow escapes in the San Francisco fires, none was closer to the "dangerous edge of things" than this. Our lives were all safe, but my transit —the only one I thought then in California, was gone. No time was left to rescue it from the burning building, and so with many valued note books which had been kept at the Institute, a respectable engineering library, and many draughting and other instruments, it was crammed into the hungry maw of the conflagration. In fact we had much ado to save ourselves. To go toward the flames or inland was impossible. But to fly straight away from them, as we were situated, had become equally so. For the streets themselves being of plank were now all on fire in that direction, and the only safety seemed in the bay. Two paths of escape had been open to us when we fell to work on the safe; but now both were cut off.

A story of a certain colored preacher in Virginia is so apposite here, that its citation may be excused. "Dar am but de two roads," he declared, "one am de broad and narrer road dat leadeth to perdishun; de oder am de narrer and de broad road dat leadeth to eternal destruction." "What's dat?" cried one of his hearers apprehensively. "Say dat again!" "De one am de broad and narrer road dat leadeth to perdishun; de oder am de narrer and de broad road dat leadeth to destruction." "If dat am de case," said the other, "dis nigger takes to de woods." *These* niggers took to the wharves; and, not until the one on which we had sought refuge had been cut away from the town with axes, were we really in a position of comparative safety. Even then constant vigilance was needful to keep the showers of sparks and blazing fragments, borne on a heavy gale of wind, from igniting the wharf; and night was fast coming on while we were still huddled on the end of the structure, blackened and begrimed from head to foot, and our clothes literally in rags, while the storm of fire still swept furiously on, and heavy explosions told from time to time how the firemen were vainly struggling, by blowing up buildings, to arrest the progress of the flames.

California is the country of countries, according to my experience, for making the best of a bad situation. Perhaps no more wretched plight could be conceived than that of the refugees on the wharf. All their personal property destroyed, their clothes in tatters, without food or drink, without money, and with nothing within reach to buy, even had they the means to purchase, their situation was doleful indeed. Yet comfort was at hand even here; and I have never ceased to recur to that time, when things around me have looked unusually dark and forbidding. On the end of the wharf were several sheds or low shanties which were barred or padlocked. One of our party, for the purpose of washing, descended by a boat ladder to the sea, and thus discovered a way of getting into these buildings from below. This was soon availed of, and there were found a great stock of ready made garments, boots, hats, in short all things requisite for a gentleman's wardrobe.

In a trice, after preliminary ablutions in the bay, the whole company were freshly attired from head to foot, the owner, I need hardly say, being compensated on his own terms afterward. Subsequently, in an adjoining building, cans of preserved meat, and baskets of claret and champagne were discovered, so that the inner man of the refugees was soon as well cared for as the outer. I chanced on a snug bench and slept for two or three hours with infinite satisfaction. On awakening, I found the sky pitchy dark. A noise came from the hovel nearest the bay, which had a second story and a glazed window. A light streamed from within, and amid the dull roar of the conflagration were heard sounds of revelry. The city on one side was a seething mass of fire; the sea, on the other, like the sky was of inky blackness. I got three barrels, and putting a board across two of them, perched the third on the platform thus made, and climbing to the top, looked in at the window.

Five or six men were within playing cards, by the light of candles stuck in empty champagne bottles, and regaling themselves at intervals from full ones. Nero playing the fiddle while Rome burned was the only parallel to it. Probably, nearly every man there was "ruined" by the fire for the half-dozenth time. But what cared they? No Frenchman was ever more ready than those early Californians to say "*vive la bagatelle.*" What must be, must be, and there was no use in crying over spilt milk. In the morning the flourishing city was a mere blackened waste. It had melted, in the words of a hackneyed, but appropriate passage "into thin air," and with Prospero we might say:

"And like the baseless fabric of this vision
The cloud capped towers, the gorgeous palaces,
The solemn temples, the great globe itself,
Yea, all which it inherit, shall dissolve,
And, like this unsubstantial pageant faded
Leave not a wreck behind."

The difference being that, in six weeks more, San Francisco was built again. Moreover, there were a great many "wrecks" in the shape of innumerable packages of merchandise, which were scattered about over the burnt district, as if they had been tossed on a sable shore by an angry sea.

An auction sale had been advertised to take place in our building within three days of the fire. It might be supposed that this was of necessity postponed; but no one would suppose so who knew the resources and indefatigable pluck of those early pioneers. Within those three days a large warehouse, built of bamboo and China mattings on the site of the old one, "rose like an exhalation." Nor were there lacking materials for the sale. The other day a representative American, of the *nil admirari* kind, happened to be in London, and was taken to the British museum. The place is now a perfect wonder-house of ancient and modern scientific and artistic curiosities. "Well," said our countryman to his companions, scratching his head, "We've got all these things in the States; only they're kind o' *scattered round.*" And so it was with the articles for the auction sale; they were all there, only they were "kind o' scattered round." Unfortunately my transit was not of the number.

On our way to the golden city we had touched at the accepted home of "Robinson Crusoe" the island of Juan Fernandez, a most picturesque and romantic spot, as the few who have seen it can testify. Such a visit was not to be forgotten, but I was especially reminded of it, not long after, by an impressive incident. Perhaps there is no more thrilling moment in the history of *Robinson Crusoe* than that in which he discovers the famous foot-print on the shore. I am certain that there was no more thrilling moment in my experience in California than that in which Friday's foot-print was brought most vividly to my mind. It was soon after the fire, and I had gone down to the beautiful region of Santa Clara, which was then, comparatively speaking, uninhabited. I was running lines, to locate certain land claims, and, having been on a previous day in a woody valley, miles from any dwelling, had agreed to meet my party, (we having separated at night to go in different directions,) at a given hour on the same spot. I was earlier than my appointment, and reached a monument of stones set up at a station covered by the compass the day before. All of a sudden I saw a foot-print. It was larger than Friday's or that of any of his tribe. I soon saw many others, indicating that the owner of the feet which made them, had been curiously inspecting our engineer's work, perhaps with a view of taking a hand in it. It cost not much reflection to persuade me that I was on the track of a huge grizzly bear, or that the straight line which represents the shortest distance from one point to another would be an excellent geometrical figure for me forthwith to describe in the expected direction of my companions. This might prove worse than the fire, since, in case of an unpleasant collision there would be no friendly wharf to fall back upon, or means of making secure the retreat. I suppose that by this time Santa Clara is as free from bears as Central Park, or rather more so; but they were then among the most serious dangers of the wayfarer. The brute who visited our station was said to have killed and maimed several men, soon after, before he was despatched. The neighborhood was also quite well provided with wild cats, and *coyotes*, the wolves of the plains, whose music lent a lively interest to one's nightly slumbers among the otherwise silent redwoods. On the whole, what with the conflagrations of the town and the wild beasts of the plains, life in California in those days did not lack the excitement of danger.

Nor were these the only sources of peril. The earlier land-surveyors had to encounter others that were unpleasantly frequent. The notions of bounds and metes entertained by the native or Mexican population at that time were singularly vague; while their views as to the treatment of persons holding different or opposing ideas on such subjects to their own, were on the other hand remarkably definite and unanimous. As a rule too, land claims overlapped each other in every direction, so that you could hardly get on a piece of ground anywhere but that there were several claimants to it. Hence the appearance in those regions of a surveyor's party with their instruments was apt to be as enlivening to the inhabitants as a red rag to a bull; and the additional interest, created by the proceedings of a generous supply of brigands, who used to plunder the expresses and stages, as well as single passengers, was hardly needed to give zest to a professional wanderer's every day life. Perhaps considering all these things, including grizzlies, it was not surprising that land surveyors should have been so proverbially scarce in the early times in California. Demand produces supply, and since then, our modern El Dorado has been quite as richly endowed with men of that calling, as other and older parts of the country.

I have glanced at these little episodes of personal adventure which I must not weary you by extending, not of course, because of their value or intrinsic importance, but only as exemplifying the opening of one among many careers which have begun at Troy, and in the Polytechnic Institute, and as affirming cordial and grateful testimony to the benefit derived from teachings here received. I could tell truly of some subsequent failures, and they might not be without their lesson. John Hunter used to say that the art of surgery would not advance until professional men had the courage to publish their failures as well as their successes; James Watt insisted that the thing most wanted in mechanical engineering was a history of failures; and Humphrey Davy declared that the most important of his discoveries had been suggested to him by his failures. However this may be, I can bear witness that while my humble successes were so largely due to the Institute, for my failures she has been in no sense responsible. In undertaking various pursuits, in various times and places, I can conscientiously say, I have always felt stronger and better for such exact science and such mental discipline as were here acquired and passed through; and, without entering upon the vexed question of the comparative advantages of classical and scientific culture, I may venture to assert that in a country like this, and for the present at least, if the thorough acquisition of both be out of the question, the master of science alone is likely to bear the palm of success from the mere proficient in classics. For the scientific work to be done in this western hemisphere is practically endless, and it is not California alone that should be an El Dorado for the American engineer, and geologist and chemist. Here is no narrow field for their energies, no limited arena for their discoveries and achievements. The whole boundless continent is theirs, and it is a peculiar glory and honor to this lovely city of Troy that she possesses a fountain head—so to say—of such knowledge and power, a school of such exceptional solidity, antiquity, and thoroughness, which sends forth its young athletes to build cities, to hew down forests, to level mountains, and to pluck forth countless riches from the bosom of the earth, to the profit and progress of our whole common country. Troy may not be a capital, indeed, but we may say to her, as the witch said to Banquo, "Thou shalt get kings, though thou be none." Though Romulus, the founder of Rome, was the son of Mars, he was likewise the offspring of Ilia. The Trojan priestess bore the child who reared the Imperial city, that "sat on the seven hills, and from her throne of beauty ruled the world." And surely it is better than imperial laurels to be the seat of a noble and constantly augmenting knowledge; the centre where come, in ever increasing numbers, young experts, who, as it is attested by the Polytechnic diploma, are rendered "competent to perform duties," and "to enter upon employments which will aid farmers, mechanics and manufacturers, in the application of science to their respective vocations, and which will contribute to the dissemination of useful knowledge among the industrious part of the rising generation."

The music of the evening was by Doring's band.

The meeting was adjourned about ten o'clock to accept the invitation referred to by President Forsyth in his opening address.

RECEPTION

BY

HON. WILLIAM KEMP.

MAYOR OF TROY.

The guests began to arrive soon after ten o'clock, and notwithstanding a heavy shower which prevailed at the time, soon formed a large assemblage. Still the Mayor's hospitality had anticipated and would gladly have provided for even a larger number.

Doring's band occupied the Library on the second floor, and discoursed some of their sweetest music, quite in keeping with the happy and fraternal feelings evident among all present.

The table was literally loaded with tempting delicacies and sweetmeats. There were numerous exquisite floral designs. A Swiss cottage made of straw was placed at each end of the table, profusely ornamented with choice fragrant flowers. In the centre of the table a miniature fountain sent forth a column of perfume, filling the room with its delightful odor. The following students assisted the sons of the Mayor as ushers: Messrs. W. P. Mason, J. L. Breese, E. A. Burdett, and C. E. Griffith.

It was already midnight before the company dispersed, with many thanks for the entertainment and pleasure of the evening, which will long be remembered in connection with the semi-centennial of 1874.

WEDNESDAY, JUNE 17.

The Alumni re-assembled in Institute Hall at ten o'clock, Vice-President Boller in the Chair. Mr. Wallace, from the committee to nominate officers for the ensuing three years, reported the following:

President.—William Gurley.

Vice-Presidents.—W. W. Walker, Frederic Grinnell, John D. Van Buren.

Secretary.—H. B. Nason.

Treasurer.—David M. Greene.

Directors.—E. Thompson Gale, Francis Collingwood, Joseph E. Platt, W. H. Doughty, R. B. C. Bement.

The nominations being approved, the above list of officers was unanimously elected.

A dispatch from Prof. James Hall was read, stating that owing to illness, he would not be able to be present and address the meeting as expected.

Hon. William Gurley, President elect, then took the Chair, thanking the association for the honor conferred upon him. Prof. Nason alluded briefly to his re-election, and wished to be allowed to resign, inasmuch as according to the constitution he could not hold the office. On motion of Hon. John H. White, the constitution was suspended, and the election thereby ratified. A. P. Boller, Esq., offered the following resolution which was unanimously adopted:

" That the thanks of the Alumni Association be tendered to Prof. H. B. Nason, Secretary, for his unwearied endeavors in organizing and carrying forward the programme of this, the semi-centennial anniversary of the Institute's life, and for watching so carefully over the comforts and pleasures of the members of this association and other visitors."

Dr. Ambler proposed a vote of thanks to Hon. A. R. Fox, for his efforts in securing the erection of the Eaton monument.

Mr. Wallace moved to include in the vote of thanks the other members of the committee, and Prof. Nason, at whose suggestion the Eaton memorial window was placed, and by whom it was also designed. Both motions were unanimously carried.

Dr. J. G. Ambler, class of 1833, presented the following resolutions, which were unanimously adopted :

Whereas, An all wise Providence has seen fit since our last meeting, to remove from this earth two of the graduates of this Institution ; and, whereas it is meet and proper that a record of such fact be made on our minutes ; therefore

Resolved, That a committee of three be appointed to draft, place on record, and send to the family of deceased, suitable resolutions expressive of our feelings on the death of Amos Westcott, M. D., of Syracuse, N. Y., a graduate of class of 1835.

Be it also *Resolved*, that a committee of three be appointed by the Chair to draft, place on record, and send to the family of deceased resolutions expressive of our feelings on the death of Prof. Anthony, of Albany, a graduate of 1840.

The following committees were appointed :

On the death of Prof. Anthony—Prof. H. B. Nason, John H. White, and A. M. Lesley.

On the death of Dr. Westcott—Dr. J. G. Ambler, Dr. S. E. Arms, and Hon. A. R. Fox.

A. M. Lesley, of New York, then spoke briefly of the time he was a pupil of Prof. Anthony, and paid a very handsome tribute to his distinguished qualifications as a teacher.

Prof. Nason read an autobiographical sketch of Prof. Anthony's life, which was prepared for the Institute records two years since.

Hon. Norman Stratton, of the Brooklyn navy yard was introduced, and addressed the alumni in regard to the history and influence of the Institute.

ADDRESS BY HON. NORMAN STRATTON,

CLASS OF 1838.

The lateness of the hour admonishes me that I must very much abridge the remarks I had intended to submit to you on this very interesting occasion, and therefore, without prelude or preface, I will at once enter upon the task assigned me.

Mr. President and Gentlemen :

The usefulness and value of an institution of learning, after having passed through a half century of existence, must be judged by a severer test than mere advertised professions. Its tenure for the future will, in a great measure, depend upon what it has already accomplished. If it has left the mark of its influence upon every decade through which it has passed ; if mankind have progressed towards a higher life by means of its teachings—if that which before was occult and useless has been brought to light, vitalized and utilized for the good of the race through its instrumentality, then it has truly demonstrated its right not only to a new lease of life, but to the earnest support of every friend of development and progress. That this institution meets and successfully answers to all such tests, severe as they are, is abundantly proven by the history of its graduates and the direct impress of their acquirements on the achievements of the past and the present.

In all the departments of the world's progress calculated by their practical utility to develop material prosperity by opening up new avenues to enterprise, and in determining new combinations of agencies to produce results before unknown, this institution has a record of which it may be justly proud. Its graduates are everywhere and always active. They are in the army and in the navy—in universities and colleges—in the halls of our legislatures, both State and National—in the laboratories of the analytical chemist—in the pulpit, in the law and in medicine—in agriculture, giving to it an elevation and a charm of intelligence which the merely plodding practical farmer never knew—in the varied and ever-varying manufacturing and mechanic arts—in intricate and careful surveys, geographical and topographical,—and in the construction of our railroads, canals and other works. Indeed so varied and polytechnic are their acquirements, that it would be difficult to find any field of practical usefulness or human enterprise where they are not found conspicuous as workers. Decided in their convictions, because thorough and practical in their deductions, they win their way to the confidence and esteem of all with whom they come in contact.

It was a graduate of this Institute who laid the first T or heavy rail, on any railroad in this State. It was a graduate of this Institute who superintended the construction of the first long, or eight wheels car which ever ran in this State. It was a graduate of this Institute who demonstrated by survey that there was no necessity for the cumbersome and tedious inclined plane on the Albany railroad, at Schenectady, and who ran a line of levels within sight of that inclined plane, establishing a grade of about fifty feet to the mile, and on which line the present track, easily traversed by an ordinary locomotive, is located. All the vast improvements in the means of intercommunication in this country with their manifold blessings and benefits to all, have been prosecuted, to a greater or less extent by our graduates. To the practical minds of our graduates we are indebted for improvements in labor-saving machinery and in instruments and apparatus of various kinds. When I entered the profession, very few of the instruments then in use were manufactured in our country, and those which were, were not considered as accurate and reliable as those imported. Our theodolites, transits, levels and drawing instruments, were all from England. Since then, intelligence, skill and enterprise have worked a complete revolution. Our home productions of these instruments have not only been augmented, but have been so improved and perfected that they excel, in finish and accuracy, those of foreign manufacture, once considered indispensable. And while I would not be invidious in naming any one particularly, to the disparagement of others, I cannot refrain from saying that this country is indebted to a graduate of this Institute, an honored citizen of this city, my valued friend, one who from boyhood has possessed a character without guile, for the establishment in this city of an extensive manufactory for the construction of implements for engineering, mathematical and philosophical purposes, which is not only a credit to this city, but to our state and nation.

All these results are natural, and not arbitrary, or by chance. These practical developments have grown out of the methods of training at this Institute. The carefully demonstrated analysis of every subject,—the knowledge of principles and their practical applications, rather than an artificial knowledge of a variety of *things*—even the habits of thought receiving an invaluable training,—these are the methods which have proved so successful in developing not only mind but character, giving to science some of its brightest ornaments, and to the nation many useful and valued citizens. And now a question very naturally interposes. If these methods are so correct and beneficial, and the results of the polytechnic plan so productive of good, why should not the number of such schools be increased all over our land; and why should its superior advantages and benefits be exclusively for one sex? The fact that many of our colleges have added to their ordinary course of instruction some of the branches of the course pursued at this Institute, is proof of the wants of the people in this respect, and shows a careful foresight on the part of such colleges, to endeavor to provide for and satisfy such wants. As to the other question, it is enough to say that the growing grace and justice of men will yet cause old prejudices, chronic and stubborn as they have been, to give way, and the time is not far distant when every school, every profession, every enterprise, will have all gates and bars removed, and access thereto be open to all, without restriction to sex. I know of no harm that would come to this Institute by admitting ladies as students. I studied botany at this Institute under the teachings of a lady professor. I refer to Miss Johnson, whose love of that science enabled her to clothe her teachings with a beauty of expression which the lapse of time has been unable to efface.

I desire to call your attention to another favorable circumstance in the history of this school. I allude to the steady progress made from its small beginnings. Very few institutions of fifty years' standing but what have had periods of declension and retrogression. With us there has been steady progress from the first. No hesitation, no faltering, no backward step. There is no time in its history when it can be said it was better five years before, but on the contrary, every five years has added to its efficiency and value. I cannot but contrast its present condition with what it was when I graduated; and more especially as regards your laboratory. I readily bring to mind our old, roughly-made wooden one, with its cheap and rude appliances, standing in Walnut Grove, on the bank of a ravine, the site of which is now occupied by the Church of the Holy Cross. You now have a laboratory of which you may justly be proud. I have never seen one more complete in all its arrangements and appliances. The contrast is equally striking in all the other departments; so that now this Institute occupies a commanding position among the institutions of learning in this country. Our graduates now excel in useful knowledge those of any college on the continent, and I might add that this knowledge is obtained at a less cost here than elsewhere, while the advantages of that knowledge, in its applications to the future of the graduate, cannot be made a subject of comparison with any school in this country. It requires a high standard of acquirements in order to gain a diploma here, and this is becoming so well-known that a diploma of this Institute is taken as conclusive evidence of the qualifications of its owner. I trust that no temptation will ever induce any lowering of the present standard.

The success of this Institute, and other institutions of learning in our country, is in my judgment solving a very important problem in relation to the schools of the general Government, supported wholly from the public treasury. The public mind is being already awakened to this subject. Nearly half a million of dollars is annually spent in their support, and an estimate shows that each graduated cadet costs the Government $15,000 for his education.

It is contended that these Government schools are wrong upon principle. It is claimed that the Government has no right to take the money of the people for the purpose of educating a select class of favored persons. Ours is a government of the people, and they should be able to provide schools for teaching every branch of knowledge needed for any department of the public service, be it army or navy, or what not.

Let the Government establish whatever qualifications it pleases, even more rigid and exacting than any now required for admission into its service, and the enterprise of our people will be equal to the emergency. Schools and departments of schools, will be started to teach the things the Government will require in order to pass the necessary examination for admission into the service; and the supply will be ample in proper men fully qualified, by their knowledge, theoretical and practical, in nautical science and the manual of arms, and this supply will be furnished without one dollar of expenditure of the public money, and better than the Government could produce at any cost. This is no partisan question. It is a question of enlightened policy, whether vast sums of the public money should be expended every year for the benefit of the favored few, without an adequate return therefor, when the objects of these schools can be accomplished in a better way, and without any cost whatever to the Government.

So much for the past and the present. The inquiry now

naturally forces itself upon us, "What of our future, and the future of this Institute?" Is that law of growth and progress, which has been so faithfully obeyed in the past, to be its leaven and its lever of power, or is that other law of deterioration and decay to govern its future? The world has made rapid strides in knowledge during the past fifty years, equal to any five hundred years of its previous history. In everything, development has followed development, in such rapid succession, while science has been unfolding new pages of her mysterious books, and throwing the light of intelligence on what was before obscure and uncertain. The heretofore inscrutable history of our race is being written in the light of scientific discoveries, not in conflict, as I believe, with the true interpretation and meaning of the Mosaic record, but in loving harmony therewith. These and kindred discoveries of science are yet to have a salutary influence upon the progress of humanity. The pernicious teachings of the past as to the utter worthlessness, vileness and depravity of man, is passing away, and as science unfolds to us the loving care of the great producing Cause, which has watched the progress of the race from its almost useless infancy to a vigorous and useful manhood, we cannot fail to feel that we have a destiny grand and glorious beyond anything we are now able to appreciate. But whatever may have been the origin of the race, whether it descended from a single pair, pure and happy in the innocence of an absence of knowledge of both good and evil, or whether it gradually evolved and developed from something lower to something higher, till through ages of intellectual chaos and twilight it at last, by almost imperceptible stages of advancement, came gradually into a clearer light,—are questions which may be named but not discussed at this time. For the present we may consider them as questions the exact solution of which is yet darkened by the clouds of mystery. But certain it is, that the race has made continual advancement from the earliest of its historical periods to the present hour; so that progress seems to be its normal condition and the most important factor of its life. What, therefore, has been so true of the past will be equally true of the future, except that each generation will use the discoveries and improvements of its predecessors as firm foundations on which to build better and more advantageously. What the discoveries and improvements of the next five decades will be, we may conjecture, but that is all.

Our fathers fifty years ago, were peering into the future, and doubtless desired to know something of its vast storehouse and its fast unfolding mysteries. If then some supernal being had told them of what the uses of steam would accomplish within the next fifty years—of the construction of roads of iron all over the country, reaching even from the Atlantic to the Pacific ocean—with what speed and luxurious comfort we could go from place to place, that even the darkness of the night would be no obstruction to this rapid transit—had told of the great improvements in the implements of agriculture and the contrivances by which man would be relieved from heavy burdens, so that science and skill would call to the multitudes of men like the Great Master of old, to leave off the heavy burdens which ignorance had imposed, and take upon them a burden that was easy.

If they had been told how light, that beautifully mysterious modification of the vital fluid, would be used in making accurate likenesses, and that the sun was to become not alone the light of the universe, but the great and accurate limner of the world.

If they had been told, of what is now so plain to us, how that destructive electricity should become a tamed agent for the transmission of messages hundreds of miles in an instant of time, and how the Atlantic ocean would be no barrier to it, but that hundreds of words should pass to and fro every hour along its uneven bed, permitting constant communications with all parts of the civilized world.

If they had been told of the startling discoveries in chemical science, and especially that a powerful anodyne would be discovered and perfected, so that it would be possible from thenceforth for the most painful operations in surgery to be performed without giving the slightest pain to the patient, who, meanwhile the operation, would be quietly reposing as in a natural slumber, thus verifying the words of the Hebrew king, "He giveth his beloved sleep." In short, if they had then been told of all the vast and mighty progressions that have taken place during the past fifty years, changing as they have, the very habits of thought of the people, and opening up channels of business enterprise before unknown, they could not have appreciated nor understood them. He who should have given such information would have been looked upon as a dreamer—a wild enthusiast, or something less complimentary.

Apply all this to our case, standing as we do to-day, looking back in contemplation and wonder of this great and glorious past, we turn our eyes to the future, and almost tremblingly ask, "What of the next fifty years?" Is there still room for other improvements as great in their changes and results as those in the past? No supernal one gives any answer to our earnest inquiries, and we are left to the dim light of analogy. We can only reason from the past. Neither the world nor the people in it will stand still. Growth and progress will be the impelling law of the future as it has been in the past. Every new development in science or art will prove accelerating forces for other and still higher developments in the same and other directions. Applications of principles to new uses and purposes will doubtless be of constant occurrence—all steadily tending, as the great first cause intended, in one direction—the beautifying of the world around us, the disenthrallment of the race from ignorance, superstition and error, and its elevation in intelligence, usefulness and happiness.

The discoveries of the past and the attainments of the present are great; the developments and achievements of the future will be glorious, far more so than we are now able to appreciate or understand, for certain it is, and you can depend upon it, that the prophetic words of the Seer of Israel are emphatically true, for, "KNOWLEDGE SHALL BE INCREASED."

Dr. Richards, a pupil of Prof. Eaton fifty-three years ago, moved a vote of thanks to Mr. Stratton for his address, which was unanimously passed.

Clark Fisher, Chief Engineer in the United States navy, made some remarks in regard the usefulness and continuance of the naval school at Annapolis, and military school at West Point, which were seconded by President Gurley.

A letter from Hon. Geo. M. Tibbits, was then read by the Secretary, expressing thanks for the invitation to be present at the various exercises of the week, and also the deep interest he has always felt in the Institution.

Professor Nason then spoke concerning the large number of students who distinguished themselves in the late war, and gave short sketches of the life and character of those for whom memorial windows have been recently placed in the library room of the Institute.

MAJOR JAMES CROMWELL, C. E.

" The good die young, but they whose hearts
Are dry as summer's dust, burn in their sockets."

James Cromwell was born at Cornwall, N. Y., January 4th, 1840. He was of Quaker parentage, and remained himself a member of that society until he joined the army. Some men are not made of common clay; and whatever may be their rank in a social point of view, God writes *noble men* on their brows, and all men pay involuntary respect. This was especially true of James Cromwell.

He entered the Institute in May, 1858, and graduated June 3rd, 1861, in advance of his class, in order to enter the service of the country he loved so dearly, that glorious cause for which he ultimately sacrificed his life. We, who knew and loved him are able to contemplate his student life with unalloyed satisfaction. Not only did he stand high in the prescribed studies of the Institute course, but those same qualities which won him respect and esteem amid the noise and bloodshed of war, made him first in the affection of his fellows in the peaceful pursuits of science. He was elected to the most popular office among the students, which he retained as long as he remained in Troy. Better than all, his character stands out prominent in its moral purity, unstained by any of those youthful excesses which are too often the accompaniments of college life. He was a gentleman in the truest, noblest acceptation of the word.

The firing on Fort Sumter aroused in James Cromwell, all the indignation natural to a heart so full of truthfulness and patriotism. He would, by entering the army, oppose the teachings of that religion under whose influence he had been educated. Nothing bade him go but the call of duty; to him that call was more than all else. "Bid me stay," he told his friends, " and there is an end of the matter, but remember, that while I obey you I will be neglecting a solemn call from God and my country, a course which would sadly affect all my after life." One answer could come to such an appeal, and one only; "Go, and God bless you." He did go; and of all our noble martyrs that have been called from "works to rewards," none went with more Christian purpose or with braver heart than James Cromwell.

He was engaged in various skirmishes, among others at Manassas Gap, November 6th, 1862, and in the more important conflicts at Fredericksburg, Va., December 14th, and 15th, 1862, at Chancellorville, Va., May 2nd, 3rd, and 4th, 1863, at Beverly Ford, Va., June 9th, 1863, and at the decisive battle of Gettysburgh, July 2nd, 1863, in which he lost his life, at the early age of twenty-three. Throughout his career as a soldier his courage was conspicuous even in that army of brave men, who purchased peace for us at such a costly price. James Cromwell seemed fully to illustrate in his brief life the familiar lines—

> "Where duty calls or danger
> Be never wanting there."

Thus responding to the call of duty, and liberty among the first, he was true to their promptings to the last; and at the age of twenty-three he had attained a position commanding respect of all. How grandly his tall figure looms up amid the smoke and blood of the battle! Patiently and heroically he had borne the heat and burden of the fight with his men—stubbornly they had held their ground amid iron storm, till the enemy wavered and were giving way—then riding forward, he turned to his men with a glad smile, and called upon them to advance, shouting Victory! At that moment the fatal shot struck him, but "he came a conqueror to his rest." Though he then departed, the glad smile still remained upon his features—victory remained; and his noble memory remains, and will ever be one of the most cherished traditions of his alma mater. In our memories he will ever be enshrined, as he last stood on that great decisive battle field of the century—a smile upon his face, his sword waving high, and shouting *Victory!*

COL. CHARLES OSBORN GRAY.

Immediately after the retreat of General Foster's forces to Newbern, it was announced through the journals of the day that one who had but recently left us had fallen in the defence of his country.

Charles Osborn Gray entered the Institute in the fall or winter of 1857, and remained until the summer of 1861, when, we believe, he was called home on account of sickness in his father's family. While here he enjoyed the confidence of his teachers and fellow students, and was generally admired for his manly conduct by all who came in contact with him. Many of his former associates were deeply affected when they heard he had fallen, and so nobly too, at the head of his regiment cheering on his men, wounded and dying in the arms of his officers, after having planted the regimental colors so noble and valiently on the Kinston bridge.

It will be remembered that his remains passed through this city on their way to their last resting place, in a neat little cemetery planned and laid out by his own hands,—and now his battered and well worn sword, the tattered and mutilated flag of his regiment, pierced by many bullets, borne so nobly through the strife of many battles are all that are left to remind us of his heroic demeanor in the cause of his country, and that he served it faithfully, by laying down his life in its cause.

Charles Osborn Gray, was born at Warrensburgh in this State, on the 24th of March, 1839, and was killed on the 14th of December, 1862, being in the 24th year of his age.

His regiment, the 96th N. Y. V., was organized at Plattsburgh, N. Y., and was mustered into the United States service February 20th, 1862, at which time he received the commission of Lieutenant Colonel, and command as Colonel, October 13th, 1862.

The following list of his engagements is inscribed upon the window: Yorktown, Williamsburgh, Fair Oaks, Seven Days' Battle, Blackwater, and Kinston.

LIEUT. OTIS FISHER.

Otis Fisher was born at Newport, Me., December 5th, 1840, but at the time of entering the Institute, was a resident of Trenton, N. J. He came to the Institute in the Fall of 1859, and remained until after the commencement of the war, in 1861. The first gun of Sumter set fire to his patriotism, and the desire to serve his country grew stronger as every appeal for soldiers came from our Capitol. He talked, dreamed, thought of nothing but the army until he received his commission. A letter written home, making known his desire, brought his father to Troy. Never can I forget the morning they came together to my room. The aged father, quite infirm, his head bowed, and his face speaking louder than his words the deep sadness of his heart, told me that, while one son was in the navy, it seemed too much to give another for the army. After stating all the case, he raised his eyes, full of anguish, and said, "Oh! can you not, by the affection he bears for you as well as for me, influence him to remain at home, at least until the need of men is greater than now?" And then came the answer that neither of us could well meet: "When will the need be greater than now, and if it is the duty of any one to go now, why is it not mine? Father I *must* go."

He soon after sought an appointment in the regular army, and by the influence of Hon. John C. Ten Eyck, U. S. Senator, received a commission as lieutenant in the Eighth U. S. Infantry. He was for a time on duty at Fort Columbus in New York harbor, and recruiting at Scranton, Pa. His regiment being ordered to Virginia, he joined them. Being desirous of more active service, he sought and obtained a staff appointment.

About the time of the second battle of Manassas, he was taken prisoner by accident. Being sent with an order, and returning to the position of his brigade, he found himself surrounded by rebel forces, who captured him and took him to Richmond, where he was confined for several months in Libby Prison. Upon his release he returned home, with very evident appearance of privation and suffering from his treatment in captivity. When he had sufficiently recovered he joined his regiment in Virginia, and was afterward put upon the sraff of Gen. Wilcox. At the battle of Gettysburg, Gen. Archer's brigade was captured by our army, and the Eighth U. S. Infantry were detailed as a guard of prisoners. Gen. Archer had captured Lieut. Fisher, and his regiment were much inclined to return in kind the severe treatment their beloved young lieutenant had received from his troops.

In the advance of Gen. Grant upon Richmond, he was in all the battles, and constantly under fire, commanding the praise of his superiors and the respect of the whole corps with which he was connected, by his gallantry. He received a slight wound, which did not disable him, and continued on duty.

At the explosion of the mine before Petersburg, among other dangerous duties, he carried an order from the Fifth to the Ninth corps, crossing the space between them, which was swept by the artillery and musketry of both sides, and narrowly escaped with his life, a bullet passing through his hat. When the last advance was made, on Friday, September 30th, below Petersburg, he volunteered to take command of a battalion of the Fourteenth New York Heavy Artillery, under Major Randall, and was wounded in the charge of the regiment, but kept command until they came out of action. For this gallant act he received the praise of all who witnessed his bravery, and the warmly expressed admiration of the soldiers he had led. The wound was in the head, and although serious, it was hoped he would recover; but on the evening of October 3d he died in hospital, and his body was forwarded to his home in Trenton.

His disposition was kind and affectionate; his manner modest and unassuming; his will firm and courageous. With such qualities, it was the fond anticipation of his many friends that he would attain the highest military honors. He has, however, fallen young, but not without leaving his record as a true soldier and patriot. Such is the brief sketch of his military life.

LIEUT. HENRY W. MERIAN, C. E.

Henry W. Merian was born in Brooklyn, N. Y., December 31, 1839. He entered the Rensselaer Polytechnic Institute in 1856, and graduated in 1858. On returning to Brooklyn he entered the engineer department of the Ridgewood Water Works, in Brooklyn, and was actively engaged in surveying, &c., until the beginning of the civil war, when he joined a New York volunteer regiment for three month's service on the upper Potomac.

After his return he was admitted to the U. S. Navy, engineer's department, in 1862, and after some service in the Brooklyn Navy Yard, was appointed Third Assistant Engineer to the U. S. Monitor Weehawken, and left in her for Port Royal, S. C., on the 19th January, 1863; thence for Warsaw Sound, Ga., where, on the 17th of June, 1863, the Weehawken had the good fortune, single-handed, to capture the rebel ram Atlanta. In July, 1863, she proceeded to Charleston harbor, and for four months was actively employed in shelling Fort Sumter, Fort Moultrie, &c. On the 6th of December, 1863, while at anchor in the bay, she foundered, and three of her engineers then on duty in the engine room, lost their lives, one of whom was Henry W. Merian. He died in the service of his country, at the age of 23 years and 11 months, universally regretted by all who knew him. In 1872, some of the remains of the lost ones on board the Weehawken were recovered, brought by order of the Navy Department to the Brooklyn Navy Yard, and there committed to earth with military honors.

MAJOR ALBERT METCALF HARPER, C. E.

Albert Metcalf Harper, born at Pittsburgh, Pa., April 22d, 1843, was the second son of John Harper and Lydia Electra Metcalf, of Pittsburgh. He was an under-graduate of the Rensselaer Polytechnic Institute, in 1861-2. He was appointed by the Governor the first Adjutant of the

139th Regiment of Pennsylvania Volunteers, August 25th, 1862. He was severely wounded in the battle of the Wilderness, May 5th, 1864. He was appointed by the President as Assistant Adjutant General of Volunteers, with the rank of Captain, by and with the advice and consent of the Senate, August 17, 1864. The President conferred on him the rank of Major by brevet, "for faithful and meritorious services," May 21, 1865.

In the month of September, 1865, he recommenced his scientific studies at the Institute, where he graduated with the degree of Civil Engineer, July 2, 1867. Subsequently, he devoted nearly a year to the faithful study of analytical chemistry. Afterward he assumed the management of a large oil refinery. In the month of October, 1869, he entered into mercantile business, as a partner in the firm of Dilworth, Harper & Co. He was unmarried. After an illness of four weeks, he died of typhoid fever, at the residence of his parents, on the evening of December 10, 1871.

Duty we know was the rule and law of his youth and manhood. What was right, what was his duty, *that* he would do. No engagement or allurement drew him aside from a recognized obligation. No companionship would succeed in persuading him to break a rule of good morals and correct life.

It is but a little while ago that our country was beginning its agony of contest for its very existence. May days so dark and perilous never come to her, nor to any of us, for her sake, again. Then, in those days, this brave boy was at his college of science. He felt the call of duty and wrote home begging permission to do that duty. He alone of his home circle had the years and physical vigor for the toil of war. He must represent his home in the ranks which were filled with so many prime youths from all our homes, rich and poor. It was not a romance, nor wild impulse; it was duty calmly measured that brought the boy home to become a soldier. The same principle carried him through three years of his service. No toil, nor peril, nor responsibility was avoided. Wounds, and their danger and suffering, were his lot; but with the first return of strength the soldier went back to his post. He was able, discreet and brave—so all testify. But so, thank God, were many others too. He was throughout, temperate, virtuous, pure, unswayed by any ill examples into any of the gross vices which too often stain the soldier's life. Would that this glory were less rare than it is. Thank God, we will to-day, that He gave this noble principle and record to this short life. Then the war over, at twenty-two years of age, the manly youth, with a wisdom not often seen in such cases, went back to his school and resumed and completed his preparation there for his maturer life. That done, he moved forward quietly and resolutely into the projects of active business. In these we all know how great and ceaseless was his energy, and how upright and courteous his acts and words were, in the market, as well as in the social circle. He has left a name and record among us, as all testify, without a blot.

JAMES R. PERCY, C. E.

Since the meeting of the Alumni, another window has been ordered for the Library, by the class of 1859, for their classmate, James R. Percy, of Fowler's Mills, Ohio, late Captain U. S. Engineers (Volunteers).

PROF. AMOS EATON.

The window for Prof. Amos Eaton is placed in the Institute Hall, in the centre of the west end of the room, and was presented by his former pupils and other members of the Alumni. It is fifteen feet in length, and five feet in breadth. In the centre is a life-size portrait, accurately copied from the original painted a short time before the death of Prof. Eaton, by our townsman and eminent artist, A. B. Moore, Esq.

Beneath the portrait is inscribed "The Republican Philosopher," which the late Mrs. Emma Willard once said would be the most appropriate inscription for his tomb. Near the top in a circle are represented the two species of plants named in honor of Professor Eaton, by Professor Gray, the Eatonia obtusata, and Pennsylvanica.

Near the bottom in a circle are represented a transit, chain and geological hammer, while at the bottom is the inscription: "Amos Eaton, born at Chatham, N. Y., May 17th, 1776; died at Troy, N. Y., May 6th, 1842. Senior Professor in this Institute from 1824 to 1842."

PROF. JOHN WRIGHT.

A window has been presented by Mrs. James Gardner, of Lansingburgh, to be placed in the east end of the hall, in memory of her brother, John Wright, M. D. Born in Troy, N. Y., February 2d, 1811; professor of botany and zoology in the Institute from 1838 to 1845. He died at Aiken, S. C., April 11, 1846.

PROF. WILLIAM ELDERHORST.

The window for Prof. William Elderhorst, presented by the alumni and friends at the semi-centennial meeting, is to be placed in the east end of the hall, and bears the following inscription: "William Elderhorst, M. D., born in Celle, Germany, Sept. 30th, 1828. Prof. of chemistry in the R. P. I. from 1855 to 1861. Died in Maracaibo, Brazil, July 28, 1861.

At two o'clock the meeting adjourned, and the alumni and former students of the Institute proceeded to Harmony Hall, where a dinner had been prepared for them and quite a large number of invited guests. The alumni were seated in the order of their classes, the president, Hon. William Gurley, presiding.

The Divine blessing was invoked by Rev. Charles E. Robinson, D. D., of Troy.

The dinner was prepared by the popular caterer, Charles F. Lucas, of Troy. After the dinner, which occupied about two hours, was finished, the president made a short speech, and called upon Dr. J. G. Ambler, of New York, class of '33, for a poem.

The Doctor disclaimed and took exception to the name of poem which had been applied to his production, for he regarded it little more than a rhyme intended as a reply to the toast of his class. The verses were received by the old graduates with a hearty relish, taking their memories back to the days of actual student life.

THE CLASS OF THIRTY-THREE.

Eighteen hundred and thirty-three !
That is the date that rouses me !
Were I but young as I was then,
How it would drive my muse's pen !
But now I must do the best I can,
For now, as you see, I'm an *aged man !*
And I respond in this humble verse,
Because in prose I might do it worse.

I was one of a class of eight,
All ambitious of something great ;
But forty years—what a time to wait !
We were but few, but some had brains,
And made the most of their mental gains ;
And that, perhaps, is the reason why
We are all alive and all so spry,
And laugh at life as the years fly by !

If, in the presidential chair,
We have not governed the nation there
And borne the burthen of public care,
We have not had the time to spare !

Or if, within some prison walls,
We have not heard our country's calls,

And done the State some service there,—
Excuse us,—we have been elsewhere !

Though virtue we have always prized,
As saints we are not canonized ;
Nor have we yet aspired so high
As by the gallows rope to die.
Not one a traitor, thief nor rogue,
(Just now so very much in vogue,)
Yet these distinctions all may win,
By patient, persevering sin !

Divinity, Medicine and Law
Have not disdained from us to draw
Recruits, their noble ranks to grace,
Each filling still an honored place ;
While, too, some hold distinguished part
In science and the works of art.

In truth, 'twere easy to be shown,
If some of us are still unknown,
Unmentioned by the "trump of fame,"
Our tutors are the men to blame !
For they instilled such *modest* ways,
Such carelessness of noisy praise,
That we have never cast our eyes
Beyond contentment's peaceful skies
To grasp such a windy prize !

No ; we were philosophic then,
And ruled ourselves like prudent men !
Our porridge then with thanks we took,
And asked no favors of a cook.
The limpid spring and simple bread,
Those luxuries before us spread,
No gout nor surfeiting to dread,
Left clear and cool the student's head !

How strange the forms of human bliss !
What contrast now, that scene and this !
Then chief the hunger of the soul,
Now other appetites control !
And this grand banquet tells us true
How much more, in this point of view,
The stomach than the head can do !

Ah ! Thirty-three, how we enjoyed
The hardest duties that employed

Our hands and hearts and spirits all,
As loyalty's of valor's call.
I well remember now a raid
That some rude, rough marauders made,
Upon our old professor's land,
When, foot to foot and hand to hand,
We made the bold intruders stand!

How rang the air with many a shout,
How poured the blood from many a snout,
While hung the dreadful strife in doubt;
Till valor, skill and bludgeons too,
Defeated there the thievish crew.

There were some noses and heads to mend,
But garden fences we must defend,
And the old professor was our friend.
So, though it was Sunday, we fought it out,
Before he knew what it was about,
But he forgave us the sinful fray
Because for him we had fought that day.

Such was the class of thirty-three!
Such, for the right, may we ever be!
Modest and valiant, strong and wise,
Noble ambition and truth the prize!

Forty years ago! How the ages slip away!
Forty of us living! Forty things to say:
But how now to go on—or even to begin,
Is as hard a doubt just now as the origin of sin!
How the truths of science then we learned to spell,
Idle rogues as we were, now 'tis hard to tell,
Though our good old mother kept us in her school,
I can well remember how we played the fool!

Our venerable founder, old Professor E——,
Upon our memory's tablet none more loved than he,
With quaint and quiet manners, odd in his attire,
How his solid science did our souls inspire!
But alas, how sadly we his pains repaid
By our inattention and the tricks we played,
With our gas explosion and sulphuric fumes,
Making it unpleasant for him in our rooms!

And I well remember one instructor there,
Whom I name with honor for his kindly care,
Generous and gentle, he would overlook

All the little mischiefs that we undertook,
Taught us all profoundly scientific lore,
And to love our studies daily more and more.
Long may he live to honor his Alma Mater's call,
Our noble state geologist, our loved Professor Hall !

Then there was sober House, now preacher in Siam,
And Smith, who first controlled and all our plans began ;
With Saunders, so sedate and innocent in face—
Yet, even in a frolic, foremost in the race ;
Rude, witty Woodruff, ever sharp and sly,
With schemes of fun and jollity lurking in his eye ;
Stout, thoughtful Crocker, studious and discreet,
Born to " go West " and fill a judge's seat ;
Van Rensselaer, a son of the old patroon,
Related also to the man i' the moon,
With many others since of wealth and fame,
But quite too numerous for me to name.
Lastly myself—but such a stammering youth,
'T was hard at times for me to speak the truth !
And much I owe to good Professor Hall,
Who helped me when *I could not speak at all.*

But all is over now, and forty years
Have closed the records of our hopes and fears,
Ambitious passions and the boisterous joys
That marked our college life when we were boys ;
Gone, those sweet visits to the neighboring school,
Where fair young ladies fell in love by rule,
While we assisted in the chemist's art,
And heard their lessons with an amorous heart ;
Or, at the church, the sermon less would prize
Than the bright glances of their sparkling eyes.

Thus memory loves to dwell upon the past,
On scenes too fragile and too fair to last,
But let us turn to that memorial stone
So lately raised for him whose virtues shone
Conspicuous along our youth's career,
And now demands a tributary tear.
Sleep, noble Eaton ! in thine honored rest,
No anxious cares to pain thy peaceful breast,
But grateful words in granite shall proclaim
Our lasting reverence for thy worthy name !

All honor to our Alma Mater, where
Grand monuments of skill their source declare.

The Pulpit, Law and Medicine here combine
And lay their laurels on her hallowed shrine.
Her Architects and Engineers with pride,
Point to their paths o'er many a roaring tide ;
Niagara and Brooklyn long will tell
How science here matures her students well,
And sends them forth to bless the waiting earth,
And make their country prouder for their birth ;
While now one brilliant more adorns her crown,
In her illustrious present chief, Charles Drowne,
And may he long enjoy his merited renown.

Professor Nason then stated that contrary to the usual order of exercises, he wished to announce and introduce first, the class of '74 graduates elect. He therefore called upon Mr. Enrique C. Zegarra of that class, who presented to the association a petition addressed to Professor W. L. Adams signed by all the students of the Institute.

" We, the undersigned members of the Rensselaer Polytechnic Institute, having the good of the Institution at heart, and believing that its best interests demand the continuance of Professor W. L. Adams in the chair of geodesy and road engineering, would respectfully request him to reconsider his reported determination to withdraw from the faculty."

The petition elicited long continued applause, showing the heart of the petitioners to be in their work, and the hearts of the assembly to be with them.

Professor Nason moved that the names of the faculty and the entire alumni association be considered as appended to the list of these petitioners.

The motion was seconded and carried with unbounded applause.

Professor Adams being called upon, said that it was as much a surprise as a pleasure to him to learn that he had succeeded so well in finding his way to the hearts of his pupils. He thanked them for the kind expression of their feelings and their interest in his continued connection with the Institute.

William Gurley, president of the association spoke in favor of the petitioners, adding that he knew of no one who could better fill the chair of Geodesy and Road Engineering than Professor Adams.

The petition was adopted as the sentiment of the entire association.

Professor Nason after giving a short sketch of the life and services of his predecessor in the chair of chemistry, Professor William Elderhorst announced his desire to have placed for him a memorial window in the Hall of the Institute. A large number of the former pupils and friends of Professor Elderhorst being present, the amount needed, $140, was immediately subscribed.

Hon. John H. White, of New York, then compared his being called upon for a speech, after this week of festivities, to another dinner after the excellent one just participated in by those present. He said, however, he would notice the fact that it appeared to him very much of a fraud to call him a graduate, when he looked over the present curriculum, for he learned in one year what the students now learn in four. He thought this looked like retrograding instead of advancing.

Speeches of congratulation, incident and reminiscences were made by W. W. Walker, and C. E. Martin, of the class of 1856, Professor E. N. Horsford, class of 1838, Clark Fisher, Chief Engineer United States navy, class of 1858, Rev. Dr. William Irvin, of Troy, Professor W. H. Searles, class of 1860, Professor David M. Greene, Division Engineer New York State Canals, class of 1851, and Frederic Grinnell, Esq., class of 1855.

Professor Nason then made a short speech, in which he alluded to the valuable services of the present Director of the Institute, Professor Charles Drowne, and paid a very handsome compliment to the former Director of the Institute, Professor B. Franklin Greene, of the Bureau of Steam Navigation at Washington, D. C.

The following committee was then appointed for the excursion to Saratoga: Hon. J. H. White, Professor E. N. Horsford, Professor D. M. Greene, Hon. Norman Stratton, and Charles P. Perkins, Esq.

A resolution was then adopted instructing the Secretary to prepare and publish as soon as convenient full records of the proceedings of this semi-centennial celebration of the Institute.

The exercises continued until a late hour in the afternoon, when the alumni and students separated with the fraternal tie that binds them together, as sons of the Rensselaer Polytechnic Institute, renewed and strengthened by this agreeable occasion of social intercourse.

The music for the occasion was furnished by Doring's band, and was all that could be desired.

RAND'S HALL, 8 O'CLOCK, P. M.

FORTY-EIGHTH ANNUAL COMMENCEMENT.

ORDER OF EXERCISES.

OVERTURE—*L'Italiana in Algeri*, ... Rossini.

Prayer by Rev. WILLIAM IRVIN, D. D.

SERENADE—*Cornet and Flute Obligato*, ... Tittl.

Report of Academic Board, Prof. CHARLES DROWNE, Director.

POLKA—*Pizzicato*, ... Strauss.

Conferring of Degrees.

FANTASIE—*Jagd*, ... Zikoff.

Address to Graduates by Hon. JAMES FORSYTH, President.

WALTZ—*Wiener Wald*, ... Strauss.

Benediction, by Rev. GEORGE N. WEBBER, D. D.

MARCH AND CHORUS—*Tannhauser*, ... Wagner.

Music by DORING'S BAND.

CANDIDATES FOR DEGREE OF CIVIL ENGINEER.

JAMES N. CALDWELL, JR., ... Carthage, O.
GEORGE W. CARNRICK, ... Troy, N. Y.
LYMAN E. COOLEY, ... Canandaigua, N. Y.
WILLIAM J. FABIAN, ... Lake Forest, Ill.
FRANK L. FORD, ... East Cleveland, O.
ALEXANDER P. GEST, ... Philadelphia, Pa.
GEORGE S. GRIFFEN, ... Phœnixville, Pa.
WILLIAM P. MASON, ... New York City.
HARRY D. PATTISON, ... Troy, N. Y.
WILLIAM H. POWLESS, ... Norwood, N. J.
ENRIQUE C. ZEGARRA, ... Piura, Peru.

ADDRESS BY HON. JAMES FORSYTH,

PRESIDENT OF THE INSTITUTE.

It is one of the positive regulations of the Institute that the president shall address the graduating class. This is the reason for detaining this audience a few minutes on topics which at this time concern the Institute, and then with a brief review of its origin, rise and progress.

Gentlemen of the Graduating Class :

The fact that there have been sixty-three men on the rolls of your class since its admission to the Institute, and that your present number is reduced to eleven, suggests matters for consideration as to the policy of the Institute. First, ought not there to be a higher requirement for admission to the Institute? Or, if that is impracticable, Second, ought not the course to be lengthened to five years? Either proposition would take off from the poorly prepared something of the severity and sharpness of the course. Third, Is the course of study really too severe? It would seem that this is not well objected, when we have so much time to devote to boating, ball playing and other games and amusements. To the second, it may be replied that all our collegiate courses of study are fixed at four years, and that it would be difficult for this school to extend its course beyond that time. It would encounter a strong prejudice in young men, who, especially in this country, regard four years as enough to be used up in getting a professional education.

Besides, the additional twenty-five per cent. of cost to the student would be a consideration of controlling effect in looking towards the Institute for his degree. Some young men of means, who are not obliged to go to work for a living immediately, may and sometimes do take the fifth year to complete the present course, to the saving of the health and strength; but the prevailing desire is to accomplish the course in four years. To the first it must be replied that the requirements for admission should be raised, at least more rigidly enforced.

Look at this slaughter of fifty-two out of sixty-three young men who ought to be here to-day to graduate! And the roll of the missing is made up entirely of those who were poorly prepared to enter. The course of study is within the reach of any young man of fair talents and industry if he is fairly prepared to enter upon it. And it is entirely beyond his reach or the reach of any one unless he has peculiar gifts and qualifications for a scientific and mathematical course, or has made preparation with reference to the course of study. It is a fearful ordeal. And the most trying of all the duties of the Faculty of the Institute is that of deciding who shall fall out after all their care and solicitude, and the anxiety of the young men to keep along even under conditions.

Those who have experience in such matters will acknowledge that it is a very difficult thing to keep up the standard of scholarship. The Faculty are not destitute of feeling and sympathy and there is a constant appeal to relax the rule. There is an amicable desire to help young men along in the different departments by marks, so as to secure a good average over the whole course. It springs from the kindliest motives. But after all it is not a mercy to the student, and it is a hurt to the Institute. It is said to be "rough" to keep a young man in the Institute for three years and a half and then tell him he cannot graduate. It is unpleasant, to say the least, for the Faculty to do such a thing, and it is not done, except it is in their judgment for the best interests of the Institute to keep up its grade of scholarship.

The Institute is a technical school, its specialty is to make civil engineers, and it was long since resolved that to entitle a man to that degree certain things indicated in the course of study must be known and shown by examination. Again, suppose the young man cannot pass and take his degree, has he lost his outlay of time and money? By no means! The Institute has given him his money's worth every day he has been in it.

Not a few of our under-graduates—those who did not get degrees—have become distinguished men in their professions, never forgetting to acknowledge the scientific teaching and drill they received at the Institute. To a man of real abilities and acquirements, what is the diploma to him? A piece of evidence which he never wants to use. But to men of the other sort, a piece of evidence which must be often paraded by them to show, for the want of other proof, that they had ever been in the Institute at all. This parchment does n't make the man—it is only evidence that he is made—and here is the pinch which we have to pass through. Shall the Institute, with just a little character to lose, jeopardize it all by conferring its degress on young men, who cannot pass its examinations, and are not worthy of it? And that, too, on the ground that they have been here so long, behaved so well, and paid their fees so promptly. How long would the Institute last at that rate? How long would any young man think it worth while to come to Troy for such a cheap thing.

We forget that the scientific life and high character of this school are of more value to the country than whole divisions of students cut off from it because they were unable to master its course. We are in a position where we can get along without students better than we can get along without character. After fifty years of building up we cannot afford to trifle with our character.

The case is different from that of the college or university. At college a liberal education is obtained, and a man may be entitled as a liberally educated man, and often takes a bachelor's degree because he is a good linguist, a good *belles-lettres* scholar, a fine writer and elocutionist, while he has accomplished only half the course, and mathematics and science have been his abomination all the way through. Such a person often gets the degree of bachelor of arts and is sent forth as a liberally educated man. At the Institute we do not propose any such sort of personage as the liberally educated man. Our objective is the civil engineer. Young men come here to be made engineers, and we must make them, and we cannot graduate half a man or one who has accomplished but half the course. Our specialty is civil engineers, and we must make a good article of its kind or we cannot rule the market.

We have a course of study which (except in tactics, gunnery and fortifications) is equal to, if not higher, than that at West Point military academy. The only capital we have is our reputation, and that has been earned by a high scientific course of study held up, and by the work and drill required to accomplish it. Nothing else will sustain us; gifts, bequests, foundations are all in vain. Some men have not the stamina for this. They may not be to blame; but the Institute is not the place for them. It cannot graduate them. If the Institute is to go down—let it go down with its standard of education full high advanced, streaming against the wind of popular clamor for an easier way to get through the Institute. Confidently asserting the principles which have blessed it with success, let it go down, if need be, with no such self-reproaches. It will have accomplished enough to secure an epitaph.

The Hon. Jonas C. Heartt, died on the 30th day of April, 1874. In this presence no eulogy could add to his stature in your estimation. He was a trustee of the Institute.

Nothing has occurred during the past year to disturb the general good order of the Institute, or the peaceful and pleasant relations existing between trustees, faculty and students. Discipline has been maintained, and the work has been thorough.

Besides these honors, as graduates, you bear with you our best wishes for your success in the world.

To the Alumni and Friends : The trustees of the Rensselaer Polytechnic Institute may as well confess that in the past fifty years' experience and practice of the school, the original idea of the founder has been widely departed from. It is not known that this is the subject of regret in any quarter. It is quite certain that no moneyed trusts have been forfeited or endangered by this departure. Natural science, botany, chemistry, zoology, mineralogy, land surveying, were at first the principal objects of the school to teach. We would now hold out to the world that we are a technical school, having one object as our specialty—the making of civil engineers. All minor degrees are discarded, maintaining that the greater includes the less. The idea of the founder was the diffusion of moderate acquirements in science, and a knowledge of the nature of soils, among his rude and illiterate tenantry on the manor of Rensselaerwyck. He saw the progress of agriculture in its lowest state among them, and he sought to bring it up. But he was also willing and anxious that his attempt should not be circumscribed. He instigated the preparation of a class of teachers in many of the counties and towns of the state, who should be able to instruct those who felt interested in scientific subjects and pursuits of the primitive and ruder sort. Those seeds of his sowing forty and fifty years ago, have been an incalculable blessing. But he never conceived of this school as it stands to-day. He died in 1839, when the school was fifteen years old, and it then was uncertain whether it had a season to live or not. His idea was a pure charity. It was for poor men who could not pay much, if any tuition.

To-day this may be considered an expensive school. Some of those here present have passed through college at less cost than some of our students expend in one year at this school. Two hundred dollars a year for tuition, is as much as some of you paid for four years' tuition at college. Board then, for forty weeks, cost $80 or $100, and books, room rent, and other things were in proportion. The patron and founder was also a pioneer, and his steps were cautious and slow, his measures simple and direct, and his instrumentalities rude and imperfect. But his idea and object was to bring science within the reach of the masses of the people, to popularize it, and extend to them its advantages and economies.

The great movement in England to popularize science, and to introduce economy and skill in the use of the materials of living among the poor, started about twenty-five years before the founding of this school, and it is not unlikely had the effect to direct attention in this country to the same subject. The Royal Institution, of London, was founded and chartered in the year 1800, and seems to have been a model of which our school was a distant imitation in a new country and amongst a comparatively poor people. It is a source of pride to us that an institution which has reflected so much of the light of science over the world, and which was in many respects the model of our own, was also founded by an American. The Royal Institution, of London, was founded by a New England man by the name of Benjamin Thompson, better known as Count Rumford in the scientific world. Thompson was born at Woburn, near Boston, Mass., in 1753, was a man of genius, and had both a checkered and brilliant career. He lived for a time and taught school in the town of Rumford, the ancient name of the present town of Concord, the capital of the State of New Hampshire. Here he married his first wife when he was only nineteen years of age. Thirty-two years later,—having meantime left his native country and become a *savant* of European reputation,—he married in Paris, for his second wife, the widow of the celebrated French chemist Lavoisier. From this town's old name he chose his title, and was made "Count Rumford" by the Elector of Bavaria in 1791. Thompson was not a rebel against King George III., but a loyalist at the opening of the strife. For some imprudent remarks on politics, his neighbors in Rumford made it unpleasant for him to reside at that place—such is toleration in war times—and he left and went abroad and entered the military service of the king, by whom he was knighted. Under these circumstances, he has never been estimated in this country for what he was worth as a scientific man. He has lately found a biographer in Boston, and a favorable notice in one of the quarterly reviews. There is no absolution for certain political sins. Even the lustre of that other great name, contemporary with him and likewise notable in science, would have been dimmed in our estimation by such a political course—even the name of Benjamin Franklin.

Rumford was an enthusiast in carrying the results of science to the aid of the poorer classes. While in Munich he wrote much on the subject of economy in the use of food and fuel. He visited London in 1795 to publish his essays, and he observed the wasteful consumption of both food and fuel in England. He looked up to the cloud of smoke overhanging London, and said that from the materials of heat thus thrown away, and made a curse instead of a blessing, he could cook all the food, warm every room, and do all the mechanical work performed by fire in the metropolis. Cuvier said of him, in view of his work in behalf of the poor, and in the advancement of science, that Rumford was the only man who took the same path for getting into heaven and into the French Academy.

In 1799, Thompson (Count Rumford), being in London, published a pamphlet of fifty pages, which led to the foundation of the Royal Institution. It was entitled, "Proposals for forming by subscriptions, in the metropolis of the British empire, a public institution for diffusing the knowledge and facilitating the general introduction of useful mechanical inventions and improvements, and for teaching, by courses of philosophical lectures and experiments, the application of science to the common purposes of life." The object was explained to be the bringing together of science and the art of workingmen, and establishing relations of helpful intercourse between philosophers and practical artisans. Agriculture, manufactures, commerce, and domestic comforts, were to be studied and improved.

Now to verify the assertion that this school was prompted by and after a sort modeled upon the plan of the royal institution of Count Rumford, let us hear the proposals of the founder of this school twenty-five years later. In the letter of the founder (Stephen Van Rensselaer) to the Rev. Dr. Blatchford, dated November 5th, 1824, he says: "I have established a school at the north end of Troy, for the purpose of instructing persons who may choose to apply themselves in the application of science to the common purposes of life. My principal object is to qualify teachers for instructing sons and daughters of farmers and mechanics, by lectures or otherwise, on the application of experimental chemistry, philosophy and natural history, to agriculture, domestic economy, the arts and manufactures. From trials which have been made, I am inclined to believe that competent instructors may be produced in the school at Troy, who will be highly useful to the community in the diffusion of a very useful kind of knowledge, with its application to the business of living." Thus it is seen the two institutions had their origin in a like impulse, both having the same object, namely: the popularization of science, or as the prospectus of the first stated it, "the application of sciences to the common purposes of life," the very words of which statement were adopted in the prospectus of the second.

At a period in history in which the intercommunication was not so rapid as now between England and this country, and the interchange and progress of ideas much slower than at present; when, according to William Cobbet, it took fifty years for an idea to penetrate the house of commons, it was no small progress made by our founder and patron, when in less than twenty-five years after the Royal Institution of London was chartered, he laid the foundation of this school. Since that time the railroad, steamship and telegraph have been added to the means of communication, and the power of the press has been immeasurably increased.

Vastly different in the circumstances of their inception were the two institutions. One opened in spacious apartments in Albemarle street, London, and was patronized by the great, wealthy and fashionable, with an admission fee of fifty guineas. And such was the rage for attending its scientific lectures, that at the end of the first year the subscription in its aid amounted to £24,000. Besides Rumford, who lived in the premises, there was Humphrey Davy, director of the laboratory, and assistant professor of chemistry, earning fame for himself, on a salary of one hundred guineas a year. And Dr. Thomas Young, styled by an Edinburgh reviewer, the apostle of the undulatory theory of light, and Dr. Thomas Garnett, with others, were on the first roll of lecturers. Subsequently, these places have been filled by such men as Michael Faraday and Professor Tyndall, who lately visited this country.

On the other hand, this school opened in 1824, "at the north end of Troy," a phrase sufficiently indefinite to indicate its uncertain and migratory character. It was, however, localized for a time in the "old bank place" on River street, near the east end of the dam,—so far as such a school as it then was, with Amos Eaton for its "senior professor" and controlling spirit, of itinerant habits and methods of studying natural science, can be said to have been localized at all—in an ill-adapted place, with only small apparatus of the ruder sort—with no subscriptions, no money, no attendants but the poor young searchers after knowledge, who followed the Professor in his botanical and mineralogical excursions across the country, and returned to the "old bank place" to find the whole faculty of the school there embodied in the person of Professor Amos Eaton—guide, philosopher and lecturer.

The lecture system, it will be observed, was the method first adopted in each. It is with science as with politics, agitation begins and an interest is awakened by talk. And in the hands of zealous, devoted, enthusiastic young men there is no subject which may not secure a hearing.

In tracing similitudes, let us not forget to mention, what has no doubt occurred to all present, in surveying the rise and progress of these two institutions, that both were in the initiatory and formative period of each, guided and controlled by men of scientific genius, eccentric in character, and enthusiasts in their profession—just that order of men who set the world ahead in whatever pursuits they may be engaged—Count Rumford and Professor Amos Eaton, both Americans.

AMOS EATON.

No apology is offered for a moment's digression, to briefly review the career of Professor Amos Eaton, so thoroughly identified with this school for the first eighteen years of its existence, before a generation of men who know his fame, but who have little knowledge of his personal history. Amos Eaton was born in the town of Chatham, Columbia County, New York, on the 17th of May, 1776. His father was a farmer and a highly respected citizen of that town. The son early manifested superior ability and high aspirations. At the age of sixteen he had made himself a practical land surveyor, making his own magnetic needle and compass case out of the rude material at hand. With the encouragement of his parents he fitted for college, and at the age of twenty-three he graduated at Williams College in 1799, with a high reputation for his scientific attainments. He commenced the study of law with Elisha Williams, in Columbia County, soon after graduating, and continued the study of law in New York in the office of Josiah Ogden Hoffman. It was in New York that he came under the instruction of Dr. Hosack and Dr. Mitchell, and became interested in botany and other natural sciences to such a degree that he never could wholly resist the sway of his enthusiasm for those pursuits. He was admitted an attorney of the Supreme Court of this State at Albany in 1802, and located as lawyer and land agent at Catskill. Here he gave his first course of popular lectures on botany, and prepared a small elementary treatise on the subject. He attended lectures at New Haven in 1815. In 1817 he returned to Williamstown and gave lectures to the students on botany, mineralogy and geology. The first edition of his "Manual of Botany" was published this year. He continued his public lectures in the large towns of New England and New York, exciting great attention and interest in the natural sciences. In 1818 Governor Dewitt Clinton invited him to Albany, and he gave a course of lectures before the members of the Legislature. In 1820 he was appointed professor of natural history in the medical college at Castleton, Vt., and delivered several courses of lectures there. About this time he seems to have settled down, and made his home in Troy, and extended his system of instruction to the people, and, with the co-operation of many of the citizens at that time, the "Lyceum of Natural History" was formed, and one of the most extensive collections of American geological specimens in the whole country was gathered and arranged. He also made geological and agricultural surveys of the counties of Rensselaer and Albany, under the patronage of the Hon. Stephen Van Rensselaer, and also a geological survey of the district of country on the line of the Erie canal, the result of which was embodied in a report of one hundred and sixty pages, published in 1824, which report has received the commendation of some of the most eminent men of the State. In 1824 Stephen Van Rensselaer established this school, and Amos Eaton was placed at the head of its faculty as senior professor, and the remainder of his life was devoted to it. During this period he published several scientific works of great value. He died in this city on the 6th of May, 1842.

Besides his habit of field explorations and actual insight, his system of teaching was peculiar and successful. He maintained that the teacher learns more in teaching than the scholar, and, therefore, he made each scholar a teacher and lecturer of his classmates. Each man was required to tell what he knew on a particular topic to his classmates in presence of the professor. Thus he awakened a zeal for investigation, and by speaking made the ready man.

Thirty years after the earth closed over him, science demanded some suitable recognition of one of its favorite sons. A monument over his grave in Oakwood and a memorial window in the great hall of the Institute, now testify to the gratitude of his pupils, and to his fame as a philosopher and teacher.

The Royal Institution, under the patronage of the crown and of the wealthy, and through its published transactions, has a world wide renown. Its sphere is in the highest walks of science and discovery, and, as an educator, comes within the reach of the few who are already learned. So changed is it from its original scope and design, that it may be doubtful whether Count Rumford revived would recognize it.

The Rensselaer School, so rude and simple in its beginnings, is likewise so changed from its original scope and design that, probably, neither the founder nor Professor Eaton would be able to recognize it were they present at its first semi-centennial celebration. "Thus it is, in the field of scientific labor, the problems which we propose to solve expand beyond the forms from which we start, and yield results as fruitful and surprising as the growth of an unknown plant from a seed cast into the ground." With devout thankfulness to the source of all blessings, we ask in humble acknowledgement and trust for the continuance of the same.

The Institute was never so prosperous as on this, the fiftieth year of its existence. Its catalogue shows an attendance at present of more than two hundred students. It is to be considered whether or not it is expedient to take students beyond that number, should they come. Our conveniences and facilities are not adequate to any more. Besides, that number seems to be the point of economy for us. If we overgo that number, it involves an increase of our faculty of instructors, to pay for which the probable small increase of students beyond that number would be insufficient. Again, we cannot always be so prosperous. The financial situation of the country is felt quite sensibly by the patrons of the Institute, and the number of students is increased or diminished by it.

The Institute, thanks to its devoted friends, is out of debt and owns a good property, well adapted to its purposes, and now pays its own way. Besides it has an invested fund of $20,000. When its friends begin to see that it has a principle of permanence in it—that it is not likely to be swept away—then they will begin to make gifts and bequests to it. Not, it is hoped, for the endowment of well paid lazy professorships, or for cheapening tuition, or for making it free

—for it tends towards indifferent work, a lack of drill and scholarship—but for the erection of buildings, for additions to the library and the supply of the latest and best apparatus and models; for we hold it to be the duty of the Institute to give to all its students the full value of their money in the very best instruction which can be obtained.

For the encouragement of those who may be in doubt about its permanence, we can only state our belief that the Institute will outlive us all. For, it has a good reputation and is popular before the country; has a large alumni of not undistinguished men in their professions and occupations. It is the pioneer school of its kind in this country, and has a system of instruction peculiarly its own, which it has not been in the power of our competitors to equal or successfully imitate. For, it is not hide-bound by any preconceived ideas or traditions, nor does it care the value of the smallest stamp for old theories about the education of young men; it claims to be up to thc times, and to be in concert with what is called " The spirit of the age," and to go forward with it. For, it puts every man upon its rolls—not in leading-strings, but upon his good behavior—and inculcates self-government in the individual, having too much to do in science and the enforcement of its course of study to be able to devote much time to elegant manners. Obeying the rules of the Institute and accomplishing its course, the student answers our requirements; beyond that, he is a denizen in our city, under the law like any citizen. For, taking it as a postulate that science is the hand-maid, and not the hater of religion—that theology is the sum of all the sciences—it is so entirely unsectarian, liberal and free to all tongues and creeds, that not only English and German speaking people, but the Latin races and people of Mexico, Cuba and South America, and the Mongolian races of China, India and Japan—Christians, Jews, Turks, infidels and heretics—all meet and mingle together and stand upon an equality as men on the rolls of the Institute. For, it is under the care and government of a board of trustees, made up principally of practical and business men of this present generation; and it proposes to do no more than it can do well, and that in its own quiet way, conducted on business principles, so that when its patronage is cut short betimes, its expenses may be reduced in corresponding ratio. For, the Institute is so grafted into the hearts of her sons, who feel a pride in it and confer a lustre upon it, that neither things present nor things to come shall be able to turn them from their filial regard and affection for it. For, lastly, the people of this city have repeatedly said in reply to the proposition to remove it: "That they will not part with it; its struggles and reverses are part of our toils and experiences; its achievements and successes all go to our renown; its blessings are our birthright and we will not sell it."

Therefore, we believe that the Institute will outlive us all, and be in time to come, as at present, a famous school—most beneficent in its influences, and the farthest and most favorably known of all the public institutions of Troy.

In view of this apparent prosperity, not a single effort is to be relaxed to promote and carry forward the Institute. It is, by no means, a complete and finished institution. It needs care and watching continually. It has, as we believe, a grand future before it, and it has a principle of growth and adaptation within it. It stands alone, like some thrifty tree, jubilant in its young strength and vigor, rooted in the soil and taking its sustenance from the land it fertilizes by its annual return of fruit and foliage.

The following gentlemen acted as ushers: Grand Marshal W. L. Fox, Messrs. C. F. Carbonell, E. V. Z. Lane, J. J. Reyes, of the class of '75; A. G. Baker, George O. Knapp, of '76; Benjamin B. Newton, Jr., W. P. Denegre, and Charles P. Griffith, of '77.

The following gentlemen had charge of the boquets and flowers: Messrs. James L. Breese, E. Ray Thompson, of the class of '75; Edward A. Burdett, of '76; C. G. Williams and Walter F. Crosby, of '77.

THURSDAY, JUNE 18.

EXCURSION TO SARATOGA.

A special train left the Union Depot at 9 A. M. It was made up of nine cars filled with a party of nearly five hundred ladies and gentlemen, composed of the alumni, faculty, students, and friends of the Institute. The trip was enlivened with music by the Institute Glee Club, while the various events of the week suggested sufficient number of topics for social chat.

Upon arrival at Saratoga, the party proceeded to the Grand Union Hotel, where a large number of rooms, its elegant parlors, spacious ball room, and still more beautiful grounds were thrown open to the guests. The morning was mostly spent in viewing the sights of the village, visiting the various hotels and springs, and drives to the lake and in other directions.

At one o'clock all returned from their wanderings and sat down to an elegant dinner, served in the spacious dining hall of the Grand Union Hotel. After dinner the party assembled in the parlor, listened to brief addresses, and were entertained with music by Lander's orchestra, of New York. Hon. J. H. White, chairman of the committee, presided. Dr. J. G. Ambler, on behalf of the committee, offered a resolution of thanks to the proprietors of the Grand Union, Messrs. Breslin, Purcell & Co., for the sumptuous and elegant manner in which the company had been received and entertained. Mr. White then said he thought it would be eminently proper for the alumni to thank the citizens of Troy for their abundant kindness and hospitality, and accordingly offered a resolution of thanks to that effect, calling upon Professor E. N. Horsford, of the class of '37, to respond.

Professor Horsford said that Professor Eaton counselled the pupils in his day to remember two things; one was not to talk without they had something to say; and the other was to stop when they had said it. He recalled the days of the Institute when he was a student, and spoke feelingly of some of the old and particular friends of it, Dr. Brinsmade, John Wright and Uri Gilbert; the kindness of the latter to the boys of his class, he said, could never be forgotten by any of them. His reference to Dr. Brinsmade was peculiarly feeling. He also referred to the conclusion of one cycle of the existence of our Institute, and the fitting memorial stone set up to Professor Amos Eaton. He made a comparison of Bernard Palissey, the discoverer of porcelain and the adornment of it with gold, and likened the efforts and devotion of Professor Eaton in behalf of the Institute, to Palissey giving his wife's wedding ring into the crucible in his experiments for the carrying out of his purpose. Eaton gave his heart's blood to the school with which his name would be ever connected. Another fine comparison was made of the bird plucking the down from its own breast to cover its young.

Rev. Mr. Brinsmade made a feeling response to the remarks which had been made complimentary to his brother.

Professor George H. Cook, State Geologist of New Jersey, and Vice-President of Rutger's College, responded to calls, and spoke of Dr. Brinsmade as one of the oldest and firmest friends of the Institute. He sometimes felt old himself when in the field, but never would he feel that the Institute was old; it was in its prime, gaining strength and power. He recalled the names of various classmates and teachers, and feelingly remarked how much the pupils in his time were obliged to Professor Eaton's wife and daughters, who seemed fully competent to instruct and answer abstruse questions for them. The Rensselaer Institute is one of the leading ones of the country, and must be sustained. He thought that the alumni and trustees should take active measures to secure an endowment, particularly in view of a bill which is before Congress at the present time, and provides that money obtained from the sale of Government lands should be appropriated to needy educational institutions. The proposition was received with applause.

Norman Stratton next spoke to the resolution telling of the warm interest the citizens of Troy always showed in the Institute during his stay there. He also gave interesting reminiscences of his classmates and teachers.

The resolution was then passed with a generous and responsive aye.

Professor Nason, on call of President White, responded for the ladies to a toast proposed to them.

A. S. Pease volunteered to respond to the resolution of thanks to Troy, in a short address.

A recess was taken here, while Lander's orchestra gave some selections of music.

In the meantime Dr. J. G. Ambler, of the class of '33, was requested to call on his classmate, Dr. Alexander Van Rensselaer, the last surviving son of the patroon and founder of the Institute. Dr. Van Rensselaer came over from Congress Hall and was introduced to the alumni and

17

friends present, and a very interesting social time was enjoyed to the close of the day.

The party left Saratoga at 4:30 P. M., arriving in Troy a little before six o'clock.

HARMONY HALL, 8 O'CLOCK, P. M.

PROMENADE CONCERT.

CONCERT PROGRAMME.

1. Ouverture—Maurer and Schlosser, ... *Auber.*
2. Fesche Geister Waltz, ... *Ed. Strauss.*
3. Potpourri La Forza Del Destino, ... *Verdi.*
4. Frühling Klange Polka, ... *A. Schmidt.*
5. Serenade—Gute Nacht, ... *Abt.*

Auld Lang Syne.

ORDER OF DANCING.

1. WALTZ—Wiener Bluet .... *J. Strauss.*
2. LANCIERS—No. 11, ... *Weingarten.*
3. GALOP—Touristen, ... *Zikoff.*
4. PROMENADE—Blumenlied Fantasia, ... *Koppitz.*
5. QUADRILLE, ... *J. Strauss.*
6. WALTZ—Ball-Promessen, ... *Ed. Strauss.*
7. LANCIERS—No. 2, ... *Weingarten.*
8. PROMENADE, ... *Selections.*
9. WALTZ—Autograph, ... *J. Strauss.*
10. QUADRILLE, ... *Strauss.*
11. GALOP—Von Hause zu Haus, ... *Zikoff.*
12. LANCIERS—Grande Duchesse, ... *Offenbach.*
13. WALTZ—Schönen blauen Donau, ... *J. Strauss.*

COMMITTEE OF ARRANGEMENTS.

H. B. Nason, Jas. W. Burden, Geo. V. Shepard,
Wm. P. Mason, Jas. L. Breese.

The music was furnished by Doring's Band, and the refreshments by C. F. Lucas, Esq.

APPENDIX.

A very large number of letters have been received from all parts of the world, from graduates, and others once connected with the Institute. These letters are not only filled with words of heartfelt interest and encouragement, but also contain many valuable hints to the future management and prosperity of the Institution.

Although these were mostly private letters, we take the liberty of making a few extracts, regretting that we have not space for more.

From letter of Strickland Kneass, of the Pennsylvania Railroad, and President of the Association of Graduates of the Rensselaer Polytechnic Institute for 1874, addressed to Wm. Gurley:

"I had hoped to be with you, and now thank you for your kind invitation. I should be most happy to meet you on our old battle ground, and possibly meet old friends. I see Stratton's name and should have been pleased to renew our acquaintance. I did hope that in my official position so kindly voted me last year, I might say something to the new graduates, impressing upon them the true appreciation of the advantages which they had over us of '39. Yet, if we in '39 had what these boys of to-day have, I fear we would have been ahead of time, for we were ready for our places, and have done some service, working up by drudgery in field and office, with the times as they progressed. If these boys of to-day, were where we were in '39, I fear their chances for rapid promotion would be discouraging. But you have much to do yet, to keep up with railroad advances. I had a short conversation with Professor Nason when here, and I say again that I feel assured that a course looking to railroad management, viz: by attaching the economics of transportation, would be attended with grand results to both the Institute and country.

"Will you say how much I regret being compelled to be away from you, as my heart is with the Institute, and as regards its standing with our company, I would say that there are some nineteen graduates who hold responsible positions with us, and they are always acceptable when opportunity offers."

From letter of General Amos B. Eaton, of Washington, D. C.:

"Although I am not an alumnus of the Rensselaer Polytechnic Institute, nor of the "Rensselaer School," as it was called in its earlier days—still it has been my intention, until to-day, to visit Troy, and to witness such of the commencement and the exercises of the semi-centennial of the Institution as might be open to me, but I find that my health is such at this time, as will not justify my leaving home.

"It is a very great satisfaction to me that the Institution that my father established, with only a few to appreciate and aid, has gained and grown until it is acknowledged throughout the whole country to rank with the best schools of science. I am especially grateful to the generous and appreciative friends of my father, that they are to erect and dedicate a monument to his memory. It is due to him from his pupils, that they should do as they propose to do, write the name *Amos Eaton* upon the granite he taught them to "spell by its component mineral factors."

"I hope during the summer to be in Troy, and then to see the "Eaton monument," and to pay my respects to President Forsyth and others of the Rensselaer Polytechnic Institute."

From letter of Rev. Marvin R. Vincent, D. D., pastor of Church of the Covenant, New York, and formerly a member of the board of trustees of the Institute:

"It will be impossible for me to be present at your meeting, but I may be allowed to express my hearty sympathy with its object. * * * I feel that the Rensselaer Institute has a legitimate claim on the liberality and confidence of your citizens, because it has always been, as it is now, a source of reputation and credit to the city. It has stood as a scientific school of the highest grade; and though the advance of science and the growth of the country have resulted in other, similar schools, yet they all still look with respect to the Rensselaer. Its graduates are filling honorable and responsible positions all over our land. Notwithstanding the multiplication of scientific schools, its number of students never was so large. And not an unimportant consideration is the fact that the Institution turns annually into Troy a very handsome revenue.

"Troy is thus, as it seems to me, only consulting her own best interests and reputation by carefully fostering this school. It is a school for the advancement of those very sciences which lie at the foundation of her manufacturing interests, the principal sources of her wealth. Nor are the manufacturing interests alone concerned. Every business man and every professional man has a personal interest in the work in which you and your colleagues are engaged. As citizens of the Republic none of us can be indifferent to the vast development of mineral wealth which is among the potent forces now shaping the civilization of the West; a development which must be largely in the ratio of the advance of science. The great truths which you illustrate, and the great discoveries for which you prepare the way, touch the realm of the physician and of the theologian as well as that of the manufacturer. And yet I know how comparatively few outside of professional circles are aware of the amount of resources necessary to keep such an institution abreast with the progress of science. Large quantities of costly and delicate apparatus, expensive models, chemicals, the best and newest scientific works and periodicals, not only accomplished Professors but able assistants, all these require a generous outlay. And such I trust the citizens of Troy will feel it for their interest to make. Surely no investment could return to the city a richer usury, both in credit and otherwise. The reputation it has already won, the respect with which it is everywhere named, the advantages occuring to your society from the residence of its accomplished Faculty, the aid it is furnishing in the development of material resources and mechanical inventions destined to re-act upon the business and manufacturing interests of the world,—all should, as it seems to me, make it your pride to cherish it and to enlarge to the utmost its facilities."

From letter of Prof. B. F. Silliman, of New Haven :

"I should have taken pleasure, had it been in my power, to have assisted at the interesting semi-centennial exercises. The Rensselaer Institute deserves abundant honor as the pioneer in this special line of professional training, in the United States, and they find it best expressed in the useful lives of their honored Alumni all over the land."

From letter of F. Collingwood, Engineer on the Suspension Bridge, New York :

"I trust that in good time the proposition brought prominently forward by Mr. Boller,—that the Alumni have a representation in the management of the Institute,—may become an accomplished fact. With proper restrictions, it can hardly result otherwise than in benefit; and I have faith to believe that the lively interest that will in time be awakened will bring also something more tangible. Though engineers as a class do not amass wealth, there must be *some* of the graduates who, in other fields of labor, will do so, and I believe that it is to such sources mainly that substantial aid should be looked for. Aside from this, the Alumni ought to know, better than any other class of men, what are the needs of the Institute, and what the wisest measures to adopt. I trust, therefore, that we shall not let another Alumni meeting pass without bringing out more pointedly the views of the members, and taking steps to press the matter upon the attention of the Trustees."

From letter of O. F. Nichols, Engineer on the Chimbote & Huaraz Railroad, Peru, S. A. :

"My friends have favored me with the newspaper reports of the semi-centennial exercises, and as I had anticipated, they passed off finely. I wish I could have been with you, but Troy and Lima are most too far apart to make such a wish practicable. I heartily approve of almost any means which have for their object the assembling of the graduates of the Institute, for I think that much of the support it obtains other than financial, depends upon the interest which the graduates take in the school, and the zeal they display in its aid. Certainly, by this time we should have given up most hope of obtaining any funds from the worthy men, rich and poor, who have received their education at the Institute. Still, if there yet be hope from the city of its birth, and the State Legislature, possibly some financial good may come out of Nazareth yet.

"Collegiate experience seems to be that individuals with large hearts, or large love of approbation and larger purses, are to be relied on, and I trust that some such individual may one day, not too far off, be found, who shall furnish Troy with the wherewithal to maintain its Institute in the position which we all wish it might hold. Now, and for long years, the high standing it has, is and has been maintained by the industry and sacrifice of its professors, aided by the record of the men, talented and deserving, of its graduates. It seems to me now that on the same elements the Institute will have to depend for many a year, for whatever of reputation it bears. The new schools, with all their wealth, do not seem to prove formidable rivals, either by diminishing the number of students at Troy, or by sending out better Engineers."

From letter of Rev. S. R. House, M. D., of the class of 1834, Missionary at Bangkok, Siam:

"I can only express my sincere regret that distance must prevent my joining my fellow graduates of the Rensselaer Institute, so honored in memory, in celebrating her semi-centennial anniversary. Be assured that few of her graduates can have greater veneration for her founders or a higher appreciation of the excellencies of her modes of instruction—or be more thankful for the delighful and profitable months spent in her halls. I have ever had reason to remember most gratefully my worthy Alma Mater, for the practical acquaintance gained of the natural sciences and applied mathematics, has been of the greatest service to me throughout my missionary life. I will mention one instance. Some lectures on chemistry with experiments given soon after my arrival here, secured for me the respect and lasting friendship of the knowledge-loving Crown Prince, who a few years after was called to the Throne and reigned for seventeen years over Siam."

(Dr. House, after leaving the Institute, graduated at Union College, and also at the College of Physicians and Surgeons in New York. While at the latter place he wrote the "Chemist's Dream" published in the *Knickerbocker Magazine.* He also made many valuable contributions to the knowledge of the natural history and geography of that little known land.)

From a letter of James T. Allen, class of 1855, written at Zurich, Switzerland :

"It may be of interest to some of the graduates to know that the father of our lamented Professor Elderhorst, Col. Elderhorst, is still living at the age of ninety-three. One of the few, who as an officer in the Hannoverian cavalry fought through Waterloo and the Peninsula. His sister, ninety-seven, his wife sixty-five, and daughter comprises the family at Hameln, Hannover. A younger brother died a few years since whom they mourn with William as though in new made graves. Two cousins about the age of the Professor wear the iron cross gained in the late French war. * *

"It would give me great pleasure to be present at the semi-centennial exercises, but as it is impossible, I propose as a toast:—" The graduates of the Rensselaer Polytechnic Institute—may they always do their level best."

ACTS OF THE LEGISLATURE,

AND PRINCIPAL DATES

RELATING TO THE

RENSSELAER POLYTECHNIC INSTITUTE.

The School was founded by Stephen Van Rensselaer, Nov. 5th, 1824. See his letter of that date to Rev. Samuel Blatchford, D. D.

1826, March 21, it was incorporated by an act of the Legislature, as "the President and Trustees of the Rensselaer School." (Laws of 1826, p. 63.) And was located at the north end of Troy, in the building called "the old Bank place."

In 1832, by an act of the Legislature, the name was changed to "The Rensselaer Institute." Laws of 1832, p. 567.

In April, 1834, the Rensselaer Institute, with the consent of Hon. Stephen Van Rensselaer, was removed to the Vanderheyden Mansion House in Troy.

In 1835, an act was passed, increasing the number of Trustees, adding the Mayor and Recorder, and also the Alderman of the Fourth ward. Laws of 1835, p. 296.

In 1837, an act was passed reviving the Troy Academy, and uniting it with the Rensselaer Institute, and giving the Regents of the University the right of visitation. Laws of 1837.

In 1843, the city of Troy gave to the Rensselaer Institute "the Infant School lot," corner of Sixth and State streets, valued at $6,500, provided Wm. P. Van Rensselaer gave a like amount in money to the Institute.

In 1844, the Rensselaer Institute was removed from the Vanderheyden Mansion House to the building erected on the Infant School lot.

In 1850, March 8, an act was passed enlarging the Board of Trustees, and adding the Mayor of Troy, *ex-officio*. Laws of 1850, p. 54.

In 1861, April 8, an act was passed changing the name, and incorporating the Rensselaer Polytechnic Institute. Laws of 1861, p. 428.

The fire of May 10, 1862, destroyed the buildings and all the furniture, appurtenances, library and cabinets, together with the records of the Board of Trustees. The School took refuge in the University on the hill (now the Provincial Seminary), until the fall of the year, when it obtained quarters in Vail's Building, corner of Congress and River streets, till May 1st, 1864, when the Rensselaer Polytechnic Institute entered into possession of the land and buildings at the head of Broadway, where it now is.

The Winslow Laboratory, named in honor of John F. Winslow, Esq., former President of the Institute, was commenced in 1865, and completed September, 1866.

INDEX.

SEMI-CENTENNIAL

CATALOGUE

—OF—

OFFICERS AND STUDENTS

—OF THE—

Rensselaer Polytechnic Institute,

1824-1874.

TROY, N. Y.:
WM. H. YOUNG, 8 & 9 FIRST STREET.
1875.

OFFICERS AND TRUSTEES

OF THE

RENSSELAER POLYTECHNIC INSTITUTE,

1824-1874.

---

*Hon. Stephen Van Rensselaer, LL. D., *Patron*, Albany, with power to appoint examiners,............................1824—39

Presidents.

*Rev. Samuel Blatchford, D. D., of Lansingburgh,...........1824—28
*Rev. John Chester, D. D., of Albany,................. .....1828—29
*Rev. Eliphalet Nott, D. D., LL. D., (President of Union College, Schenectady,)..................................1829—45
*Rev. Nathan S. S. Beman, D. D., LL. D., Troy,..............1845—65
Hon. John F. Winslow, Troy,.......................... ...1865—68
*Thomas C. Brinsmade, M. D., Troy,.......................1868—68
Hon. James Forsyth, Troy,................................1868

Vice Presidents.

*Orville L. Holley, Troy, (Surveyor General of the State of New York), 1st Vice President,.......................1824—31
*T. Romeyn Beck, M. D., Albany, 2d Vice President,..........1824—28
*Hon. David Buel, Jr., Troy, 2d Vice President,..............1829—60
*Rev. N. S. S. Beman, D. D., Troy,...... .. . .1842—45
William P. Van Rensselaer, Greenbush, ...1845—64
*Thomas C. Brinsmade, M. D., Troy,.... ....1864—68
*Hon. George Gould, Troy, ...1868—68
E. Thompson Gale, C. E., Troy, ...1869—72
Hon. William Gurley, C. E., Troy,... 1872

Secretaries.

*Moses Hale, M. D., ... 1824—35
*Rev. E. Hopkins, ... 1835—41
*Hon. Isaac McConihe, ... 1841—42
Hon. Joseph White, ... 1842—49
Stephen Wickes, M. D., ... 1849—54
Rev. John B. Tibbits, ... 1854—61
Hon. William Gurley, C. E., ... 1861—72
William H. Doughty, C. E., ... 1872

Treasurers.

*Hon. Hanford N. Lockwood, ... 1824—44
*Thomas C. Brinsmade, M. D., ... 1844—47
Hon. Day Otis Kellogg, ... 1847—50
William H. Young, ... 1850

Trustees.

*Rev. Samuel Blatchford, D. D. .... 1824—28
*Elias Parmelee, ... 1824—34
*Hon. John Cramer, ... 1824—48
*Hon. Guert Van Schoonhoven, ... 1824—44
*Hon. Simeon DeWitt, ... 1824—28
*T. Romeyn Beck, M. D., ... 1824—28
*Hon. John D. Dickinson, LL. D., ... 1824—40
*Jedediah Tracy, ... 1824—25
*Hon. Richard P. Hart, ... 1825—44
*Gen. Nicholas F. Beck, ... 1828—31
*Judge Jesse Buel, ... 1828—35
Philip S. Van Rensselaer, ... 1833—44
*Rev. Phineas L. Whipple, ... 1833—37
*Rev. Eliphalet Nott, D. D., ... 1842—45
*Hon. David Buel, Jr., ... 1842—44
*Hon. H. W. Strong, (*Ex Officio*), ... 1842—44
D. G. Egleston, " .... 1842—44
*Rev. N. S. S. Beman, D. D., LL. D., ... 1842—65
*Rev. W. B. Sprague, D. D., ... 1842—44
*John Holme, Esq., ... 1842—56
Rev. A. T. Twing, D. D., ... 1842—68
*Hon. Isaac McConihe, LL. D., ... 1842—67
*Hon. Jonas C. Heartt, (*Ex Officio*), ... 1843—43
*Hon. Gurdon Corning, " .... 1843—68
Stephen Bowman, " .... 1843—44
*Rev. Reuben Smith, ... 1843—45

Hon. A. B. Olin, (*Ex Officio*), ... 1844—48
Jared S. Weed, " .... 1844—45
*Thomas C. Brinsmade, M. D., ... 1844—68
William P. Van Rensselaer, ... 1845—49
*Luther Tucker, ... 1845—49
*Hon. Daniel D. Barnard, ... 1845—50
*James Dana, (*Ex Officio*), ... 1847—49
Hon. Francis N. Mann, (*Ex Officio*), ... 1847—50
Stephen Wickes, M. D., ... 1847—54
*Benjamin P. Johnson, ... 1849—66
Alexander Van Rensselaer, M. D., ... 1849—68
*John Wilkinson, ... 1849—55
Hon. J. M. Warren, ... 1849
Le Grand B. Cannon, ... 1849—64
D. Thomas Vail, ... 1849
*Hiram Slocum, ... 1849—65
*Orsamus Eaton, ... 1849—59
Rev. John B. Tibbits, ... 1849—68
Hon. Joseph White, ... 1850—55
Hon. Day Otis Kellogg, (*Ex Officio*), ... 1850—50
*Amos Dean, ... 1850—53
*Hon. Hanford N. Lockwood, (*Ex Officio*), ... 1850—51
Hon. Joseph M. Warren, " .... 1851—52
*Hon. George Gould, " .... 1853—53
Hon. Foster Bosworth, " .... 1853—53
Hon. Elias Plum, " .... 1853—54
*Thomas W. Blatchford, M. D., ... 1854—66
Hon. Jonathan Edwards, ... 1854—68
*Hon. John A. Griswold, (*Ex Officio*), ... 1855—56
B. Franklin Greene, ... 1855—59
Hon. William Gurley, ... 1855
*Jonathan E. Whipple, ... 1856—66
*Hon. Hiram Slocum, (*Ex Officio*), ... 1856—57
Hon. Alfred Wotkyns, M. D., (*Ex Officio*), ... 1857—58
*Hon. Arba Read, " .... 1858—60
Hon. John F. Winslow, ... 1860—68
E. Thompson Gale, ... 1860
*Hon. John A. Griswold, ... 1860—72
Hon. Isaac McConihe, Jr., (*Ex Officio*), ... 1860—67
Hon. George B. Warren, Jr., " .... 1861—62
William H. Young, ... 1861
Hon. Lyman Wilder, ... 1861
*Hon. Arba Read, ... 1861—63
Albert E. Powers, ... 1861
*Rev. Peter Bullions, D. D., ... 1862—64

Hon. James Thorn, M. D., (*Ex Officio*)....................1862—63
Hon. William L. Van Alstyne, " ....1863—64
Hon. James Thorn, M. D., (*Ex Officio*)....................1864—65
Rev. Duncan Kennedy, D. D.,....................1864—68
*Hon. Jonas C. Heartt,....................1864—74
*Hon. George Gould,....................1864—68
David Cowee,....................1865
Alexander L. Holley,....................1865—67
Hon. Uri Gilbert, (*Ex Officio*)....................1865—66
*F. B. Leonard, M. D.,....................1866—69
James S. Knowlson,....................1866
Hon. Uri Gilbert,....................1866
Hon. David A. Wells, LL. D.,....................1866
*Hon. J. L. Flagg, (*Ex Officio*,)....................1866—68
Hon. Charles R. Ingalls,....................1868
Rev. Marvin R. Vincent, D. D.,....................1868—70
William A. Shepard,....................1868
Hon. Francis S. Thayer,....................1868
Hon. James Forsyth....................1868
Joseph W. Fuller,....................1868
Hon. William Kemp,....................1868
Azro B. Morgan,....................1868—69
Hon. Miles Beach, (*Ex Officio*)....................1868—78
Rev. J. Ireland Tucker, D. D.,....................1869
Alexander L. Holley,....................1870
Clarence E. Dutton, U. S. A.,....................1870
Hon. Uri Gilbert, (*Ex Officio*)....................1870—71
Henry C. Lockwood,....................1871
William H. Doughty, ...1871
Hon. Thomas B. Carroll, (*Ex Officio*)....................1871—73
Hon. William Kemp, " 1873

FACULTY AND OTHER INSTRUCTORS.

Senior Professors.

*Amos Eaton, A. M.,....................................1824—42
George H. Cook, C. E., B. N. S.,..........................1842—46
Charles Drowne, C. E., A. M.,..............................1859—60

Directors.

B. Franklin Greene, C. E., A. M.,..........................1847—59
*Rev. N. S. S. Beman, D. D., LL. D.,.........................1859—60
Charles Drowne, C. E., A. M.,.......................... 1860

Junior Professors.

*Lewis C. Beck, M. D.,....................................1824—29
*Hezekiah H. Eaton, A. B., (r. s.)..........................1829—30
*Paul Eugene Stevenson, A. B., (r. s.).......................1830—35
*Ebenezer Emmons, A. M., M. D., (N. Y. State Geologist),......1835—39

Professors of Geology.

*Amos Eaton, A. M.,.....................................1824—35
*Ebenezer Emmons, M. D.,................................1835
George H. Cook, C. E., A. M.,.............................1842—46
Edward A. H. Allen, C. E.,...............................1851—54
James Hall, LL. D., (N. Y. State Geologist),................1854

Professors of Chemistry.

*Amos Eaton, A. M.,.....................................1824—35
James Hall, A. M.,......................................1835—37
*William Elderhorst, M. D.,..............................1855—61
Charles A. Goessmann, Ph. D.,............................1861—64
Henry B. Nason, A. M., Ph. D.,...........................1864

Professors of Botany.

*Amos Eaton, A. M., ... 1824—38
R. Halsted Ward, A. M., M. D., ... 1869

Professors of Botany and Zoology.

*John Wright, M. D., (State Botanist of Michigan), ... 1838—45
*Frederick B. Leonard, M. D., ... 1845—48

Professors of Natural History.

*Lewis C. Beck, M. D., ... 1824—29
Edward A. H. Allen, C. E., ... 1854—55
Henry B. Nason, A. M., Ph. D., ... 1858—64

Professors of Mechanics.

B. Franklin Greene, C. E., A. M., ... 1847—59
Charles Drowne, C. E., A. M., ... 1859

Professors of Mathematics and Astronomy.

Charles Drowne, C. E., ... 1851—55
Dascom Greene, C. E., ... 1857

Professors of Descriptive Geometry and Drawing.

G. Gustavus Berger, ... 1851—51
S. Edward Warren, C. E., ... 1853—72
Dwinel F. Thompson, B. S., ... 1872

Professors of Geodesy, Road Engineering and Topographical Drawing.

Charles Drowne, C. E., (Professor of Geodesy and Road Engineering), ... 1851—55
David M. Greene, C. E., ... 1856—61
William H. Searles, C. E., ... 1862—64
Charles McMillan, C. E., ... 1865—71
William L. Adams, C. E., ... 1872

Professor of Mental Philosophy.

*Rev. N. S. S. Beman, D. D., LL. D., ... 1854—65

Professors of Modern Languages.

*George F. Struvé,....................................1854—56
Louis Cousin, B. L. and S., de la Faculté de Paris,...........1856—59
Philip H. Baermann,.......... ....1861—66
J. H. C. Lajoie de Marceleau, A. B.,............. ....1869—73

Professors of English Composition.

James T. Allen, B. S.,..................................1855—58
T. Newton Wilson, A. M.,................ .. ..1859—59

Professor of Metallurgy and Practical Mining.

George W. Maynard, A. M.,..............................1867—71

Adjunct Professors of Mathematics.

Charles Drowne, C. E.,..................................1849—51
Dascom Greene, C. E.,... ....1853—57
*T. Orlando Hopkins, C. E.,.............................1857—59
William Fenton, C. E.,........... ....1864—70

Instructors in Mathematics.

Charles Drowne, C. E.,..................................1847—49
George W. Plympton, C. E.,..............................1850—50
Dascom Greene,..1852—53
De Volson Wood,... ....1856—57
Joseph G. Fox, C. E.,...................................1861—62
Horace Loomis,..1862—63
William Fenton, C. E.,..................................1863—64
George M. Hunt, C. E.,.................. ....1864—67

Instructors in Descriptive Geometry and Drawing.

David Hathaway, C. E...................... ....1847—50
S. Edward Warren, C. E.,.......................... ...1852—53
Albert G. Emery,..1855—58

Instructors in Physics or Mechanics.

Charles Drowne, C. E.,..................................1847—49
*James W. Bradshaw, C. E.,... ....1850—51
William Tweddale, C. E.,................................1852—54
George L. Moody,..1854—54

B

C. Whitman Boynton, C. E., ... 1856—57
Albert H. Gallatin, M. D., ... 1866—67
Arthur W. Bower, C. E., ... 1871
Henry A. Rowland, C. E., ... 1872

Instructors in Geodesy.

George B. Roberts, ... 1850—51
*Joseph A. Moak, ... 1854—55
David M. Greene, C. E., ... 1855—56
Charles C. Martin, C. E., ... 1856—57
William L. Adams, C. E., (Acting Professor), ... 1864—65
Charles E. Smith, C. E., (Acting Professor), ... 1871—72

Instructors in Botany.

*Jose Tell Ferrao, B. S., ... 1850—51
Lewis G. Lowe, C. E., M. D., ... 1854—55
R. Halsted Ward, A. M., M. D., ... 1867—69

Instructors in Modern Languages.

Paul Edward Von Thun, ... 1852—54
*John B. Luce, A. M., ... 1860—61
J. H. C. Lajoie de Marceleau, A. B., ... 1866—69
Jules Godeby, A. B., ... 1873

Instructors in English Composition.

*James R. Percy, B. S., ... 1858—59
Charles E. Illsley, A. B., ... 1866—67
Alexander G. Johnson, A. M., ... 1869

Assistants in Chemistry.

Edward Suffern, ... 1835—36
D. S. Smalley, ... 1835—36
Jonathan R. Powell, C. E., ... 1847—48
Lewis G. Lowe, C. E., ... 1849—50
*Jose Tell Ferrao, ... 1850—51
James T. Allen, (Instructor), ... 1854—55
Matthieu Darmstadt, Ph. D., ... 1866—68
Irving A. Stearns, M. E., ... 1868—69
Edward Nichols, B. S., ... 1871—73
Alfred S. Bertolet, M. E., ... 1873—75

Adjuncts and Assistants to the Senior Professor.

(Appointed for a Single Term or Year.)

Fay Edgerton, ... 1828
Thomas E. Ripley, ... 1828

Daniel A. Comstock,..................................... 1829
John W. Barrows,..................................... 1829
James E. Booth,..................................... 1831
Samuel W. Williams,..................................... 1832
Alexander Van Rensselaer,..................................... 1833
D. Cady Smith,..................................... 1833

Adjuncts and Assistants to the Junior Professors.

(Appointed for a Single Term or Year.)

*Timothy Dwight Eaton,..................................... 1827
*Orlin Oatman,..................................... 1827
*Douglass Houghton,..................................... 1830
James B. Dungan,..................................... 1830
Abram Sager,..................................... 1831
Abel Storrs,..................................... 1832
James Hall,..................................... 1833

Janitors.

Asahel Gilbert,..................................... 1826—35
Lloyd Harper,..................................... 1855—69
Julius Bethmann,..................................... 1869

FACULTY AND OTHER INSTRUCTORS
1874.

HON. JAMES FORSYTH, PRESIDENT.

CHARLES DROWNE, C. E., A. M., DIRECTOR.
Professor of Theoretical and Practical Mechanics.

JAMES HALL, LL. D., N. Y. STATE PALÆONTOLOGIST.
Professor of Theoretical, Practical and Mining Geology.

DASCOM GREENE, C. E.
Professor of Mathematics and Astronomy.

HENRY B. NASON, A. M., PH. D.
Professor of Chemistry and Natural Science.

WILLIAM L. ADAMS, C. E.
Professor of Geodesy, Road Engineering, and Topographical Drawing.

DWINEL F. THOMPSON, B. S.
Professor of Descriptive Geometry, Stereotomy, and Drawing.

R. HALSTED WARD, A. M., M. D.
Professor of Botany.

ALEXANDER G. JOHNSON, A. M.
Instructor in the English Language and Literature.

ARTHUR W. BOWER, C. E.
Assistant Professor of Mathematics and Instructor in Mechanics.

HENRY A. ROWLAND, C. E.
Assistant Professor of Physics.

JULES GODEBY, A. B.
Instructor in French.

ALFRED S. BERTOLET, M. E.
Instructor in Analytical Chemistry.

GRADUATES OF THE INSTITUTE.

(r. s.) Denotes Rensselaer School. * Deceased.

CLASS OF 1826.

Stillman E. Arms, A. B. (r. s.,) M. D., Physician,..... *Elizabethtown, N. J.*

*Abner Benedict, A. B. (r. s.,) Attorney and Counsellor at Law,..................................... *New York City.*

*Albert Danker, A. B. (r. s.,) Civil Engineer,............... *Troy, N. Y.*

*Hezekiah H. Eaton, A. B. (r. s.,) late Assistant Professor of Chemistry in the Medical Department of Transylvania University,.. *Lexington, Ky.*

*Timothy Dwight Eaton, A. B. (r. s.,) late Assistant Professor of Natural History in Rensselaer Polytechnic Institute,.............. *Troy, N. Y.*

*Ebenezer Emmons, A. B. (r. s.,) A. M., M. D., late Professor of Geology and Mineralogy in Williams College, and State Geologist of North Carolina,....................................... *Williamstown, Mass.*

Addison Hulbert, A. B. (r. s.,) —— ——

Philip C. W. T. McManus, A. B. (r. s.,) Agriculturist,... *Brunswick, N. Y.*

*William S. Pelton, A. B. (r. s.,) M. D., Physician,......... *Ithaca, N. Y.*

Bennet F. Root, A. B. (r. s.,) M. D., Physician,......... *Manchester, Mich.*

CLASS OF 1827.

*Jonathan Chandler, A. B. (r. s.,) M. D., Physician,...... *Bennington, Vt.*

John J. Davey, A. B. (r. s.,) —— *Malaga, Spain.*

Francis G. Drew, A. B. (r. s.,) —— *Drewsville, N. H.*

Asa Fitch, Jr., A. B. (r. s.,) M. D., Physician, and N. Y. State Entomologist, ... *Salem, N. Y.*

George F. Horton, A. B. (r. s.,) M. D., Physician, late President of Pennsylvania State Medical Society,........................ *Terrytown, Pa.*

Samuel C. Jackson, A. B. (r. s.,) —— ——

John C. Keeney, A. B. (r. s.,) Clergyman, ——

*Orlin Oatman, A. B. (r. s.,) Merchant,.......... *Port Washington, Wis.*

*Edward Sanford, A. B. (r. s.,) Attorney and Counsellor at Law,.. *New York City.*

Charles L. Weston, A. B. (r. s.,) Attorney and Counsellor at Law,....................................... *Burlington, N. J.*

CLASS OF 1828.

*HIRAM ARNOLD, A. B. (r. s.,) ——— *Amsterdam, N. Y.*
*GARDNER BULLARD, A. B. (r. s.,) ——— ———
*FAY EDGERTON, A. B. (r. s.,) late Professor of Chemistry and Natural History in Utica High School,........................*Utica, N. Y.*
THOMAS EMORY, JR., A. B. (r. s.,) ——— ———
WILLIAM HENRY, A. B. (r. s.,) ——— ———
THOMAS C. RIPLEY, A. B. (r. s.,) Attorney and Counsellor at Law,........ ....*Saginaw, Mich.*

CLASS OF 1829.

JOHN M. BARROWS, A. B. (r. s.,) A. M., ——— ———
CYRUS BRYANT, A. B. (r. s.,) Agriculturist,.................*Princeton, Ill.*
*JOSEPH B. CLARKE, A. B. (r. s.,) ——— ———
*DANIEL O. COMSTOCK, A. B. (r. s.,) Horticulturist,........*Lockport, N. Y.*
MINER GOLD, A. B. (r. s.,) A. M., ——— ———
JAMES S. HORTON, A. B. (r. s.,) M. D., Physician,..........*Goshen, N. Y.*
*DOUGLASS HOUGHTON, A. B. (r. s.,) M. D., late State Geologist of Michigan, ...*Detroit, Mich.*
*LYSANDER H. KINGMAN, A. B. (r. s.,) ——— *Norfolk, Va.*
*JEREMIAH B. METCALF, A. B. (r. s.,) Civil Engineer,.....*Sandwich Islands.*
*ALANSON J. PRIME, A. B. (r. s.,) M. D., Physician,... *White Plains, N. Y.*
*JOHN L. RIDDELL, A. B. (r. s.,) M. D., Physician and Chemist,........... ....*New Orleans, La.*

CLASS OF 1830.

RUFUS B. BEMENT, A. B. (r. s.,) ——— ———
*THEODORE W. DECKER, A. B. (r. s.,) Agriculturist and Manufacturer,...... ....*Blooming Grove, N. Y.*
ALBERT R. FOX, A. B. (r. s.,) Glass Manufacturer,.......*Sand Lake, N. Y.*
LEMUEL G. OLMSTEAD, A. B. (r. s.,) A. M., LL. D., Archæologist,.......... ....*Moreau Station, N. Y.*
*GEORGE K. OSBORN, A. B. (r. s.,) Attorney and Counsellor at Law,....... ....*Troy, N. Y.*
SAMUEL J. PIKE, A. B. (r. s.,) ——— ———
*MERRITT PLATT, A. B. (r. s.,) late Superintendent of Milford High School, ...*Milford, Conn.*
RUSH SHERRILL, A. B. (r. s.,) Merchant,.................*New York City.*
*P. EUGENE STEVENSON, A. B. (r. s.,) A. M., Principal of Passaic Classical Institute,..*Paterson, N. J.*
JOSEPH THOMAS, A. B. (r. s.,) A. M., M. D., Physician,....*Philadelphia, Pa.*
*WILLIAM WILKINSON, A. B. (r. s.,) Attorney and Counsellor at Law,..... ....*Poughkeepsie, N. Y.*

CLASS OF 1831.

*James C. Cobb, A. B. (r. s.,) M. D., Physician, ... *San José, Cal.*
*Edward Devol, A. B. (r. s.,) Merchant, ———
Augustus G. Hill, A. B. (r. s.,) ——— ———
Abraham Sager, A. B. (r. s.,) A. M., M. D., Professor of Obstetrics, etc., in the University of Michigan, ... *Ann Arbor, Mich.*
Abel Storrs, A. B. (r. s.,) Agriculturist, ... *Lebanon, N. H.*

CLASS OF 1832.

William H. Boyd, A. B. (r. s.,) Merchant, ... *Monroe, Mich.*
James Hall, A. B. (r. s.,) LL. D., N. Y. State Palæontologist, and Professor of Theoretical, Practical, and Mining Geology in Rensselaer Polytechnic Institute, ... *Albany, N. Y.*
*John H. Philip, A. B. (r. s.,) M. D., Physician, ... *Mellenville, N. Y.*
Samuel W. Williams, A. B. (r. s.,) D. D., LL. D., Missionary, *Pekin, China.*

CLASS OF 1833.

John G. Ambler, A. B. (r. s.,) M. D., Dentist, ... *New York City.*
Edwin B. Crocker, A. B. (r. s.,) Justice of the Supreme Court, ... *Sacramento, Cal.*
Henry J. Mabbett, A. B. (r. s.,) ——— ———
William S. Sanders, A. B. (r. s.,) ——— *Shushan, N. Y.*
David C. Smith, A. B. (r. s.,) ——— ———
Alexander Van Rensselaer, A. B. (r. s.,) M. D., — *New York City.*
Bleeker B. Woodworth, A. B. (r. s.,) ——— ———

CLASS OF 1834.

Theron R. Hopkins, A. B. (r. s.,) C. E., Merchant, ... *San Francisco, Cal.*
Samuel R. House, A. B. (r. s.,) M. D., Missionary, ... *Bangkok, Siam.*
*Philo D. Whittelsey, A. B. (r. s.,) Merchant, ... *New York City.*

CLASS OF 1835.

Caleb Briggs, B. N. S., C. E., M. D., Physician, ... *Ironton, O.*
William H. Clement, C. E., Agriculturist, ... *Morrow, O.*
Joseph B. Cottman, B. N. S., ——— ———
*Jacob F. Eddy, C. E., ——— *Chicago, Ill.*
Robert G. McKee, C. E., ——— ———
D. S. Smalley, B. N. S., C. E., Principal of Classical School, ... *Jamaica Plain, Mass.*
Edward Suffern, C. E., Agriculturist, ... *Wilmington, Ill.*
*Michael Tuomey, B. N. S., late State Geologist of South Carolina and Alabama, ———
*Amos Westcott, C. E., B. N. S., M. D., Dentist, ... *Syracuse, N. Y.*
Worthington B. Williams, C. E., ——— ———

CLASS OF 1836.

James S. Drayton, B. N. S., —— ——
Tyrus W. Hurd, C. E., M. D., Physician,............*Bullion City, Nev.*
Aaron G. McKee, C. E., Agriculturist,.............. *West Arlington, Vt.*
Israel Slade, C. E., B. N. S., —— *Springfield, W. Va.*
Sherman Van Ness, C. E., B. N. S., City Surveyor,........*Hudson, N. Y.*
*Nathan R. Wilde, C. E., B. N. S., —— *Worthington, Ind.*

CLASS OF 1837.

Lorenzo M. Arnold, B. N. S., C. E., —— *New York City.*
Henry Baker, C. E., —— ——
B. Franklin Buck, C. E., —— *West Arlington, Vt.*
Charles R. Cook, C. E., —— ——
E. Thompson Gale, C. E., President of the United National Bank,... ....*Troy, N. Y.*
*Leman B. Garlinghouse, C. E., Manufacturer,.......*Canandaigua, N. Y.*
Fletcher J. Hawley, C. E., B. N. S., D. D., Clergyman,..*Danbury, Conn.*
George Johnson, C. E., B. N. S., —— ——
Levi L. Lockling, C. E., B. N. S., —— *San Diego, Cal.*
James Oakey, C. E., —— ——
Aaron B. Olmstead, C. E., B. N. S., A. M., President Saratoga Savings Bank, ...*Saratoga Springs, N. Y.*
Stephen V. R. Patterson, C. E., Broker,...............*New York City.*
Horace N. Rogers, C. E., —— ——
Henry R. Snyder, C. E., Chief Engineer of the Atlantic and Ontario Railroad,... ....*Johnstown, N. Y.*
James P. Wallace, C. E., President of the N. Y. Guaranty and Indemnity Company,...................... ....*New York City.*
Levi H. Warren, C. E., —— ——
*Charles Whipple, C. E., M. D., Physician,...............*Nyack, N. Y.*
John Woodworth, Jr., C. E., —— ——

CLASS OF 1838.

*Henry J. Avery, B. N. S., M. D., —— ——
George W. R. Bayley, C. E., Chief Engineer and General Superintendent of the New Orleans, Mobile, and Texas Railroad,....*New Orleans, La.*
William C. Bailey, B. N. S., A. M., M. D., Physician, *Chatham Village, N. Y.*
Ezra S. Carr, C. E., B. N. S., M. D., —— *Oakland, Cal.*
Charles S. Cross, C. E., —— ——
*Charles S. Field, C. E., Civil Engineer, —— *Texas.*
Eben N. Horsford, C. E., A. M., —— *Cambridge, Mass.*
*Jerome B. Howard, C. E., Artist,......................*New Haven, O.*
*David Kendall, C. E., Manufacturer of Thermometers and Barometers, ...*Rochester, N. Y.*

*William G. Lapham, C. E., Superintendent of the Western Division of the New York Central and Hudson River Railroad,.......*Syracuse, N. Y.*
George B. Lent, C. E., ——— *Poughkeepsie, N. Y.*
Edward Mynderse, C. E., ——— ———
Allen Pearce, C. E., ——— ———
George Putnam, C. E., ——— ———
*John A. Robison, B. N. S., Contracting Engineer,.......*Santiago, Cuba.*
Norman Stratton, C. E., Civil Engineer, U. S. Navy,.....*Brooklyn, N. Y.*
Albert A. Thompson, B. N. S., ——— ———
Stephen T. Whipple, C. E., Manufacturer,................*Pittsfield, Mass.*

CLASS OF 1839.

Benjamin W. Bours, C. E., Banker,.......................*Stockton, Cal.*
Edward Brinley, Jr., B. N. S., C. E., Civil Engineer, and Surveyor-General of East New Jersey,........................*Perth Amboy, N. J.*
George H. Cook, C. E., B. N. S., Ph. D., LL. D., Vice President of, and Professor of Chemistry and Natural Philosophy in Rutger's College, and State Geologist of New Jersey,.........*New Brunswick, N. J.*
*Elihu W. Cotes, C. E., Merchant,........................*Warren, O.*
George R. Dennis, B. N. S., ——— ———
*Henry J. Drayton, C. E., ——— ———
William Gurley, C. E., Manufacturer of Mathematical Instruments,...... ....*Troy, N. Y.*
Strickland Kneass, C. E., Assistant to the President of the Pennsylvania Railroad Co.,..................................*Philadelphia, Pa.*
*John Van Ness Philip, B. N. S., late Lieut. in the U. S. Navy,.......... ....*Claverack, N. Y.*
*James H. Post, C. E., ——— ———
George C. Potter, C. E., City Engineer,............*San Francisco, Cal.*
William J. Powell, C. E., ——— ———
Orrin Stebbins, C. E., B. N. S., ——— ———
James Tilghman, B. N. S., C. E., ——— ———
Peter Van Rensselaer, B. N. S., C. E., ——— ———
*Augustus P. Van Schaick, C. E., Civil Engineer,....*Lansingburgh, N. Y.*
Francis G. Woodward, C. E., Mechanical Engineer, ... *Worcester, Mass.*

CLASS OF 1840.

*Charles H. Anthony, B. N. S., A. M., late Principal of Classical School, ...*Albany, N. Y.*
Charles Collins, C. E., B. N. S., Chief Engineer of the Lake Shore and Michigan Southern Railroad,......................*Cleveland, O.*
Edward N. Dauchy, C. E., Merchant,......................*Troy, N. Y.*
Anson Durham, C. E., ——— *Galesville, N. Y.*
Abel N. Haskin, B. N. S., C. E., Manufacturer,........*Battenville, N. Y.*

ALFRED B. HASKIN, C. E., B. N. S., Manufacturer,......*Battenville, N. Y.*
*WILLIAM LEWIS, C. E., B. N. S., M. D., Druggist,......*Burlington, Wis.*
AUSTIN F. PARK, C. E., B. N. S., A. M., Solicitor of Patents,...*Troy, N. Y.*
SAMUEL B. PARSONS, C. E., ——— ———
GEORGE H. STARBUCK, C. E., Manufacturer of Steam Engines, etc.,........ ....*Troy, N. Y.*
*WILLIAM G. VOUGHT, C. E., B. N. S., ——— *Victory, N. Y.*
GURDON B. WALLACE, C. E., Druggist,....................*Troy, N. Y.*
JOHN H. WHITE, C. E., Attorney and Counsellor at Law,....*New York City.*

CLASS OF 1841.

JOSEPH R. BRADWAY, C. E., B. N. S., ——— ———
ELDRIDGE G. BUSWELL, B. N. S., C. E., M. D.,——— *North Adams, Mass.*
*NATHAN COTTERELL, 2d, C. E., Agriculturist,........*Hoosick Falls, N. Y.*
JOEL B. HARRIS, C. E., Manufacturer of Car Wheels,........*Rutland, Vt.*
LEONARD W. HASKIN, C. E., Manufacturer,............*Battenville, N. Y.*
CHARLES B. HYDE, C. E., Civil Engineer, ———
DOUGLASS W. HYDE, C. E., Manufacturer,..............*Pittstown, N. Y.*
JOSEPH H. JENNY, C. E., Manufacturer,....................*Troy, N. Y.*
EDWARD R. KELLOGG, C. E., B. N. S., Real Estate Agent,....*New York City.*
NATHAN KELLOGG, C. E., Merchant,......................*Malden, N. Y.*
LOUIS LA COSTE, C. E., ——— ———
SENECA H. MARLETT, C. E., B. N. S., Civil and Mining Engineer, and Surveyor-General of Nevada,......................*Carson City, Nev.*
SOLOMON V. R. MILLER, C. E., Agriculturist,..........*Schaghticoke, N. Y.*
HENRY POMEROY, C. E., B. N. S., A. M., ——— ———
LODOWICK STANTON, JR., C. E., ——— ———
GEORGE TIBBITS, C. E., Manufacturer,.....................*Troy, N. Y.*
ROBERT H. VAN BERGEN, C. E., A. M., Agriculturist,......*Coxsackie, N. Y.*

CLASS OF 1842.

REED B. BONTECOU, B. N. S., M. D., Physician, ...*Troy, N. Y.*
DAVID COLLIN, JR., C. E., B. N. S., Agriculturist,......*Fayetteville, N. Y.*
HENRY W. DANFORTH, C. E., Assistant Assessor, U. S. Internal Revenue,... ....*Troy, N. Y.*
B. FRANKLIN GREENE, C. E., B. N. S., A. M., Professor of Mathematics, U. S. Navy, Bureau of Navigation,....... ....*Washington, D. C.*
FITZ EDWARD HALL, C. E., A. M., D. C. L., Professor of Hindustani and Hindu Law in King's College,................*London, England.*
AARON L. LINDSLEY, C. E., A. M., Clergyman,..........*Portland, Oregon.*
JOHN MCCAUGHIN, C. E., ——— ———
*IRA R. PRATT, C. E., B. N. S., ——— *Prattsburgh, N. Y.*
JAMES WADE, JR., C. E., Attorney and Counsellor at Law,....*Cleveland, O.*

CLASS OF 1843.

James Campbell, Jr., B. N. S., Manufacturer of Linseed Oil Varnish,...... *Dayton, O.*

Clarkson N. Potter, A. M., C. E., Attorney and Counsellor at Law,...... *New York City.*

*Thomas B. Small, B. N. S., C. E., M. D., Physician,... *Schaghticoke, N. Y.*

CLASS OF 1844.

John Henry Brodt, C. E., B. N. S., A. M., Clergyman,.................. *Williamsburgh, N. Y.*

Jonathan B. Rider, B. N. S., C. E., Agriculturist,........ *Chatham, N. Y.*

Gilbert T. Taylor, C. E., B. N. S., General Freight Agent on the Aspinwall and Panama Railroad,........................ *Panama, C. A.*

CLASS OF 1845.

Joseph E. Clark, B. N. S., M. D., Physician,............ *Brooklyn, N. Y.*

Lewis E. Gurley, C. E., A. B., Manufacturer of Mathematical Instruments, ... *Troy, N. Y.*

*Stephen E. Haskell, B. N. S., C. E., Manufacturer,.. *Lansingburgh, N. Y.*

Goodwin Lowrey, C. E., B. N. S., ——— ———

Thomas B. Rider, C. E., Agriculturist,.................. *Chatham, N. Y.*

James A. Skilton, B. N. S., LL. B., Attorney and Counsellor at Law,...... *Brooklyn, N. Y.*

CLASS OF 1846.

Jabez P. Bloss, B. N. S., M. D., Physician,................. *Troy, N. Y.*

Samuel S. Greele, A. B., C. E., Civil Engineer, and Superintendent of a Manufactory,...................................... *Chicago, Ill.*

*William Hall, C. E., B. N. S., Civil Engineer,............ *Mobile, Ala.*

William A. Ingham, C. E., B. N. S., LL. B., Attorney and Counsellor at Law,.. *Philadelphia, Pa.*

Alexander M. Lesley, B. N. S., Merchant............... *New York City.*

John E. May, B. N. S., C. E., Merchant,................... *Boston, Mass.*

Jonathan R. Powell, C. E., B. N. S., Agriculturist,...... *Chatham, N. Y.*

James A. Penfield, B. N. S., Superintendent of Iron Works,............ *Crown Point, N. Y.*

Percival Roberts, B. N. S., C. E., Builder of Iron Bridges, and Manufacturer of Car Axles,............................ *Philadelphia, Pa.*

James H. Salisbury, B. N. S., A. M., M. D., Physician, and Professor of Physiology, Histology, and Pathological Anatomy in Cleveland Charity Hospital Medical College,............................ *Cleveland, O.*

Samuel W. Sutherland, C. E., Agriculturist,............ *Bloomington, Ill.*

CLASS OF 1847.

ROBERT G. COOK, B. N. S., ——— *Dalles, Oregon.*

CHARLES DROWNE, C. E., B. N. S., A. M., Director of, and Professor of Mechanics in Rensselaer Polytechnic Institute, ... *Troy, N. Y.*

RICHARD EDWARDS, JR., B. N. S., C. E., LL. D., Principal of State Normal University, ... *Normal, Ill.*

*GEORGE A. GALE, B. N. S., Agriculturist, ... *Northborough, Mass.*

JOHN W. MURPHY, B. N. S., C. E., Civil Engineer, Bridge Builder, and Contractor, ... *Philadelphia, Pa.*

GEORGE W. PLYMPTON, C. E., A. M., Professor of Physical Science in Brooklyn Collegiate and Polytechnic Institute, ... *Brooklyn, N. Y.*

*AUGUSTUS ROSSMAN, C. E., Agriculturist, ... *Claverack, N. Y.*

ADRIAN VAN SINDEREN, B. N. S., C. E., A. M., Attorney and Counsellor at Law, ... *New York City.*

J. FORMAN WILKINSON, C. E., Assistant Superintendent of the New York Central and Hudson River Railroad, ... *Syracuse, N. Y.*

JOEL R. WOODRUFF, C. E., Chief Engineer of the——Railroad, *St. Louis, Mo.*

*ALFRED A. WOTKYNS, C. E., B. N. S., A. B., Merchant, ... *Troy, N. Y.*

CLASS OF 1848.

*JASPER N. BALL, C. E., A. B., Clergyman, ... *Grand Rapids, Mich.*

A. LAMONT CHUBB, C. E., B. N. S., Manufacturer of Agricultural Implements, ... *Grand Rapids, Mich.*

C. FREDERIC CREHORE, C. E., M. D., Physician, ... *Boston, Mass.*

J. FRANKLIN HOUGHTON, C. E., Capitalist, ... *Sacramento, Cal.*

ISAAC G. JOHNSON, B. N. S., C. E., Manufacturer of Malleable Iron, ... *Spuyten Duyvil, N. Y.*

ELMER H. LOCKE, B. N. S., ——— ———

LEWIS G. LOWE, C. E., B. N. S., A. M., M. D., ——— *Bridgewater, Mass.*

J. G. NICKERSON, B. N. S., ——— *Lynn, Mass.*

HENRY SEDLEY, C. E., Associate Editor of the New York Times, ... *New York City.*

JAMES G. THOMPSON, B. N. S., Clerk of Chenango County, . . *Norwich, N. Y.*

CLASS OF 1849.

THOMAS W. BAILEY, C. E., ——— *Wapello, Ia.*

CHARLES A. CUMMINGS, B. N. S., C. E., Architect, ... *Boston, Mass.*

JOSEPH S. FISHER, C. E., ——— *Memphis, Tenn.*

JAMES H. FROTHINGHAM, B. N. S., C. E., Merchant. . . . . . . *New York City.*

*GEORGE M. HALL, C. E., Merchant, ... *Bastrop, Texas.*

*HOLLAM L. PECK, C. E., Civil Engineer, ... *Schenectady, N. Y.*

GEORGE B. ROBERTS, C. E., B. N. S., First Vice President of the Pennsylvania Railroad Co., ... *Philadelphia, Pa.*

PORTER ROCKENSTYNE, C. E., ——— ———

JULIUS A. SKILTON, B. N. S., A. M., M. D., U. S. Consul General, ... *Mexico City, Mex.*
GEORGE A. STEARNS, C. E., Merchant, ... *Boston, Mass.*
*BENJAMIN TURNER, C. E., late Chief Engineer of the Nicaragua R. R., ... *Nicaragua.*
ALFRED WILKINSON, C. E., Banker, ... *Syracuse, N. Y.*

CLASS OF 1850.

EDWARD A. H. ALLEN, C. E., Principal of Sawin Academy, . *Sherborn, Mass.*
JOHN F. BARNARD, C. E., General Superintendent of the Kansas City, St. Joseph, and Council Bluffs Railroad, ... *St. Joseph, Mo.*
*JAMES W. BRADSHAW, C. E., Civil Engineer, ... *Lansingburgh, N. Y.*
*JOSÉ TELL FERRAO, B. S., Principal of School for Young Ladies, ... *Bahia, Brazil.*
CORNELIUS S. MASTEN, C. E., Chief Engineer of the Rochester and State Line Railroad, ... *Rochester, N. Y.*
NATHANIEL MORTON, C. E., Manufacturer, ... *Plymouth, Mass.*
R. WILLARD WARE, C. E., Resident Engineer on the Delaware Division of the Erie Railroad, ... *Port Jervis, N. Y.*

CLASS OF 1851.

WILLIAM H. BURRALL, C. E., Mechanical Engineer, ... *Springfield, Mass.*
DAVID M. GREENE, C. E., Deputy Engineer of the State of New York, ... *Troy, N. Y.*
*CHARLES L. LOOMIS, C. E., late Division Engineer on the Minneapolis and Cedar Valley Railroad, ... *Northfield, Minn.*
S. EDWARD WARREN, C. E., Professor of Descriptive Geometry, Stereotomy, and Drawing in Massachusetts Institute of Technology, .. *Newton, Mass.*

(In consequence of the extension of the Courses of Study, none were graduated in the year 1852.)

CLASS OF 1853.

JOHN A. BAGLEY, C. E., Civil Engineer, ... *New York City.*
FREDERIC O. BURHANS, B. S., Assistant Superintendent of a Manufactory, ... *Warrensburgh, N. Y.*
DASCOM GREENE, C. E., Professor of Mathematics and Astronomy in Rensselaer Polytechnic Institute, ... *Troy, N. Y.*
CHARLES M. OSBORNE, C. E., Attorney and Counsellor at Law, ... *Rock Island, Ill.*
WILLIAM TWEEDDALE, C. E., City Engineer, ... *Topeka, Kan.*
GEORGE C. WATRISS, C. E., Draftsman, Pacific Iron Works, ... *San Francisco, Cal.*

CLASS OF 1854.

CALVIN ACKLEY, C. E., Civil Engineer,............ ....*Kinderhook, N. Y.*
*THOMAS K. BALTZELL, C. E., late Assistant Engineer on the —— R. R., ...*Tallahasse, Fla.*
J. MORTON CLINCH, C. E., Manufacturer of Chronometers and Astronomical Clocks,..*Boston, Mass.*
HENRY CURTIS, C. E., Attorney and Counsellor at Law,... *Rock Island, Ill.*
*JOSEPH A. MOAK, C. E., Civil Engineer,............*Richmond, Va.*

CLASS OF 1855.

JAMES T. ALLEN, B. S., Associate Principal of the English and Classical School,.... ....*West Newton, Mass.*
FRANCIS COLLINGWOOD, C. E., Assistant Engineer on the East River Suspension Bridge,..*New York City.*
*CHARLES E. CROSS, C. E., late Capt. U. S. Engineers,.....*Lawrence, Mass.*
FREDERIC GRINNELL, C. E., President and Joint Proprietor of the Providence Steam and Gas Pipe Co.,...................*Providence, R. I.*
HENRY HOLMES, C. E., Merchant,........ ....*Salem, Mass.*
AUGUSTO DE LACERDA, B. S., Agent for the U. S. and Brazil Mail Steamship Co.,...*Bahia, Brazil.*

CLASS OF 1856.

C. WHITMAN BOYNTON, C. E., Manufacturer,........... *Woodbridge, N. J.*
LEICESTER BURNETT, C. E., Superintendent and Chief Engineer of Fremont, Elk Horn Valley, and Missouri River Railroad,....*Missouri Valley, Ia.*
*NICHOLAS H. CHAMBERLAINE, C. E., Civil Engineer,..........*Keokuk, Ia.*
JOHN M. CLARKE, C. E., Merchant,..........................*Chicago, Ill.*
JOSEPH P. DAVIS, C. E., Principal Assistant Engineer on the St. Louis Water Works,...*St. Louis, Mo.*
JOHN D. ESTABROOK, C. E., Engineer of Construction, Fairmount Park,.... ....*Philadelphia, Pa.*
GEORGE F. ELLS, C. E., Manufacturer,.................*Long Eddy, N. Y.*
CHARLES C. MARTIN, C. E., Principal Assistant Engineer on the East River Suspension Bridge,..............................*Brooklyn, N. Y.*
WILLIAM H. MARTIN, C. E., Bridge Builder on the California Pacific Railroad,.......................................*San Francisco, Cal.*
HIRAM F. MILLS, C. E., Hydraulic Engineer,..............*Lawrence, Mass.*
JOHN H. QUACKENBUSH, C. E., Manufacturer,................*Troy, N. Y.*
GILMAN TRAFTON, C. E., Civil Engineer, and member of the Louisville Bridge and Iron Co.,..................................*Louisville, Ky.*
WILLIAM W. WALKER, C. E., Chief Engineer of Burlington, Cedar Rapids, and Minnesota Railroad, and President of Sioux City and Pembina Railroad Co.,...................................*Cedar Rapids, Ia.*

JOHN A. WILSON, C. E., Chief Engineer of Bennett's Branch Extension of the Allegheny Valley Railroad,..................*Philadelphia, Pa.*

EDMUND YARDLEY, C. E., —— ——

CLASS OF 1857.

FREDERIC Y. DABNEY, C. E., —— *Dry Grove, Miss.*

ROBERTO ESCOBAR, C. E., —— *New York City.*

*T. ORLANDO HOPKINS, C. E., late Civil Engineer and County Surveyor,.... .... *Alvarado, Cal.*

G. FREDERIC KIRBY, C. E., Banker,..........................*Chicago, Ill.*

GABRIEL LEVERICH, C. E., Mechanical and Consulting Engineer,.......... ....*New York City.*

CHARLES MACDONALD, C. E., Engineer and Contractor for the Construction of Iron and Wooden Bridges,....................*New York City.*

*JOHN OSTROM, A. B., C. E., Civil Engineer,........ *Virginia City, Nev.*

WILLIAM M. PRATT, C. E., Manufacturer,................. *Meriden, Conn.*

WASHINGTON A. ROEBLING, C. E., Chief Engineer of the East River Suspension Bridge,..............................*Brooklyn, N. Y.*

*FRANCISCO TRUJILLO, C. E., First Assistant Engineer on the Havana Railroad,.......................................*Havana, Cuba.*

HEZEKIAH WATKINS, C. E., A. M., LL. B., Attorney and Counsellor at Law, ...*New York City.*

DE VOLSON WOOD, C. E., A. M., Professor of Mathematics in Stevens Institute of Technology, ...*Hoboken, N. J.*

CLASS OF 1858.

JAMES C. COIT, A. B., C. E., Planter,......................*Cheraw, S. C.*

THEODORE COOPER, C. E., Second Assistant Engineer in the U. S. Navy, ... *Steamer "Nyack," South Pacific.*

WILLIAM HOWARD DOUGHTY, C. E., —— *Troy, N. Y.*

ALBERT H. EMERY, C. E., Civil Engineer,................*New York City.*

CLARK FISHER, C. E., Manufacturer,.......................*Trenton, N. J.*

HENRY HARLEY, C. E., Merchant,......................*New York City.*

GEORGE HUNT, C. E., Civil and Mining Engineer,.........*Gold Hill, Nev.*

JOSEPH M. KNAP, C. E., Vice President of the Fort Pitt Foundry Company,. ....*Pittsburgh, Pa.*

WILLIAM METCALF, C. E., Joint Proprietor of the Crescent Steel Works,.... ....*Pittsburgh, Pa.*

*HENRY W. MERIAN, C. E., late Third Assistant Engineer in the U. S. Navy, ...*Steamer "Weehawken."*

ARIO PARDEE, JR., C. E., Superintendent Coal Mines,........*Hazleton, Pa.*

GEORGE H. PEIRCE, C. E., Mining Engineer,..............*Montreal, C. E.*

*JOSEPH G. RICE, C. E., Civil Engineer, and Superintendent of Silver Mines, ...*Bear Valley, Mariposa Co., Cal.*

L. FREDERIC RICE, C. E., Chief Engineer of —— Railroad,..——, *Ga.*

RICHARD P. ROTHWELL, C. E., M. E., Editor of Mining and Engineering Journal, ... *New York City.*
J. GARDNER SANDERSON, C. E., Civil Engineer,.............. *Scranton, Pa.*
JOSEPH M. WILSON, C. E., Engineer of Bridges and Buildings, Pennsylvania Railroad,.................................. *Philadelphia, Pa.*
CHARLES W. WINSLOW, C. E., Assistant Engineer on the Canada Southern Railroad,........................... *St. Thomas, Ontario, Canada.*

CLASS OF 1859.

ALEXANDER J. CASSATT, C. E., General Manager of the Pennsylvania Railroad, ... *Philadelphia, Pa.*
José N. CASANOVA, B. S., ——— *Cardenas, Cuba.*
WALTER CRAFTS, C. E., Superintendent Shelby Iron Works,.............. .... *Columbiana, Ala.*
ORMOND W. FOLLIN, B. S., ——— *San Francisco, Cal.*
ALBERT S. GREENE, C. E., Chief Engineer in the U. S. Navy, in charge of Boiler Experiments,.... ... . *Newburgh, N. Y.*
GEORGE M. GREENE, C. E., Passed Assistant Engineer in the U. S. Navy, ——
THEODORE I. HEIZMANN, C. E., Chief Engineer, Maintenance of Way, Pennsylvania Railroad,........................... *Philadelphia, Pa.*
*JAMES R. PERCY, C. E., late Capt. U. S. Engineers, (Volunteers,)........ .... *Fowler's Mills, O.*
HARRISON A. ROYCE, C. E., Manufacturer,.................. *Boston, Mass.*
RUSSELL SAGE, 2d, C. E., Superintendent of the Chicago Division of the Milwaukee and St. Paul Railroad,.................. *Milwaukee, Wis.*
ARTHUR B. DE SAULLES, B. S., First Assistant Mining Engineer, Schuylkill Coal Co., ... *Woodside, Pa.*
FRANK G. SMITH, C. E., Captain and Brevet Major 4th U. S. Artillery,. ——
ROBERT I. SLOAN, C. E., Civil Engineer,.................. *Trenton, N. J.*
LORENZO J. DE VISCARRONDO, C. E., Chief Engineer of the Cordova and Malaga Railroad,............................... *Malaga, Spain.*
NORMAN A. WILLIAMS, C. E., Manufacturer, ... *Utica, N. Y.*

CLASS OF 1860.

JAMES W. BIRDSALL, T. E., Merchant,...... .... *New York City.*
ALBERTO DE CASTRO, T. E., Municipal Architect of Havana,.. *Havana, Cuba.*
LUIZ DA R. DIAS, JR., T. E. Assistant Engineer on the Don Pedro II. Railroad,............... .. .. *Rio de Janeiro, Brazil.*
RICHARD D. DODGE, C. E., Civil Engineer,.... .... *Jersey City, N. J.*
EDWARD M. GRANT, C. E., Engineer and Contractor for Machinery, Bridges, and Grant's Patent Wrought Iron Piers,................ *Macon, Ga.*
HENRIQUE HARRIS, T. E., C. E., Merchant,... .... *New York City.*
GEORGE C. HOLTON, C. E., Merchant,.................... *Belleville, C. W.*
RAMON MATAS, T. E., Civil Engineer,.................. *Barcelona, Spain.*

CHARLES McMILLAN, C. E., Professor of Civil and Mechanical Engineering in Lehigh University,.. ....*South Bethlehem, Pa.*
CALVIN PARDEE, B. S., Assistant Superintendent of Coal Mines, *Hazleton, Pa.*
JOHN PEMBERTON, JR., C. E., Second Assistant Engineer in the U. S. Navy, and Assistant Professor of Natural and Experimental Philosophy in U. S. Naval Academy,............................ ....*Annapolis, Md.*
WILLIAM H. SEARLES, C. E., Consulting Civil and Mechanical Engineer,..... ....*New York City.*
*AURELIO SERRANO, C. E., late Assistant Engineer on the Croton Water Works,..*New York City.*
WILLIAM S. SIMPSON, B. S., ——— *Baltimore, Md.*
CHARLES E. SMITH, C. E., LL. B., Civil Engineer,.............*Troy, N. Y.*
FELIX R. R. SMITH, C. E., Planter,...................*Arkansas Post, Ark.*
*CHARLES B. THOMPSON, B. S., Banker and Manufacturer,....*Rockford, Ill.*
JOHN D. VAN BUREN, JR., C. E., Assistant Engineer, Department of Docks, ...*New York City.*

CLASS OF 1861.

WILLIAM L. BALDWIN, C. E., M. D., Physician,..............*Utica, N. Y.*
ALFRED P. BOLLER, A. M., C. E., Civil and Consulting Engineer, and Bridge Architect,................. ....*New York City.*
*EBENEZER P. BUCKINGHAM, C. E., late Superintendent of Oil Wells,....... ....*Mt. Vernon, O.*
*JAMES CROMWELL, C. E., late Major U. S. Infantry, (Volunteers,)......... ....*Cornwall, N. Y.*
RUFUS H. EMERSON, C. E., Merchant,........... ....*Pittsburgh, Pa.*
WILLIAM FENTON, C. E., ——— ———
JOSEPH G. FOX, C. E., A. M., Professor of Civil and Topographical Engineering in Lafayette College,............................*Easton, Pa.*
ESTÉVAN A. FUERTES, C. E., Professor of Civil Engineering in Cornell University,..*Ithaca, N. Y.*
BURDETT GOWING, C. E., Passed Assistant Engineer in the U. S. Navy,..... ....*Troy, N. Y.*
WILLIAM L. HASKIN, C. E., Captain and Brevet Major 1st U. S. Artillery,.. ....*Charleston, S. C.*
WARREN T. KELLOGG, C. E., Manufacturer,..................*Troy, N. Y.*
JAMES LALLY, C. E., Merchant,.........................*New York City*
ANTHONY T. E. MULLIN, C. E., Passed Assistant Engineer in the U. S. Navy, ...*New Orleans, La.*
ROBERT NEILSON, C. E., Superintendent of Elmira and Canandaigua Division of Northern Central Railroad,......................*Elmira, N. Y.*
T. GUILFORD SMITH, A. M., C. E., Secretary of Union Iron Co., *Buffalo, N. Y.*
THADDEUS S. SMITH, C. E., Assistant Engineer on the St. Louis Water Works, ...*St. Louis, Mo.*

MOSHER A. SUTHERLAND, C. E., Manufacturer,............*New York City.*
WILLIAM N. SYMINGTON, C. E., Superintendent of the American Barytes Co., ...*Alexandria, Va.*

CLASS OF 1862.

WILLIAM L. ADAMS, C. E., Professor of Geodesy, Road Engineering, and Topographical Drawing in Rensselaer Polytechnic Institute,......... ....*Troy, N. Y.*
WILLIAM S. AUCHINCLOSS, C. E., Vice President of the Jackson and Sharp Car and Coasting Vessel Building Co.,............ *Wilmington, Del.*
*NATHAN W. BUCKHOUT, C. E., Civil Engineer,..........*Burkesville, Ky.*
RICHARD H. BUEL, C. E., Consulting Mechanical Engineer,.*New York City.*
HORACE CROSBY, C. E., Civil Engineer,........... ..*New Rochelle, N. Y.*
ARBA R. HADDOCK, C. E., Merchant,.................. *Brooklyn, N. Y.*
ANICETO G. DE MENOCAL, C. E., Engineer Navy Yard,.. *Washington, D. C.*
JOHN C. UNDERWOOD, C. E., Chief Engineer and Superintendent of Bridges, ...*Bowling Green, Ky.*
PETER D. VROOM, JR., C. E., 1st Lieut. 3d U. S. Cavalry,.*Fort McPherson, Neb.*

CLASS OF 1863.

FRANCIS E. APPLETON, C. E., Assistant Engineer on the Union Pacific Railroad,..*Omaha, Neb.*
VAN BRUNT BERGEN, C. E., Assistant Engineer on the Brooklyn Water Works, ...*Brooklyn, N. Y.*
*PERCY T. BROWNE, C. E., late Division Engineer on the Union Pacific Railroad,..*Omaha, Neb.*
JAMES P. GOULD, C. E., Chief Engineer of the Delhi and Middletown Railroad,..*Delhi, N. Y.*
FRANK HINCKLEY, C. E., Assistant Engineer on the Western Pacific Railroad, ...*San Francisco, Cal.*
FRANCISCO R. NARANJO, C. E., Civil Engineer,...........*Coquimbo, Chile.*
AUGUSTUS E. W. PAINTER, C. E., Assistant Superintendent of Iron Works,. ....*Pittsburgh, Pa.*
BENJAMIN C. POTTS, C. E., Attorney and Counsellor at Law, *Newark, N. J.*
GEORGE T. STODDER, C. E., —— ——
EDWIN THACHER, C. E., Assistant Engineer, Louisville Bridge Co.,....... ....*Louisville, Ky.*
IGNACIO M. DE VARONA, C. E., —— *New York City.*
FREDERIC W. VAUGHAN, C. E., Principal Assistant Engineer, Louisville Bridge Co.,..*Louisville, Ky.*

CLASS OF 1864.

PETER H. FOX, C. E., —— *Harrisburgh, Pa.*
RALPH G. PACKARD, C. E., Civil Engineer and Contractor, .*Brooklyn, N. Y.*

ROBERT VAN BUREN, C. E., Assistant Engineer on the Brooklyn Water Works, ... *Brooklyn, N. Y.*

CHRISTOPHER C. WAITE, C. E., Chief Engineer and Superintendent of the Cincinnati and Muskingum Valley Railroad,........... *Zanesville, O.*

DRAKE WHITNEY, C. E., Joint Proprietor of Cataract House,.. *Niagara Falls, N. Y.*

HENRY W. WILSON, C. E., Assistant Engineer, Construction Department of the Pennsylvania Railroad,..................... *Philadelphia, Pa.*

CLASS OF 1865.

GEORGE B. BRAINERD, C. E., Civil Engineer,............. *Brooklyn, N. Y.*

SAMUEL BUEL, JR., C. E., Civil Engineer,................ *New York City.*

CLIFFORD BUXTON, C. E., U. S. Assistant Engineer,.... *Gloucester City, N. J.*

THOMAS M. CLEEMANN, A. M., C. E., Civil Engineer,...... *Philadelphia, Pa.*

HENRY H. FARNUM, JR., C. E., Chief Engineer of the South Side Railroad of Long Island,.................................. *Brooklyn, N. Y.*

JOHN W. GRISWOLD, B. S., Superintendent of a Manufactory, *Philadelphia, Pa.*

HORACE LOOMIS, C. E., Principal Assistant Engineer on the New York and Erie Railroad,.................................. *Hoboken, N. J.*

MARSHALL H. MALLORY, C. E., Proprietor of the "Churchman,".. *Hartford, Conn.*

José R. DA S. PIRAJÁ, JR., C. E., Assistant Engineer on the Don Pedro II. Railroad,................................ *Rio de Janeiro, Brazil.*

THOMAS C. RAYMOND, C. E., —— *Boston, Mass.*

JOHN C. THOMPSON, C. E., Superintendent of the Railroad Department of Crown Point Iron Co.,..................... *Crown Point, N. Y.*

ALFRED T. WHITE, C. E., Merchant,.................... *New York City.*

CLASS OF 1866.

*ALEXANDER ADDISON, C. E., late Student of Mining Engineering,.. *Clausthal, Prussia.*

CHARLES C. CRAFT, C. E., Civil Engineer,................. *Pittsburgh, Pa.*

THEODORE N. ELY, C. E., Superintendent of the Machine Shops of the Pennsylvania Railroad, ... *Altoona, Pa.*

HERBERT C. FELTON, C. E., Engineer, Manchester and Camden Railroad,.. *Camden, N. J.*

JOHN Q. A. FORD, C. E., Second Assistant Engineer in the U. S. Navy,.. *Steamer "Pensacola."*

WILLIAM P. HARRIS, C. E., Contractor for Public Works,..... *Chicago, Ill.*

GEORGE M. HUNT, C. E., Teacher,.................. *North Argyle, N. Y.*

THOMAS L. KNAP, C. E., General Superintendent of the Fort Pitt Foundry, ... *Pittsburgh, Pa.*

BENJAMIN N. LILIENTHAL, C. E., Superintendent of the New York Mill, for the Golden Chariot Co.,.................... *Silver City, Idaho.*

ALBON P. MAN, Jr., A. B., C. E., Civil Engineer,.......... *La Crosse, Wis.*

CHARLES P. PERKINS, A. M., C. E., Assistant Engineer on the Elmira and Canandaigua Division of Northern Central Railroad,... *Elmira, N. Y.*

JOSEPH C. PLATT, Jr., C. E., President of the Mohawk & Hudson Co., Manufacturers of the Eddy Patent Valve and Bailey Patent Hydrant,...... *Waterford, N. Y.*

CHARLES W. RAE, C. E., Second Assistant Engineer in the U. S. Navy, U. S. Flagship ——.......... *European Squadron.*

JOHN S. SCHAEFFER, C. E., First Assistant Engineer, Newark Aqueduct,.... *Newark, N. J.*

HOLLAND N. STEVENSON, C. E., Second Assistant Engineer in the U. S. Navy, ——

FRANK N. TREVOR, C. E., Manufacturer of Machinery,..... *Lockport, N. Y.*

WILLIAM H. WILEY, C. E., Superintendent Tunnel Hill Coal Co.,......... *Zanesville, O.*

CLASS OF 1867.

A. W. FERREIRA D'AGUIAR, A. M., C. E., Civil Engineer,... *New York City.*

PALMER H. BAERMANN, C. E., Civil Engineer,.......... *Albany, N. Y.*

ARTHUR BEARDSLEY, C. E., Professor of Civil Engineering and Industrial Mechanics in the University of Minnesota......... *St. Anthony, Minn.*

ABRAHAM B. COX, Jr., A. M., C. E., Resident Engineer, Leighton Bridge and Iron Works,.......... *Rochester, N. Y.*

*JOSÉ ESCOBAR, C. E., —— *Trinidad, Cuba.*

SAMUEL J. FIELDS, C. E., Engineer, Niagara Bridge Works,.. *Buffalo, N. Y.*

MAX L. GOLDSTEIN, C. E., —— ——

CÁRLOS GUERRERO, B. S., C. E., Chief Engineer, Sagua Railroad,.......... *Sagua la Grande, Cuba.*

*ALBERT M. HARPER, C. E., Merchant,.................. *Pittsburgh, Pa.*

FRANK J. HEARNE, C. E., Joint Proprietor of Riverside Furnace,.......... *Wheeling, W. Va.*

JOSÉ HERNANDEZ, C. E., Civil Engineer,........... *New Brunswick, N. J.*

CHARLES E. ILLSLEY, A. M., C. E., First Assistant City Engineer,......... *St. Louis, Mo.*

ERNESTO L. LUACES, A. B., C. E., —— *Puerto Principe, Cuba.*

GEORGE B. MALLORY, C. E., Marine Engineer, ... *Philadelphia, Pa.*

THOMAS F. MARSHALL, A. B., C. E., Engineer on the Northern Pacific Railroad,.......... *Rock Island, Ill.*

ALBERT H. MILLET, C. E., Civil Engineer to the Republic of Ecuador, S. A., ... *Quito, Ecuador.*

FRANK L. MOORE, C. E., Real Estate Agent,................ *Denver, Col.*

CHARLES H. MOSS, C. E., Bloomfield Iron Mines,...... *Roaring Spring, Pa.*

C. VALLETTE PETTIBONE, C. E., Merchant, ... *Fond du Lac, Wis.*

JOHN SALTAR, Jr., C. E., Civil Engineer to the Republic of Ecuador, S. A., ... *Quito, Ecuador.*

POMPEYO SARIOL, C. E., —— *Cordova, Mex.*

Francis H. Saylor, A. M., C. E., Engineer and Bridge Builder,............ .... *Philadelphia, Pa.*

Milo A. Smith, C. E., Manufacturer, ... *Detroit, Mich.*

William B. Stilson, C. E., Assistant Engineer on the Delaware Division of the Erie Railroad,.......................... *Port Jervis, N. Y.*

Cyrus R. Stone, C. E., Assistant Engineer on the Lake Superior and Mississippi River Railroad,........................... *Hinckley, Minn.*

CLASS OF 1868.

Joseph J. Albright, M. E., Real Estate and Securities,.. *Washington, D. C.*

Thomas Appleton, C. E., Civil Engineer,.................. *Portland, Me.*

José J. A. de Barcellos, B. S., C. E., Sugar Cane Planter,........... .... *Campos, Brazil.*

Stephen W. Barker, M. E., Merchant,.............. *White Creek, N. Y.*

Virgil G. Bogue, C. E., Division Engineer on the Callao, Lima, and Oroya Railroad, Peru, S. A.,.............................. *Lima, Peru.*

Roswell E. Briggs, C. E., Civil and Hydraulic Engineer,............... .... *Fall River, Mass.*

Leffert L. Buck, C. E., Engineer in charge of the Verrugas Viaduct, Callao, Lima, and Oroya Railroad, Peru, S. A.,......... *Surco, Peru.*

Joseph H. Campbell, M. E., Superintendent Iron Works,...... *Ironton, O.*

Gaspar F. de Ceballos, C. E., ——— *Remedios, Cuba.*

Mordecai T. Endicott, C. E., Civil Engineer, U. S. Navy Yard,......... .... *Philadelphia, Pa.*

Francis F. Fay, M. E., ——— *Troy, N. Y.*

George T. Hall, C. E., Assistant Engineer on the Eastern Division of the New York State Canals, ... *Whitehall, N. Y.*

Benjamin R. Lawrance, B. S., Merchant, ... *New Orleans, La.*

Alter Megear, C. E., Assistant Superintendent of the Edge Moor Iron Works, ... *Edge Moor, Del.*

William W. Mills, C. E., Civil Engineer,............... *New York City.*

Othniel F. Nichols, C. E., Assistant Engineer on the Callao, Lima, and Oroya Railroad, Peru, S. A.,....... .... *Lima, Peru.*

Harwood V. Olyphant, C. E., Acting President of the Delaware and Hudson Canal Co.,................................. *Albany, N. Y.*

Ambrose V. Powell, C. E., Civil Engineer,........... *Battle Creek, Mich.*

C. Ridgely Schott, C. E., Assistant Engineer, Bureau of Civil and Topographical Engineering, Department of Public Parks,.............. .... *New York City.*

George S. Skilton, C. E., Civil Engineer,............ *Mexico City, Mex.*

Theodore S. Smith, Jr., C. E., Assistant Engineer on the Jersey City and Albany Railroad,........... .... *Stony Point, N. Y.*

Irving A. Stearns, M. E., Civil and Mining Engineer,..... *Wilkesbarre, Pa.*

CLASS OF 1869.

TRUMAN H. ALDRICH, M. E., Miner and Shipper of Coal,... *Montevallo, Ala.*
ROBERTO ANZOLA, C. E., *La Palma, New Granada.*
EDWARD W. ARMS, C. E., Manufacturer of Mathematical Instruments,..... .... *Troy, N. Y.*
ROBERT B. C. BEMENT, C. E., Chief Engineer of the Chicago, Dubuque, and Minnesota Railroad,................................ *Dubuque, Ia.*
ALEXANDER M. BLACK, C. E., Kensington Iron Works,..... *Pittsburgh, Pa.*
FREDERICK J. BOLLER, C. E., Civil Engineer,............. *New York City.*
HENRY BURDEN, JR., M. E., Burden Iron Works,............ *Troy, N. Y.*
WILLIAM N. BURGESS, M. E., Resident Engineer on the Davenport and St. Paul Railroad,.................... .... *Davenport, Ia.*
ROBERT FORSYTH, C. E., Manager of the Bessemer Department, North Chicago Rolling Mill,.................................... *Chicago, Ill.*
HENRY G. MCCLELLAN, C. E., Chief Engineer of the Southern Railroad of Ecuador, S. A.,................................. *Quito, Ecuador.*
JOSEPH MULLIN, JR., C. E., Attorney and Counsellor at Law,............ .... *Watertown, N. Y.*
WILLIAM A. PECK, A. M., C. E., Assistant Engineer on the New York and Canada Railroad,............................... *Keeseville, N. Y.*
ROBERT C. PEEBLES, C. E., Assistant Engineer on the Pittsburgh Division of the Pennsylvania Railroad,....................... *Pittsburgh, Pa.*
JOHN PIERPONT, M. E., Assistant U. S. Engineer on Improvement of River Navigation,................................... ...... *Chicago, Ill.*
JOHN SQUIRES, C. E., Assistant Engineer on the Buffalo and Jamestown Railroad,... *Buffalo, N. Y.*
ARTHUR B. STARR, C. E., Assistant Engineer on the Philadelphia and Erie Railroad,... *Erie, Pa.*
LOWELL H. STONE, C. E., Civil Engineer,.............. *West Troy, N. Y.*
WILLIAM A. THOMPSON, C. E., Chief Engineer of the Sussex Railroad,... .... *Newton, N. J.*
CHARLES H. UTLEY, M. E., Merchant,.................... *Buffalo, N. Y.*
THEODORE VOORHEES, C. E., Superintendent Rensselaer and Saratoga Division, Delaware and Hudson Canal Co.,.............. *Saratoga, N. Y.*

CLASS OF 1870.

HENRY N. BABCOCK, M. E., Assistant U. S. Engineer in charge of Coast Improvements, ... *Newport, R. I.*
*JOSEPH T. BAILY, C. E., ——— *St. Louis, Mo.*
ANTHONY H. BLAISDELL, C. E., Assistant U. S. Engineer in charge of the Survey and Improvement of Osage River,............ *St. Louis, Mo.*
ARTHUR E. BOARDMAN, C. E., City Engineer,...... .... *Macon, Ga.*
JUAN GONZALEZ, JR., C. E., ——— *Matanzas, Cuba.*
JACOB E. HEYL, B. S., Chemist at Sugar Refinery, ...*Philadelphia, Pa.*
*GEORGE H. MANN, C. E., Civil Engineer,............. *New Haven, Conn.*

CHARLES R. MATHER, M. E., Assistant U. S. Engineer on the Coast Survey, ... *Newport, R. I.*

THOMAS O'NEIL MORRIS, C. E., Assistant Engineer on the Indianapolis and St. Louis Railroad,.................................. *Indianapolis, Ind.*

ROBERT C. NEAL, M. E., Mining Engineer,.............. *Bloomsburgh, Pa.*

GEORGE D. NICKEL, M. E., Deputy U. S. Surveyor of Public Lands,...... .... *Denver, Col.*

EDWARD PARRISH, JR., C. E., Assistant Engineer, Construction Department of the Pennsylvania Railroad,.................... *Philadelphia, Pa.*

JOHN H. RANDOLPH, C. E., Planter,.................. *Bayou Goula, La.*

JAMES D. REYNOLDS, C. E., Consulting and Executive Engineer,.......... .... *Chicago, Ill.*

HENRY A. ROWLAND, C. E., Assistant Professor of Physics in Rensselaer Polytechnic Institute,................................ *Troy, N. Y.*

NATHANIEL E. RUSSELL, C. E., Assistant U. S. Engineer in charge of the Improvement of River Navigation,.. .... *Appleton, Wis.*

CHARLES H. SCOTT, M. E., ——— *Philadelphia, Pa.*

JUSTUS M. SILLIMAN, M. E., Professor of Mining Engineering and Graphics in Lafayette College,................................ *Easton, Pa.*

*EDWARD SOTHERS, M. E., ——— *Valparaiso, Chile.*

WILLIAM C. STRAWBRIDGE, M. E., Attorney and Counsellor at Law,...... .... *Philadelphia, Pa.*

CLASS OF 1871.

FEDERICO M. ALCOVER, C. E., Civil Engineer,..... *Sagua la Grande, Cuba.*

MIGUEL DE T. ARGOLLO, C. E., Civil Engineer,...... *Rio de Janeiro, Brazil.*

WILLIAM L. BAKER, C. E., Assistant Engineer, Detroit Bridge and Iron Works,.. *Detroit, Mich.*

WILLIAM S. BATES, M. E., Student at Law,.... .... *Cincinnati, O.*

ALFRED S. BERTOLET, M. E., Instructor in Analytical Chemistry in Rensselaer Polytechnic Institute,.......................... *Troy, N. Y.*

HENRY M. BOARDMAN, C. E., Country Surveyor,............ *Boardman, O.*

ARTHUR W. BOWER, C. E., Assistant Professor of Mathematics and Instructor in Mechanics in Rensselaer Polytechnic Institute,........ *Troy, N. Y.*

MILTON W. ENSIGN, C. E., Assistant Engineer on the Galveston, Harrisburgh, and San Antonio Railroad,.. .... *Flatonia, Tex.*

ALBERT W. FOSTER, C. E., ——— *Madison, Ga.*

FRED. L. GARLINGHOUSE, C. E., Assistant Engineer on New York and Erie Railroad,.. *Buffalo, N. Y.*

ALBERTO V. DE GOICOURIA, C. E., Broker,... .... *New York City.*

CHARLES L. GRIMES, C. E., Manufacturer of Farming Implements,... ... . *Mansfield, O.*

ALFRED P. KIRTLAND, C. E., Resident Engineer on the West Pennsylvania Division of the Pennsylvania Railroad,.............. *Blairsville, Pa.*

George C. MacGregor, C. E., Assistant Engineer, Construction Department of Pennsylvania Railroad,......................*Altoona, Pa.*

M. William Mansfield, C. E., Civil Engineer,.............*Zanesville, O.*

*J. Harrod Marks, C. E., Assistant Engineer on the Southern Pacific Railroad,..*Jefferson, Tex.*

Henry G. Morse, C. E., Assistant Engineer, Wrought Iron Bridge Co.,..*Canton, O.*

Edward Nichols, B. S., Assistant Superintendent Steel Works,..*Lewiston, Pa.*

John B. Otto, C. E., Civil Engineer,..................*Williamsport, Pa.*

Richard Prescott, M. E., Adjunct Professor of Natural Science in Albany Free Academy,....................................*Albany, N. Y.*

Spencer V. Rice, C. E., Instructor in Graphics and Field-Work in Lehigh University,..................................*South Bethlehem, Pa.*

Charles G. Roebling, C. E., Wire Rope Manufacturer,.....*Trenton, N. J.*

Charles F. Ropes, M. E., Merchant,..................*Indianapolis, Ind.*

Richard Schermerhorn, C. E., Assistant Engineer, Park Avenue Railroad,...*Brooklyn, N. Y.*

Russell D. Walbridge, C. E., Superintendent of Metallurgical Works,...*Brooklyn, Cal.*

Thomas M. Williamson, M. E., Superintendent of the Coal Department of the Grand Tower Mining, Manufacturing, and Transportation Co.,...*Grand Tower, Ill.*

CLASS OF 1872.

William A. I. Aikin, C. E., A. M., Mining Engineer,........*Pioche, Nev.*

John F. Alden, C. E., Assistant Engineer, Leighton Bridge and Iron Works,...*Rochester, N. Y.*

George Burnham, Jr., C. E., Assistant Engineer, Fairmount Park,..*Philadelphia, Pa.*

William H. Burr, C. E., Assistant Engineer, Phillipsburgh Bridge Co.,...*Phillipsburgh, N. J.*

W. Lee Church, C. E., Ludlow Valve Works,.............*Troy, N. Y.*

Federico G. Garcia, C. E., ——— *Lima, Peru.*

Harvey M. Geer, C. E., Civil Engineer and Contractor,......*Troy, N. Y.*

George H. Lea, C. E., ——— *Philadelphia, Pa.*

Graham Macfarlane, C. E., Assistant Engineer of Mines, Fall Brook Coal Co.,..———, *Pa.*

Elias P. Mann, C. E., Civil Engineer,.....................*Troy, N. Y.*

William Marling, C. E., ——— *Moncton, N. B.*

David Reeves, C. E., Clark, Reeves & Co., Builders of Wrought Iron Bridges,.......................................*Phœnixville, Pa.*

William B. Sherman, C. E., Civil and Hydraulic Engineer, *Fall River, Mass.*

Ellery Stowell, C. E., ——— ———

ALEXANDER J. SWIFT, C. E., A. M., Assistant Engineer on the Troy Bridge, ... *Troy, N. Y.*

ALFRED WALTER, C. E., Assistant Engineer in charge of the Swamp Division of Bennet's Branch Extension of Alleghany Valley Railroad,....... .... *Jefferson Line, Pa.*

JONAS F. YOUNG, C. E., ——— *Niagara Falls, N. Y.*

CLASS OF 1873.

ARTHUR L. BAKER, C. E., Assistant Professor of Civil Engineering in Lafayette College,.................................... *Easton, Pa.*

JAMES E. BELL, C. E., Assistant Engineer on the Cleveland, Columbus, Cincinnati, and Indianapolis Railroad,................ *Cincinnati, O.*

ABRAHAM BLUN, B. S., C. E., ——— *New York City.*

*FRED M. BRYANT, C. E., Late Assistant Engineer on the Hoosac Tunnel, ... *North Adams, Mass.*

CHARLES CAMPBELL, C. E., ——— *Ironton, O.*

JOHN H. CURTIS, C. E., Division Engineer, 1st Division of the Southern Railroad of Ecuador, S. A.,............... *Milagro, Ecuador, S. A.*

JAMES DUANE, C. E., Assistant U. S. Engineer,............ *Portland, Me.*

ARTHUR J. FRITH, C. E., Instructor in Civil and Mechanical Engineering in Lehigh University,....... .... *South Bethlehem, Pa.*

CHARLES P. HARRIS, C. E., Dealer in Lumber, and Manufacturer of Doors, Blinds, &c.,.. *Rutland, Vt.*

JOHN G. HUMPHREYS, C. E., ——— *Hartford, Conn.*

NORMAN B. KELLOGG, C. E., Civil Engineer, ... *San Francisco, Cal.*

THOMAS J. LONG, C. E., ——— *New York City.*

MANUEL A. PELAEZ, A. B., C. E., ——— *New York City.*

B. WALKER PETERSON, A. M., C. E., ——— *Wheeling, W. Va.*

JAMES REED, Ph. B., C. E., Assistant Engineer on the Pennsylvania Railroad,... *Altoona, Pa.*

WILLIAM H. REEVES, C. E., Clark, Reeves & Co., Builders of Wrought Iron Bridges,.. *Phœnixville, Pa.*

PEDRO J. SOSA, C. E., ——— *New York City.*

THEODORE STEINACKER, C. E., Architect,.................... *Chicago, Ill.*

D. AUGUSTUS TOMPKINS, C. E., Assistant Superintendent of Bessemer Steel Works,.. *Bethlehem, Pa.*

HERMAN VOORHEES, C. E., ——— *New York City.*

T. CHESTER WALBRIDGE, C. E., Vice-President of Mohawk & Hudson Manufacturing Co.,..... .... *Waterford, N. Y.*

CLASS OF 1874.

JAMES N. CALDWELL, Jr., C. E., Assistant Engineer on the Cleveland and Sandusky Railroad,.............. .... *Cleveland, O.*

GEORGE W. CARNRICK, C. E., Assistant Engineer on Hudson River Improvements,..................................... *Troy, N. Y.*

LYMAN E. COOLEY, C. E., Professor of Civil Engineering in Northwestern University, ...*Evanston, Ill.*

WILLIAM J. FABIAN, C. E., Assistant U. S. Engineer on Improvement of Connecticut River Navigation,....................*Hartford, Conn.*

FRANK L. FORD, C. E., Assistant Engineer on the Cleveland and Sandusky Railroad, ...*Cleveland, O.*

ALEXANDER P. GEST, C. E., Assistant Engineer on the Northern Central Railroad,..*Canton, Pa.*

GEORGE S. GRIFFEN, C. E., Under instruction in the Works of the Phœnix Iron Co.,.... ....*Phœnixville, Pa.*

WILLIAM P. MASON, C. E., —— *Troy, N. Y.*

HARRY D. PATTISON, C. E., —— *Troy, N. Y.*

WILLIAM H. POWLESS, C. E., Assistant Engineer on Roanoke River Improvements,.......... ....*Norfolk, Va.*

ENRIQUE C. ZEGARRA, C. E., Assistant Engineer on the Chimbote Canal,... .... *Peru, S. A.*

MEMBERS OF THE INSTITUTE

Who did not Complete the Full Course.

The years denote the time of entering, without regard to Class, or length of time in attendance.

1824-9.

Augustus Bagley, ... Staten Island.
John R. Bigelow, ... Cummington, Mass.
Nathan Brockway, ... Oswego.
John Howard Bryant, ... Cummington, Mass.
Samuel Buel, ... Troy.
Daniel B. Cady, ... Schoharie.
March Chase, ... Drewsville, N. H.
Lewis T. Cobb, ... Cummington, Mass.
Daniel O. Comstock, ... Lockport.
Augustus Collins, ... Sparta, Ga.
William Cornell, ... Troy.
Luther Cross, ... Grafton, N. H.
Amos B. Eaton, ... Troy.
Thomas H. Eaton, ... Randolph, Mass.
Jonathan Ely, A. M., ... Chittenango.
Bela Foster, A. B., ... Hanover, N. H.
Darwin Gibson, ... Sandy Hill.
Richard H. Hale, M. D., ... Troy.
William G. Haniford, ... Enfield, N. H.
Oscar Hanks, ... Troy.
William A. Hitchcock, M. D., ... Orwell, Vt.
Ferris Jacobs, ... Schoharie.
*William A. King, ... Philadelphia, Pa.
John E. May, ... Pittstown.
Robert McManus, ... Troy.
Robert Peter, Jr., ... Pittsburgh, Pa.
*Augustus Pitcher, ... Albany.
John H. Philip, ... Kinderhook.
George Philip, ... Claverack.
Thomas W. Pratt, ... Boston, Mass.
Benjamin Richards, ... White Creek.

Joseph Richards, M. D.,................White Creek.
George W. Seward,....................Warwick.
Charles Sherwood,................. Elmira.
George Smith,.........................Henrietta.
James M. Trimble,....................Hillsboro, O.
Courtland Van Rensselaer, A. B.,.......Albany.
George Williams,.....................Troy.
John Wright,.........................Troy.
George W. Weston,...................Sandy Hill.
Richard H. Williams..................Middlesex.

1829-31.

William Aiken, M. D.,.................Onondaga.
James C. Booth,.....................New York.
Franklin Bradley, M. D.,..............Manchester, Vt.
LeGrand B. Cannon,..................Troy.
John Cassidy,.........................New York.
Eliphalet Cramer,....................Troy.
Martin Crandall,......................Sandlake, N. Y.
Charles S. Disbrow,..................Troy.
James B. Dungan,.....................Canandaigua.
Charles Duval, M. D.,................Schaghticoke.
William B. Eaton,....................Troy.
Charles H. Fellows,..................Troy.
Asa E. Foster,.......................Erie, Pa.
William H. Freeland,.................Claverack.
John F. French,.......................Hartford.
Charles Gardner,.....................Troy.
John H. Haynes,......................Nassau.
Calvin Hollister,.....................Pawlet, Vt.
Amos S. Hutchinson,..................Ackworth, N. H.
Hollister Lathrop,....................Sherburne, Mass.
Rev. Mr. Leavenworth,................Missionary,
Philander Moore,....................Fort Ann.
George M. Noble,.....................Tinmouth, Vt.
James Pickett,.......................Pittstown.
Franklin Pierce,......................Ontario.
F. W. Powell,.........................Middlebury, Vt.
Charles Robertson,...................Curracoa, W. I.
Augustus Slingerland,................Albany.
John Thomson,.......................Albany.
Charles F. Tuttle,....................Troy.
E. Van Allen,.........................Bloomingdale.
Joseph M. Warren,....................Troy.
Daniel Williams,.....................Troy.
Edwin Wilmarth,......................Salem.

1832-3.

Elmer W. Adams,......................Canton, Conn.
Orla Beals,...........................Lansingburgh.
William H. Bears,......................Newbern, N. C.
William W. Brockway,..................Troy.
John G. Buel,..........................Troy.
Daniel H. Burtis,......................Troy.
Eliam E. Barney,.......................Lowville.
Samuel Buel, A. B.,....................Troy.
Theodore E. Clark,....................———
George H. Cramer,.....................New York.
Edward O. Eaton,......................Troy.
David S. Eigenbrodt, M. D.,............Jamaica, L. I.
A. W. Fisher,..........................Halifax, Vt.
Charles Freiot,........................Troy.
Joseph Gary, Jr.,......................Troy.
Thompson Hollister,....................Troy.
William Hollister,.....................Troy.
Calvin Huntington,.....................Vermont.
Ferris Jacobs, M. D.,..................Washington, D. C.
Henry Lane,............................Troy.
William Lansing,.......................Lansingburgh.
Francis R. Livingston,.................Red Hook.
James S. May,..........................Pittstown.
John K. Myers,.........................Whitehall.
William H. Norton,.....................Nassau.
*Charles L. Prescott,..................Troy.
Albert E. Powers,......................Lansingburgh.
William L. Read,.......................Pittstown.
Rev. George Scarborough,...............Brooklyn, Conn.
William R. Schuyler,...................Ovid.
Charles Sherwood,......................Elmira.
Charles Smith,.........................Coeymans.
Isaac Smith,...........................New York.
John W. Sprague,.......................Troy.
Henry M. Swift,........................Georgia.
Josiah M. Talbot,......................Maine.
Asa P. Thayer,.........................Troy.
Charles C. Tracy,......................Troy.
James W. Underhill,....................Troy.
Stephen Wickes,........................Jamaica, L. I.
John H. Willard,.......................Troy.
Joseph L. White,.......................Cherry Valley.

1834-5.

*Oliver A. Arnold, ... Troy.
Hall Jackson Birgin, ... Athenstown, N. H.
*Peter A. Burden, ... Troy.
William Hollis Cades, ... Albany.
Charles A. Cook, ... Troy.
Garret Drake, ... Troy.
Cuvier Eaton, ... Troy.
Zina Pitcher Egleston, ... Troy.
Peter Fellows, ... Greenbush.
Nathan D. Garnsey, ... Clifton Park.
Joseph S. Gary, ... Troy.
William S. Haight, ... Troy.
Joseph Abel Haskins, ... Brunswick.
Lansing Hodgeman, ... Stillwater.
*Arthur Hanks, ... Troy.
Charles Henry Lindley, ... Troy.
Charles Nichols Lockwood, ... Troy.
Peter George Philip, ... Claverack.
Lewis L. Southwick, ... Troy.

1835-6.

Henry G. Adams, ... Brunswick.
Nelson B. Betts, ... Troy.
Jacob Henry Dater, ... Troy.
Walton W. Evans, ... New Brunswick, N. J.
William R. Guest, ... New York.
Henry W. Hewitt, ... Troy.
Charles Miller, ... Truxton.
David Price, ... Troy.
Charles H. Russell, ... Hebron.
Samuel Sherrerd, ... Belvidere, N. J.
H. Martin Smith, ... West Troy.
Joseph O. Smith, ... Caledonia.
Warren S. Smith, ... New Brunswick, N. J.
James A. Suffern, ... Haverstraw.
Thomas A. Tillinghast, ... Troy.

1836-7.

Henry Andrews, ... ———
Royal Wheeler Baker, ... Fort Ann.
John T. Blatchford, ... Troy.
Theodore F. Boudinot, ... Parsippany.
Josephus C. Brockway, ... Middlebury, Vt.
John Bull, ... Canandaigua.

Nathan H. Camp, ... Troy.
William B. Constable, ... Schenectady.
Andrew B. Cross, ... Saratoga.
Andrew A. Douglass, ... Stephentown.
William Hillhouse, ... Watervliet.
John Hooper, ... Troy.
Isaac Law, ... Salem.
Jonathan H. Merritt, ... Half Moon,
Samuel J. Mills, ... Guilford, Conn.
Silas C. Newton, ... Glens Falls.
Jacob Painter, ... Middletown, Pa.
Peter H. Rice, ... Whitehall.
Stoughton N. Taylor, ... Ballston.
Westerlo Van Rensselaer, ... Albany.
Addison G. Williams, ... Pompey.
*Charles M. Yvonnett, ... Troy.

1837-8.

Charles O. Benedict, ... Saratoga.
Cyrus Bentley, ... New Lebanon.
Albert W. Curtis, ... Sheffield, Mass.
Matthew Dorr Clark, ... West Bloomfield.
James T. Cornell, ... Wilton.
Preston Denton, ... Saratoga.
Rutger L. Drake, ... Troy.
Mark S. Dickerman, ... Troy.
*Theodore D. Judah, ... New York.
Nathan K. Masten, ... Troy.
Charles R. Mallory, ... Austerlitz.
James Oakey, ... Schaghticoke.
Edward E. Spoor, ... Avon, Conn.
W. W. Theobald, ... Albany.
John George Whittaker, ... New York.

1838-9.

Samuel C. Bigelow, ... Troy.
James A. Brazelton, ... Newmarket, Tenn.
Reuben Buck, ... Waterford.
James L. Cramer, ... Northumberland.
John C. Cramer, ... Waterford.
Isaac Drake, ... Troy.
J. Humboldt Eaton, ... Troy.
Richard H. Franchot, ... Butternuts.
George N. Gates, ... Louisiana.
*Charles S. Heartt, ... Troy.

Peter A. Ladieu, ... Troy.
Gerritt G. Lansing, ... New York.
William Mills, ... Troy.
Robert W. Rutherford, ... Lodi, N. J.
Sylvester E. Spoor, ... Troy.
William S. Stedman, ... Troy.

1839-40.

William H. Cole, ... Watervliet.
Hugh Connity, ... Waterford.
Ira Ford, ... Hoosack.
*Robert Lay, ... Springfield.
Hial Kenyon Parsons, ... Colebrook, N. H.
William McManus Storm, ... Eaton.
*William G. Vought, ... Victor.
Herman Whipple, ... Shaftsbury, Vt.
John D. Yates, ... Schenectady.

1840-1.

Sewell W. Hall, ... Troy.
Ezra E. Howard, ... Williamsvillo.
William A. Lee, ... Granville.
William H. Pratt, ... Chatham.
George N. Sharp, ... Troy.
John B. Tibbitts, ... Troy.

1841-2.

Elijah Bryan, 2d, ... Schaghticoke.
John H. Cook, ... Hanover, N. J.
G. Merriam Fisher, ... Lansingburgh.
Erastus Geer, ... Troy.
John P. Reilay, ... Troy.
William H. Rossiter, ... Troy.
John Shaw, ... Troy.
James H. Sherrill, ... New Hartford.
Graham R. Wickes, ... Troy.

1842-3.

William Bonesteel, ... Grafton.
Clarence Buel, ... Troy.
John G. Buswell, ... Troy.
George E. Douglass, ... New York.
Johnson H. Eaton, ... Troy.
Francis K. Field, ... Malden.
Derrick Lane, ... Troy.

Sidney W. Park, ... Troy.
Nathaniel B. Powers, ... Lansingburgh.
Adam R. Smith, ... Troy.
Stephen Sweet, ... Watervliet.
Braine Walsh, ... Lansingburgh.

1843-4.

Richard D. Bloss, ... Troy.
Oliver T. Burt, ... Syracuse.
Charles E. Callender, ... Manlius.
James R. Chamberlin, ... Troy.
Charlton H. Davis, ... Troy.
Joseph K. Downing, ... Bristol, Pa.
George H. Eaton, ... Troy.
Isaac M. McConihe, ... Troy.
William R. Shaw, ... Troy.

1844-5.

H. W. Brinsmade, ... Troy.
Theodore Brooks, ... Brunswick.
William H. Bull, ... Troy.
John S. Crary, ... Salem.
John W. Dorlon, ... Troy.
Louis A. Fellows, ... Troy.
Lusher Gay, ... Troy.
George C. Hall, ... Troy.
Henry S. Hatch, ... Troy.
Jonas S. Heartt, ... Troy.
Albert Holton, ... Troy.
Edward Hubbell, ... Troy.
Henry G. Landon, ... Troy.
William W. McConihe, ... Troy.
Robert F. Silliman, ... Troy.
John H. Warren, ... Troy.
John P. Willard, ... Troy.

1845-6.

Halsey Brainard, ... Troy.
William F. Burden, ... Troy.
William H. Burtis, ... Troy.
Matthias M. Cook, ... Hanover, N. J.
Charles R. Goodrich, ... Lansingburgh.
James A. Gray, ... Herkimer.
John S. Mallary, ... Troy.
Hiram McChesney, ... Troy.

Samuel L. Palmer, ... Chatham.
George Peacock, ... Troy.
William Powers, ... Lansingburgh.
Jedediah Randall, ... Norwich.
Robert M. Randall, ... Syracuse.
James T. Sargent, ... Sandy Hill.
Nicholas G. Van Meerten, ... Paramarabo.
Nicholas Van Namee, ... Pittstown.
John E. Warren, ... Troy.

1846-7.

John A. E. Abbott, ... Waltham, Mass.
Nathaniel F. Allen, ... Northboro, Mass.
Nathaniel T. Allen, ... Medfield, Mass.
James H. Ball, ... Nassau.
George L. Barker, ... New Lebanon.
John A. Goodwin, ... Bridgewater, Mass.
John Hammond, ... Crown Point.
T. Charlton Henry, ... Syracuse.
Thomas B. Heermans, ... Syracuse.
Charles M. Holton, ... Brunswick.
John F. Kidder, ... Syracuse.
Gardner Landon, Jr., ... Troy.
Daniel Marble, ... Troy.
Charles D. Rossiter, ... Brooklyn.
L. A. Rousseau, ... Troy.
J. Dayton F. Smith, ... Hamilton.
H. E. Thayer, ... Troy.
John I. Thompson, ... Troy.

1847-8.

Charles S. Abbott, ... Bath, N. H.
Thomas D. Cammack, ... New Orleans.
Augustus P. Chamberlain, A. B., ... Salem, Mass.
Henry Clum, ... Brunswick.
D. Cady Eaton, ... New Haven, Conn.
George H. Everest, ... New Lebanon.
William B. Guernsey, ... Norwich.
Benjamin Marble, ... Troy.
W. Henry Merriam, ... Troy.
John J. Moffatt, ... Stephentown.
James Neal, ... Portland, Me.
John W. Osborn, ... Watervliet.
David B. Parsons, ... Hoosick Falls.
A. B. Strawbridge, ... New Orleans.

J. A. Sullivan, ... Boston, Mass.
William S. Thomas, ... Norwich.
Henry B. Warren, ... Troy.

1848-9.

John C. Bell, ... Roxbury, Mass.
Richard Bloss, Jr., ... Troy.
Calvin Bush, ... Nassau.
W. O. Carpenter, ... Troy.
Bloomfield W. Caswell, ... Herkimer.
Harvey B. Dauchy, ... Troy.
Nathan Dauchy, ... Troy.
John Edson, ... Bridgewater, Mass.
F. A. Goodnough, ... Troy.
J. P. Hoag, ... Sandy Hill.
James Irvine, ... Kingsbury, Ala.
Francis Irvine, ... Kingsbury, Ala.
Edward R. Johnson, ... Albany.
John N. Miller, ... Niskayuna.
George A. Murdock, ... Brookline, Mass.
Achilles J. Rousseau, ... Troy.
Frederick D. Tator, ... Troy.
Samuel M. Vail, ... Troy.
Edward Wade, ... Watervliet.
Louis H. Weaver, ... Troy.
J. Clifford Yeager, ... Philadelphia, Pa.
Lewis E. Yorke, ... Salem, N. J.

1849-50.

Horatio Ames, Jr., ... Falls Village, Ct.
John E. Baker, ... Schaghticoke.
Hampden Buel, ... Troy.
John G. Buel, ... Troy.
James A. Burden, ... Troy.
Charles W. Burrage, ... Leominster, Mass.
Aaron Burt, ... Syracuse.
H. M. Chase, ... Plattsburgh.
O. W. Clary, ... Syracuse.
William B. Cogswell, ... Syracuse.
Hiram Cole, ... Kingsbury, Ala.
*Silas T. Covell, ... Troy.
Thomas Davis, ... Templeton, Mass.
Jacob A. Diver, ... Melrose.
William L. Drowne, ... Canaan.
J. D. Fouquet, ... Plattsburgh.

John M. Fouquet, ...Plattsburgh.
Eugene Hodson, ...Florida.
Joseph H. Howard, ...Brooklyn.
M. E. Hutton, ... Troy.
Samuel L. Irish, ...Chatham.
J. H. Knickerbacker, ...Schaghticoke.
John M. Landon, ...Nassau.
Augustus Lane, ...Key West, Fla.
James R. Larkin, ...St. Louis, Mo.
Albert L. Lee, ...Fulton.
Henry Lester, ...Syracuse.
Abiel T. Loomis, ...Fulton.
A. W. McMurray, ...Lansingburgh.
H. A. Middleton, Jr., ...Charleston, S. C.
George H. Nettleton, ... Springfield, Mass.
Richard B. Noyes, ...Southport, Wis.
E. A. Putnam, ...Syracuse.
Simon P. Schermerhorn, ...Mohawk.
C. E. Dudley Tibbitts, ...Troy.
Augustus W. Twing, ...Lansingburgh.
Charles H. Warren, ...Pittstown.
Charles S. Warren, ...Troy.
Charles Wellington, ...Syracuse.
P. White, ...Troy.
P. P. Wintermute, ...Elmira.
William E. Young, ...New York.

1850-1.

*Augustus E. Babcock, ...Troy.
James G. Balton, ...Troy.
Ripley R. Calkins, ...Avoca.
Abijah C. Curtis, ...Great Barrington, Mass.
Samuel D. Davis, ...Troy.
James A. Eddy, ...Troy.
Titus C. Eddy, ...Troy.
Charles S. Hicks, ...Troy.
William P. Hubbard, ...Bangor, Me.
George T. Lane, ...Troy.
Horatio Lloyd, ...Salem.
Alexander C. Low, ...Dover, N. H.
J. R. Mallary, ...Troy.
Horace Maxwell, ...Louisville, Ky.
Robert E. Meyer, ...Troy.
George L. Moody, ...Boston, Mass.

J. Henry Nicholson, ... Buffalo.
James G. Patton, ... Brunswick.
*T. H. Pierce, ... Williamsburg.
Frederick R. Stowe, ... Troy.
William A. Thompson, ... Troy.
H. H. Ward, ... Brooklyn.
William S. Williams, ... Syracuse.

1851-2.

Daniel Atwood, ... Boston, Mass.
Charles H. Ballard, ... Charlemont, Mass.
Nathaniel T. Bartlett, ... Plymouth, Mass.
George C. Bell, ... Amsterdam.
Edward H. Brown, ... Syracuse.
John Otis Burt, ... Syracuse.
John C. Clifford, ... Buffalo.
Frederick W. Coleman, ... New York.
Charles H. Fisher, ... Lansingburgh.
Isaac D. Fisher, ... Boston, Mass.
Nathaniel Fisher, Jr., ... Northboro, Mass.
Edmund B. French, ... Troy.
Job P. Grant, ... Schaghticoke.
Bryan Grant, ... Schaghticoke.
George B. Hunt, ... Huntsville, Conn.
George E. Kimberly, ... Chicago, Ill.
John H. Leavitt, ... Charlemont, Mass.
John H. Maxon, ... Adams.
Samuel McConihe, ... Troy.
George H. Moon, ... Hillsdale.
Reuben Nickerson, ... Bangor, Me.
Myron Platt, ... Glens Falls.
Duane Simmons, ... Glens Falls.
James G. Smith, ... Chicopee, Mass.
Walter M. Smith, ... Newark, O.
Tench F. Tilghman, ... Oxford, Md.
Eugene L. Williams, ... Syracuse.
Preston C. F. West, ... Philadelphia, Pa.
B. Franklin Woodford, ... Mt. Morris.

1852-3.

Robert T. Adriance, ... Poughkeepsie.
Stephen E. Babcock, ... Troy.
*Edward D. Barton, ... Troy.
*John P. Beach, ... Troy.

MANNING C. BLACKSTONE, ... Adams.
OLIVER P. BUEL, ... Troy.
ELIAS E. CORYELL, ... New Hope, Pa.
HEBER CRANE, ... Detroit, Mich.
CHARLES D. CURTIS, ... Adams.
BURR DAUCHY, ... Troy.
DANIEL CADY EATON, ... New Haven, Conn.
NEWTON EDDY, ... Waterford.
A. PARK HAMMOND, ... Rockville, Conn.
HENRY F. HAYWARD, ... Kingston, C. W.
ROMANUS HODGMAN, ... Chelmsford, Mass.
HENRY LOHNES, ... Schaghticoke.
*GEORGE A. MASON, ... Chicago, Ill.
G. W. MEYLERT, ... Milford, Pa.
FRANCIS K. MIDDLETON, ... Charleston, S. C.
JOHN M. MOTT, Jr., ... Lansingburgh.
FRANKLIN A. MORSE, ... East Poultney, Vt.
MATTHEW P. MYERS, ... Troy.
WILLIAM P. OPENHEIMER, ... Ponce, Porto Rico.
M. PELTON, ... Syracuse.
CHARLES H. RICHARDS, ... Warrensburgh.
ALEXANDER H. SHARPE, ... Salem.
OVID T. SIMMONS, ... Saugerties.
CLEMENT H. SINNICKSON, ... Salem, N. J.
*JAMES S. THORN, ... Troy.
CORNELIUS L. TWING, ... Lansingburgh.
B. C. McVICKAR, ... Chicago, Ill.
J. WATSON WEBB, Jr., ... New York.
J. WATSON WEBB, 2d, ... New York City.
J. BECKWITH WEST, ... Washington, D. C.

1853-4.

JAMES BAPTISTE, ... Troy.
HENRY F. BIRGE, ... Troy.
FREDERICK BRAEM, ... Poughkeepsie.
ROBERT T. BURNS, ... Toronto, C. W.
JOHN CAMP, Jr., ... Norwalk, Conn.
EDWARD CAMPBELL. Niagara, C. W.
JAMES CARPENTER, ... Demorestville, C. W.
JEROME M. CHAPMAN, ... Farmington, Ill.
H. S. CHATFIELD, ... New York.
HENRY S. CHURCH, ... Troy.
FREDERICK R. CURTIS, ... New York.
FRANCIS C. DRAPER, ... Toronto, C. W.
LEBBEUS EGERTON, Jr., ... Troy.

Benjamin Franklin, ... Lansingburgh.
Byron F. Frisbie, ... Watertown.
H. S. Gatzmer, ... Philadelphia, Pa.
Edwin R. Gridley, ... Hudson.
Joseph Greer, ... New York.
J. L. Hickes, ... New York.
George P. B. Hill, ... New York.
Edward Harleston, ... Charleston, S. C.
William W. Henry, ... Grand Rapids, Mich.
Eustis Huger, ... Fort Munroe, Va.
William D. Jarvis, ... Toronto, C. W.
David T. Jenkins, ... Vernon.
Hayward Jones, ... Troy.
William P. Kellogg, ... Lansingburgh.
Carolan J. Kinsey, ... Clifton Mills.
Antonio F. de Lacerda, ... Bahia, Brazil.
Robert C. Laisdell, ... Lansingburgh.
Joseph B. Livingston, ... Trenton, N. J.
George W. Lyle, ... Athens.
Charles Macguire, ... West Troy.
G. Elliott Macomber, ... Ballstown.
John J. Macpherson, ... Charleston, S. C.
Charles W. Mann, ... San Francisco, Cal.
Edmund H. Murney, ... Belleville, C. W.
Austin B. Paige, ... Unity, N. H.
James H. Place, ... Rochester, N. H.
William D. Powell, ... Niagara, C. W.
Longworth Powers, ... Florence, Italy.
Charles C. Pope, ... Syracuse.
Charles M. B. Prioleau, ... Charleston, S. C.
Manuel Quintana, ... Havana, Cuba.
William Radenhurst, ... Toronto, C. W.
*William A. Robertson, ... Rahway, N. J.
John Roff, ... Watervliet.
Charles E. Rowland, ... Charleston, S. C.
John W. Ross, ... Troy.
George H. Sanford, ... Ballston.
J. Sterling Smith, ... Geneseo.
James M. Tyler, ... Hillsdale.
Robert B. Thurston, ... Huntington, L. I.
James G. Tracy, ... Syracuse.
Artemas Wood, ... Lansingburgh.
E. H. Welch, ... Lambertville, N. J.

1854-5.

John A. Abert, ... Washington, D. C.
Aruna M. Adsit, ... Troy.
George W. Boutelle, ... Bennington, Vt.
A. E. Browning, ... Trenton, N. J.
Charles D. Burrus, ... West Troy.
Jehiel W. Cheney, ... Massena.
D. E. Cornell, ... Hoosick.
Benjamin E. Crane, ... Athens, Ga.
Dan. B. Dorsey, ... Watertown.
John D. P. Douw, ... Greenbush.
Oliver B. Filley, ... Lansingburgh.
Henry P. Gerrish, ... Newburyport, Mass.
G. R. Giddings, ... Jefferson, O.
Edwin R. Gridley, ... Hudson.
Charles Harris, ... New York.
DeWitt C. Hayes, ... Watertown.
J. W. Heimstreet, ... Troy.
E. Pearce Horne, ... Milledgeville, Ga.
Richard Hurley, ... Troy.
Benjamin F. Johnson, ... Belleville.
George P. Johnson, ... Plymouth, Mass.
Charles Henry Jones, ... Reading, Pa.
Beverly R. Keim, ... Reading, Pa.
William S. Kimball, ... Lawrence, Mass.
Benton L. Kingsbury, ... Towanda, Pa.
John C. Kinzie, Jr., ... Chicago, Ill.
Robert T. Luce, ... Yonkers.
R. L. Maxon, ... Stowell's Corners.
Frederick G. McKean, ... Baltimore, Md.
Frederick Mercur, ... Towanda, Pa.
J. Caldwell Newton, ... New York.
George Paddock, ... Watertown.
Frederick Shelly, ... Troy.
Theodore D. Selleck, ... Norwalk, Conn.
William C. Starr, ... Trenton, N. J.
*Clifford Stickney, ... Chicago, Ill.
Charles A. Stetson, Jr., ... New York.
L. M. Swift, ... Cornwall, Conn.
Charles Ten Eyck, ... Schodack.
Egbert Ten Eyck, ... Schodack.
Thomas W. Thurston, ... Huntington, L. I.
Edward A. Trotter, ... New York.
Albertus Webb, ... Trenton, N. J.

William D. Wells, ... Troy.
Malcolm E. Williams, ... Syracuse.

1855-6.

Richard L. Annesley, ... Albany.
Hill Barker, ... Bangor, Me.
R. M. Benedict, ... New York.
David H. Buel, ... Poughkeepsie.
I. Townsend Burden, ... Troy.
W. F. Cornish, ... Bethlehem, N. J.
Wilson Crosby, ... ———
George S. Dawson, ... Albany.
Richard H. Doughty, ... Troy.
Richard P. H. Durkee, ... New York.
*Thomas Eaton, ... Troy.
William Gilbert, ... Troy.
*Charles O. Gray, ... Warrensburgh.
Henry M. Heller, ... Clintonville.
J. Lawrence Hicks, ... Flushing.
Emelio M. Hidalgo, ... Cienfuegos, Cuba.
Baron Higman, ... Newport, R. I.
Theodore Hubbell, ... Troy.
A. Mayor Lawvere, ... Freeport, Ill.
N. B. Lord, ... Nassau.
James MacDonald, ... Albany.
Francis H. Parker, ... Oswego.
V. A. Pugsley, ... Amenia.
Henry Redmund, ... Orange, N. J.
Carlos E. Sauvalle, ... Havana, Cuba.
Daniel F. Schenck, ... Oswego.
Justino Nunes de Sento-Se, ... Bahia, Brazil.
Pliny T. Sexton, ... Rochester.
Alexander Smith, ... Orange, N. J.
Francis K. Stevens, ... Poughkeepsie.
Frederick W. Trippe, ... Newark, N. J.
Jay Westinghouse, ... Schenectady.
Thomas G. Wood, ... Albany.

1856-7.

Henry S. Adams, ... Chicopee, Mass.
Frank P. Amsden, ... Scranton, Pa.
William P. Anderson, ... Cincinnati, O.
Milton S. Bradshaw, ... Lansingburgh.
James D. Butler, ... Groton, Mass.
William B. Chapman, ... New York.

Daniel Carhart, ...Clinton, N. J.
John B. Carpenter, ... Wyoming, Pa.
Eugene M. Copeland, ...Fort Ann.
Fred F. Durand, ...New York.
Cyrus F. Emery, ... Mexico.
Charles R. Floyd, ...St. Marys, Ga.
Henry F. Greene, ...Syracuse.
Chauncy E. Ives, ...Lansingburgh.
*Thomas L. Johnston, ...Troy.
Nathan N. Keeler, ...Salem.
T. Ellery Lord, ...Albany.
William G. Myers, ...Canton, Miss.
Dudley Olcott, ...Albany.
James H. Perry, ...Troy.
M. S. Prudhomme, ...Opelousas, La.
Robert F. E. Redington, ...Troy.
William W. Rousseau, ...Troy.
Thomas Rowland, ...Alexandria, Va.
Francisco R. Sabat, ...St. Johns, P. R.
James C. Stodder, ...Boston, Mass.
John H. Taylor, ...Newark, N. J.
Edward L. Topp, ...Memphis, Tenn.
Rush Vanleer, ...Nashville, Tenn.
Isaac P. Wodell, ...Ellisburgh.
John Wylie, ...Iroquois, C. W.

1857-8.

Antonio S. Casanova, ...Cienfuegos, Cuba.
Charles H. Dauchy, ...Troy.
Charles D. Fisher, ... Lansingburgh.
James M. Hawley, ...Troy.
John R. Halsey, ...Newark, N. J.
George P. Herthel, ...St. Louis, Mo.
*Edgar Horsefall, ...Schenectady.
Stewart Ives, ...Lansingburgh.
Jordan W. Lockwood, ...Martindale.
Joseph D. Lomax, ...New York.
Edward T. Maidment, ...Albany.
Francisco A. Payrol, ...Villa Clara, Cuba.
William H. Scranton, ...Scranton, Pa.
John H. Strader, ...Cincinnati, O.
Edmund L. Tyler, ...Norwich, Conn.
Marin F. Yznaga, ...Trinidad, Cuba.

1858-9.

Henry W. Bill, ... Philadelphia, Pa.
Albion M. Christie, ... Savannah, Ga.
Churchill Crittenden, ... San Francisco, Cal.
J. Caldwell Crombie, ... Rochester.
Edgar M. Cullen, A. B., ... Brooklyn.
Hanford Day, ... Lansingburgh.
E. T. Eddy, ... Troy.
*Otis Fisher, ... Trenton, N. J.
Leonard Goodwin, ... Morris, Conn.
Henry P. Gregory, ... Plattsburgh.
William H. Gulick, ... Blossburg, Pa.
Franklin S. Hall, ... Fredericksburgh, Va.
Marshall Hastings, ... Benicia, Cal.
Ira Harris, Jr., ... Albany.
William T. Hart, ... Union Point, Ga.
William B. Hyde, ... Benicia, Cal.
Llewlyn M. Kaufman, ... Leesport, Pa.
Jacob Lippman, ... Savannah, Ga.
George W. Miller, ... Johnsonville.
Joseph Ridgeway, Jr., ... New York.
Augustus Sackett, ... Warren, Conn.
E. Sheldon Scribner, ... Janesville, Wis.
Abraham J. Storm, ... Stormville.
Charles F. Turnbull, ... Charleston, S. C.
James D. Warner, ... Albany.
William Zimmermann, ... Buffalo.

1859-60.

Henry M. Adams, ... Amherst, Mass.
John T. Carroll, ... Troy.
*Walter O. Dunbar, ... Preble.
William H. Gillett, ... Buffalo.
Nathaniel Irish, ... Pittsburgh, Pa.
James G. Knap, ... Brownville.
George W. Lane, ... Troy.
Leonard March, ... Bangor, Me.
Reuben W. Petrikin, ... Lock Haven, Pa.
Franklin C. Prindle, ... Arlington, Vt.
Lewis Y. Schermerhorn, ... Greenwich.
Thomas Van Valkenburgh, ... Lockport.

1860-1.

Francisco E. Anido, ... Villa Clara, Cuba.
Thompson H. Doughty, ... New York.

George B. Hickman, ... West Chester, Pa.
Charles McC. Lord, ... Lyme, Conn.
Edwin C. Moncure, ... Hinds Co., Miss.
J. Lawrence Rathbone, ... Albany.
Mortimer H. Roberts, ... Glens Falls.
Nicholas Tanco, ... Havana, Cuba.
Sinclair G. Turnbull, ... Westchester.

1861-2.

Miguel de Arostegui, ... Puerto Principe, Cuba.
George H. Bierce, ... Circleville, O.
Edmund L. Cole, ... Troy.
Theodore W. Davis, ... Poughkeepsie.
Arthur J. Dillon, ... St. Louis.
Edward H. Hammond, ... Waltham, Mass.
Andrew S. Hughes, ... St. Joseph, Mo.
Walter James, ... New York.
Freeborn G. Jewett, Jr., ... Poughkeepsie.
Ervin B. Kenyon, ... Hoosick.
Frederick Mason, ... Taunton, Mass.
C. Stewart Maurice, ... Sing Sing.
John C. McMurray, ... Lansingburgh.
William J. Myers, ... Pittsburgh, Pa.
Montague P. Neff, ... Cincinnati, O.
Christopher L. Painter, ... Pittsburgh, Pa.
William W. Parrish, ... Philadelphia, Pa.
Edward R. Satterlee, Jr., ... New York.
Charles H. L. Smith, ... New York.
William Wheelwright, ... London, Eng.
George T. Wicks, ... Poughkeepsie.
Thomas F. Witherbee, ... Port Henry.

1862-3.

Francis Babcock, A. B., ... New York.
Charles W. Bebee, ... Ravenswood, L. I.
Julius N. Beemer, ... Newton, N. J.
James Bettner, ... Yonkers.
Charles E. Burrall, ... Rock Island, Ill.
George O. Catlin, ... Troy.
Robert S. Church, ... Brooklyn.
Charles Davison, ... New York.
Bertram Delafield, ... Staten Island.
Johnston L. De Peyster, ... Tivoli.
Asahel Edgington, ... Edgington, Ill.
S. De Puy Freer, ... Cortland.

Thomas Gordon, ...New York.
Edward M. Green, ...Troy.
Charles R. Hicks, ...Troy.
Samuel B. Judah, ...Vincennes, Ind.
John F. Marsh, ...Chicago, Ill.
James T. Munn, ...New York.
George H. Munson, ...Amsterdam.
G. Frederick Oliver, ...Troy.
Alexander S. Palmer, Jr., ...Stonington, Conn.
Melvin Stephens, ...Brooklyn.
Plowdon Stevens, ...Grafton.
Robert H. Thompson, ...Troy.

1863-4.

Whitfield B. Abbott, ...Fort Lee, N. J.
*Edward L. Archer, ...Brooklyn.
Satterlee Arnold, ...Sandlake.
Frederick A. Apelles, ...West Point.
Justo M. del Cañal, ...Pinar del Rio, Cuba.
Pablo B. Cantero, ...Trinidad, Cuba.
Gideon W. Carmichael, ...Sandlake.
William G. Cochrane, ...New York.
William H. Coughlin, ...Brooklyn.
Walter E. Cox, ...Bethlehem, Pa.
L. Huntley Cramer, ...Saratoga.
B. Dalton Dorr, ...Philadelphia, Pa.
Augustus H. Eaton, ...Troy.
Francis W. Elston, ...Crawfordsville, Ind.
Alfred De F. Gale, ...Troy.
Charles C. Gerard, ...Newburgh.
Guillermo P. Gonzalez, ...Havana, Cuba.
Nelson J. Harris, ...Hamilton.
Alfred W. Higgins, ...Buffalo.
Charles P. Howell, ...Goshen.
H. Reeve Ingalls, ...Troy.
Amasa C. Jackson, ...New York.
J. Ross Jackson, ...Paterson, N. J.
George M. King, ...Morristown, N. J.
William Knight, ...Yonkers.
J. Hamilton Langworthy, ...Stonington, Conn.
Edward H. Morrison, ...Newark, N. J.
Charles W. Musgrave, ...Bay Ridge.
Julien S. Ogden, ...New York.
Robert E. Packer, ...Mauch Chunk, Pa.
Juan Perez, ...Consolacion, Cuba.

Jose Ponce, ... Trinidad, Cuba.
George V. Shepard, ... Troy.
Charles L. Snow, ... Brooklyn.
Orison B. Smith, ... Ravenswood.
N. Henry Starbuck, ... Troy.
*Charles Underhill, ... Sing Sing.
David H. Valentine, ... Greenpoint.
Eugene Vanderpool, ... Newark, N. J.
*William A. Vandervoort, ... New York.
Frank Warren, ... Louisville, Ky.
William Waters, ... Franklin.

1864-5.

*Diego A. de Aguero, ... Puerto Principe, Cuba.
George P. Atwill, ... New York.
Joseph N. Balestier, Jr., ... New York.
Mills W. Barse, ... Olean.
Frank O. Bennet, ... Bellport.
Felix A. Campuzano, ... Matanzas, Cuba.
Alexander H. Caryl, Jr., ... Groton, Mass.
J. Wakefield Cortlan, ... Baltimore, Md.
Frederick S. Cozzens, ... Yonkers.
Antonio E. Desvernine, ... Havana, Cuba.
Samuel L. Dolsen, ... Middletown.
Franklin Dwelle, ... Rushville.
Fernando M. Figueredo, ... Bayamo, Cuba.
Teofilo Gimbernat, B. S., ... New York.
David H. Gould, ... Bergen.
J. Leslie Gregg, ... Wilmington, Del.
Albert W. Hubbard, ... Birmingham, Conn.
Frederick H. Humphrey, ... Auburn.
Ambrosio D. Lamadriz, ... Matanzas, Cuba.
Pedro Malibran, ... Trinidad, Cuba.
H. Frederick Merwin, ... Brooklyn.
Maximo E. Mora, ... Havana, Cuba.
Luis M. Morejon, ... Matanzas, Cuba.
Jose R. Nadal, ... Mayagues, Porto Rico.
Andrew Onderdonk, ... Sherwood, N. J.
Worth Osgood, ... Troy.
Carl F. Palfrey, ... Belfast, Me.
Thomas O. B. Pott, ... Pottsville, Pa.
*Robert B. Reading, ... Philadelphia, Pa.
Cornelius Roosevelt, ... New York.
Clinton F. Stephens, ... Auburn.
Warner Underwood, ... Bowling Green, Ky.

Leopoldo Valdes, ... Havana, Cuba.
Wesley Vandercook, ... Fremont, O.
Charles K. Wead, ... Malone.

1865-6.

Robert W. Aborn, Jr., ... Orange, N. J.
Robert F. Adams, ... New York.
Rodolfo Adan, ... Puerto Principe, Cuba.
Moses Atwood, ... Pittsburgh, Pa.
Phineas Barnes, Jr., ... Portland, Me.
Andrew Barry, ... Hillsboro, O.
Lewis L. C. Bartlett, ... Providence, R. I.
Thomas Bradford, ... New Brighton, Pa.
Samuel Brady, ... Detroit, Mich.
Edmund Canfield, ... Dover, N. J.
Charles G. Cooper, ... Mt. Vernon, O.
St. Clair Denny, ... Pittsburgh, Pa.
William R. Freeman, ... New York.
Alexander Gray, ... Wilkesbarre, Pa.
Orrin S. Gridley, ... Buffalo.
George S. Gunnison, ... Brooklyn.
Eugene J. Hall, ... Brandon, Vt.
George B. Hall, ... Detroit, Mich.
Gideon Hawley, ... Albany.
William T. Hull, ... Philadelphia, Pa.
Josiah W. Jenkins, ... Vernon.
Julius J. Larrinaga, ... San Juan, P. R.
William N. Lee, ... Detroit, Mich.
Gardner MacGregor, ... Mac Gregor, Ia.
Frederico J. Marquetti, ... Havana, Cuba.
Thomas G. McKell, ... Chilicothe, O.
Pablo Mendive, ... Havana, Cuba.
Thomas H. Mitchell, ... Cincinnati, O.
Raimundo Navarro, ... Monterey, Mex.
Jose A. Nunez, ... San Juan, P. R.
William G. Park, ... Pittsburgh, Pa.
Frank Place, ... Cincinnatus.
Matthew Preston, ... Pittsburgh, Pa.
Manuel E. Rivas, ... Matanzas, Cuba.
James Rockwell, Jr, ... Utica.
Arthur A. Rogers, ... Utica.
George B. Rogers, ... Williamsburgh.
Julian A. Rogers, ... Utica.
Antonio Sanchez, ... Puerto Principe, Cuba.
William Sanderson, ... Milwaukee, Wis.

Charles W. Schanck, ... New York.
Jesse M. Smith, ... Detroit, Mich.
John W. Trott, ... Niagara Falls.
Hiram F. Willis, ... Eldred, Pa.
Teofilo Zambrano, ... Monterey, Mex.

1866-7.

Caetano F. D'Almeida, ... Rio Janeiro, Brazil.
Joao J. Alves, ... Bahia, Brazil.
William D. Baber, ... Pottsville, Pa.
Willis H. Ballance, ... Peoria, Ill.
Charles J. Bates, ... Cincinnati, O.
Robert Bell, ... Rochester.
Henry E. Brown, ... Warren, Pa.
S. Matthews Cary, ... Houlton, Me.
T. Chalmers Clarkson, ... Pittsburgh, Pa.
James P. Coleman, ... Pemberton, N. J.
Cornelius M. Comegys, ... Cincinnati, O.
Edward B. Crane, ... Dorchester, Mass.
Clay Crawford, ... Cleveland, O.
Honorato F. de Cueto, ... Cienfuegos, Cuba.
William H. Fitch, ... New Salem.
John H. Gardinier, ... Springfield.
Thomas A. Hamilton, ... Athens, Ga.
Archibald P. Law, ... Carbondale, Pa.
Sherman H. LeRoy, ... Staatsburg.
Judson Medenhall, ... Lewistown, Pa.
Edward G. Morton, ... Newburgh.
Alberto J. Nadal, ... Mayagüez, Porto Rico.
Merritt Peckham, Jr., ... Utica.
Frank W. Quereau, ... Brooklyn.
George Taylor, ... Fremont, O.
Charles H. Thatcher, ... Hartford, Conn.
Alexander R. Thompson, ... Newark, N. J.
*Frederick Tinker, ... Newark, N. J.
George W. Worcester, ... Hollis, N. H.
Sabas J. Yturbide, ... Mexico, Mex.

1867-8.

Samuel H. Aby, Jr., ... New Orleans, La.
William P. Allendorph, ... Troy.
William H. Barry, ... Cincinnati, O.
John W. Beaman, ... North Hadley, Mass.
Richard Blackstone, ... Connellsville, Pa.
Isaac F. Bosworth, ... Troy.

Orin S. Bixby, ...Milford.
Robert C. P. Coggeshall, ...New Bedford, Mass.
Charles L. Du Bois, ...Washington, D. C.
Wright Gardner, ...Lansingburgh.
Frank A. Lindsay, ...Troy.
James D. Mason, ...Providence, R. I.
Robert P. Paulding, ...Cold Spring.
Joseph H. Peters, ...Amesbury, Mass.
William C. Roberts, ... Baltimore, Md.
Gustave Roullier, ...New York.
Henry G. Sandkuhl, ...Poughkeepsie.
Charles E. Sayles, ...Elmira.
Thomas E. Vermilye, Jr., ...Utica.
Harry E. Woodrow, ...Cincinnati, O.
William M. Woollett, ...Watervliet.
Charles D. Wright, ...Orwell, Vt.

1868-9.

William A. Adams, ...Cincinnati, O.
Antonio A. Aguirre, ...Havana, Cuba.
Juan P. Arriola, ...Trinidad, Cuba.
Juan B. Berriozabal, ... Mexico, Mex.
Alexander C. Chenoweth, A. B., ...Carlisle, Pa.
George B. Chenoweth, A. B., ...Carlisle, Pa.
Pedro A. Cardona, ...Manzanillo, Cuba.
Lucas A. de Castro, ...Trinidad, Cuba.
Stewart F. Chisholm, ...Cleveland, O.
William H. Coffin, ...Washington, D. C.
Clarence L. Cook, ...Brooklyn.
Melville Curtis, ...West Farnham, C. E
Mark L. Filley, ...Lansingburgh.
Emilio Giro, ...Santiago, Cuba.
Pedro F. Hernandez, ...Matanzas, Cuba.
George C. Johnson, ...Brunswick.
Leopoldo del Junco, ...Cienfuegos, Cuba.
Frank R. Kellogg, ...Ashland, O.
James D. Ketchum, ...Washington, D. C.
Domingo L. Lamadriz, ...Matanzas, Cuba.
Gustavus A. Longnecker, ...Mechanicsburgh.
John K. Longnecker, ...Mechanicsburgh.
Arthur MacArthur, ...Troy.
*Henry R. Massey, ...San Francisco, Cal.
Charles E. Perkins, ...Akron, O.
Rafael J. Rua, ... Matanzas, Cuba.
John W. Sinnickson, ...Salem, N. J.

Manning L. Spooner, ... Reading, O.
George M. Thornton, ... Pawtucket, R. I.
Walter F. Upson, ... Tallmadge, O.
Howard S. Winslow, ... Cincinnati, O.
Charles C. Woods, ... Washington, Conn.

1869-70.

Frank P. Abercrombie, ... Roslyn, L. I.
George S. Andrus, ... Brooklyn.
Frank R. Blackinton, ... North Adams, Mass.
William B. Carroll, ... Troy.
Thomas Charlton, ... Ironton, O.
Chauncey C. Edson, ... New York.
Frank A. Fletcher, ... Indianapolis, Ind.
Ramon Guillot, ... Havana, Cuba.
James P. Harrison, ... Fayette, Miss.
William Harrison, ... Troy.
Charles A. Ingraham, ... Cambridge.
Charles C. Kneisly, ... Dayton, O.
Charles M. Marsh, ... Woodstock, Vt.
Charles W. McMaster, ... Troy.
William T. Miller, ... Buffalo.
Alexander G. Pendleton, ... Washington, D. C.
Emilio Pritchard, ... New York.
Solon B. Prindle, ... Troy.
Thomas J. Rodman, ... Rock Island, Ill.
Edward I. Rogers, ... New Castle, Del.
Roswell D. Sawyer, ... Dover, N. H.
Charles H. Schimpf, ... Allentown, Pa.
Francis Shippen, ... Burlington, N. J.
Michael M. Shoemaker, ... Cincinnati, O.
Edgar G. Stoney, ... Cedar Rapids, Ia.
Charles T. Sutton, ... Tunkhannock, Pa.
George H. Tilden, ... New Lebanon.
Jose M. Tribino, ... Guayaquil, Ecuador.
G. Norman Weaver, ... Newport, R. I.
Edward B. Welling, ... North Bennington, Vt.
Edwin L. Westermann, ... Sharon, Pa.

1870-1.

Sidney W. Beauclerk, ... Louisville, Ky.
Edward D. Blackwell, ... Norristown, Pa.
George B. Coe, ... Oxford.
Hugh Cooper, ... Mt. Vernon, O.
John A. Corliss, ... Waterford.

FRANK A. DICKSON,........................New Haven, Conn.
HENRY GOOLD,............................Albany.
EDWARD T. GOULD,........................Troy.
SAMUEL HALL,............................Evansville, Ind.
JOHN T. HALLIDAY,.......................Brooklyn.
CHARLES M. HUBBARD,.....................London, O.
S. WARREN INGALLS,......................North Adams, Mass.
EUGENE B. JONES,........................Washington, Mo.
JOHN R. KALEY, A. B.,...................Albany.
HARRY A. LA PAUGH,......................Utica.
EUGENE S. LARKIN,.......................Bridgeport, Conn.
JOSEPH S. LYBRAND,......................Philadelphia, Pa.
JOSE YGNACIO MARTINEZ,..................New York.
WALTER P. McCULLOCH,....................Greenbush.
EDMUND S. MILLS, Jr.,...................Hastings-upon-Hudson.
WILLIAM R. MYGATT,......................Oxford.
WILLIAM L. OTIS,........................Cleveland, O.
G. L. M. PINTO,.........................Rio Janeiro, Brazil.
P. PORTER POINIER,......................Newark, N. J.
JOHN E. ROBINSON,.......................Mt. Clement, Mich.
WILLIAM H. SHIRLAND,....................San Francisco, Cal.
FREDERICK W. SNOW,......................Ramapo.
ETHELBERT A. STANLEY,...................Schuylerville.
*FLOYD S. THAYER,.......................Mendota, Ill.
LESLIE J. WATSON,.......................Paterson, N. J.
CHARLES H. WICKHAM,.....................Tioga, Pa.
EDWARD A. WIKIDAL,......................Canton, O.
GEORGE E. WINSLOW,......................Bay Ridge.
THOMAS S. WOTKYNS,......................Troy.

1871-2.

ONWARD BATES,...........................St. Louis, Mo.
LE GRAND L. BENEDICT,...................New York.
RUDOLPHUS R. BOURLAND,..................Peoria, Ill.
JULIUS R. BURNHAM,......................Glens Falls.
SAMUEL K. CASS,.........................Pittsburgh, Pa.
MICHAEL E. DEVLIN,......................West Chester.
HENRY E. DRAYTON,.......................Philadelphia, Pa.
HARRY A. ELLIOTT,.......................Des Moines, Ia.
WARREN EWEN, Jr.,.......................Lima, Peru.
FRANKLIN FIELD, Jr.,....................Troy.
WILLIAM H. FLOYD, Jr.,..................St. Joseph, Mo.
EDWARD B. GUTHRIE, A. B.,...............Buffalo.
THEODORE W. H. HAUSCHILD,...............Spragueville, Ia.
CHARLES H. KING,........................Troy.

HENRY MACTIER, ... Philadelphia, Pa.
HENRY C. PARSONS, ... Albany.
OVERTON PRICE, ... Hillsboro, O.
GREGORIO C. QUESADA, ... San Jose, C. R.
THORNTON A. RODEFER, ... Bellaire, O.
PATTERSON H. RORER, ... Lynchburg, Va.
JOHN H. SOLLENBERGER, ... Louisville, O.
WILLIAM A. TIBBAL, ... Hartford, Conn.
WILLIAM WHEATLEY, Jr., ... New York.
FRANK W. WHITLOCK, A. B., ... Great Barrington, Mass.
ALBERT M. WILSON, ... Brooklyn.

1872-3.

CLARK S. BAILY, ... Utica.
JOSEPH W. BURDEN, A. B., ... Troy.
RICHARD E. CHISM, ... Norristown, Pa.
ROBERT C. CLAPP, ... Fort Hamilton.
FRANK M. CLARKSON, ... Rochester.
*EDWARD H. CONKLING, ... Bennington, Vt.
JAMES F. D'WOLF, ... Bristol, R. I.
LOUIS H. EVANS, ... Chicago, Ill.
ISAAC P. FLAGLER, ... La Grange.
PAUL A. FLEURY, ... Upper Falls, Md.
EDGAR FREEDMAN, ... New York.
FRANCIS C. GAMBLE, ... Toronto, C. W.
JOHN K. HALL, ... New York.
WILLARD HARLEY, ... New York.
JOSE J. C. MALCHER, ... Para, Brazil.
NESTOR J. NARVARTE, ... Lima, Peru.
GOUVERNEUR OGDEN, ... Troy.
WILLIAM C. ROSS, ... Troy.
FREDERICK F. SCHEINER, ... Newark, N. J.
DANIEL L. SLATAPER, ... Pittsburgh, Pa.
CHARLES M. SMITH, ... Hardwick, Mass.
JOHN B. UNDERHILL, ... New York.
H. GLYDE WILKENS, ... Detroit, Mich.

MEMBERS OF THE INSTITUTE
1874.

CLASS OF 1874.

James N. Caldwell, Jr., C. E.,......... Carthage, O.
George W. Carnrick, C. E., ...Troy.
Lyman E. Cooley, C. E.,................Canandaigua.
William J. Fabian, C. E.,..............Lake Forest, Ill.
Frank L. Ford, C. E.,..................East Cleveland, O.
Alexander P. Gest, C. E.,...... ......Philadelphia, Pa.
George S. Griffen, C. E.,...............Phoenixville, Pa.
William P. Mason, C. E.,...............New York City.
Harry D. Pattison, C. E.,....... ......Troy.
William H. Powless, C. E., ...Norwood, N. J.
Enrique C. Zegarra, C. E., ...Piura, Peru.

CLASS OF 1875.

Samuel Alexander,...................Cohoes.
R. Edward Ball, ...Jamaica.
Adolfo E. Besosa,.....................Ponce, Porto Rico.
Henry L. Binsse,.................. ...New York.
James L. Breese, ...New York.
Charles F. Carbonell,... ....Havana, Cuba.
Walter E. Dauchy, ...Crescent.
Richard V. W. Du Bois, ...Hudson.
Edward W. Eckert, ...Pittsburgh, Pa.
John A. Ferriss, Jr.,..................Troy.
Tucker H. Fisher,....................Columbia, S. C.
William L. Fox, ...Philadelphia, Pa.
John W. Gray, ...Harrisonburgh, Va.
Warren Greene, ...Louisville, Ky.
James A. Hutchison, Jr., ...Pittsburgh, Pa.
Charles T. Judson,....................Lansingburgh.
William G. Kay,....... ....Chicago, Ill.
Edward V. Z. Lane, ...New York.
Henry C. Lay, Jr.,................ ...Easton, Md.
*Charles McAlester,....................Florence, Ala.
William B. Maxwell, ...Nassau, Bahamas.

Charles S. Pease, ...Tarrytown.
Frank Pond, ...Worcester, Mass.
Harry L. Richardson, ...Great Barrington.
Palmer C. Ricketts, ...Princeton, N. J.
Frank L. Rowland, ...Mystic River, Conn.
H. De Witt Smith, ...Marshall, Tex.
Robert S. Taylor, ...Richmond, Va.
E. Ray Thompson, ...Troy.
Thomas W. Todd, ...Louisville, Ky.
Joseph R. Underwood, ...Nashville, Tenn.
John A. L. Waddell, ...Cobourg, Canada.
J. Tripler Wainwright, ...Philadelphia, Pa.
George B. Wellington, ...Troy.
George E. Winslow, ...Bay Ridge.

CLASS OF 1876.

W. Clinton Adams, ...Washington, D. C.
J. Frank Aldrich, ...Chicago, Ill.
William M. Allaire, ...New York.
James C. Anderson, ...Newton, N. J.
Frederic S. Bagley, ...Meadville, Pa.
Arthur G. Baker, ...Decorah, Ia.
Thomas F. Barry, A. B., ...Rochester.
Tarlton Bates, ...St. Louis, Mo.
L. Harvie Blanton, ...Frankfort, Ky.
Edward A. Burdett, ...Troy.
William H. Byram, ...Detroit, Mich.
Edward C. Carter, ...Jacksonville, Ill.
Josiah R. T. Davis, ...Philadelphia, Pa.
Charles A. Draper, ...Sing Sing.
S. Waters Fox, ...Louisville, Ky.
Isaac W. Frank, ...Pittsburgh, Pa.
Harold A. Freeman, ...Philadelphia, Pa.
Edward G. Geuder, ...Cleveland, O.
N. Audinet Gibert, ...New York.
Fred H. Goodrich, ...St. Paul, Minn.
Arturo Guerra, ...San Juan, Port Rico.
William Henderson, ...Troy.
Joseph B. Hoeing, ...Lexington, Ky.
William W. Huntington, ...Brooklyn.
Lay Huntley, ...Troy.
John P. Kelly, ...Troy.
James C. Kingsley, ...Brooklyn.
George O. Knapp, ...Hartford, Conn.
William A. Langridge, ...Muscatine, Ia.

Samuel B. Low, ... Jersey City, N. J.
Souichiro Matsmoto, ... Ogaki, Japan.
John McLean, ... Rochester, Minn.
John W. Nier, ... Detroit, Mich.
John B. Parkinson, ... Boston, Mass.
Henry B. Patten, ... Enfield, Conn.
George F. Penfield, ... New Rochelle.
Arthur S. Potter, ... Adams.
De Forest Pruyne, ... Belleville.
E. Ogden Ross, ... Troy.
George P. Scriven, ... Chicago, Ill.
Henry C. Shaw, ... Pittsburgh, Pa.
C. Sooy Smith, ... Maywood, Ill.
Willis G. Smith, ... St. Paul, Minn.
Edward A. Spilsbury, ... Baltimore, Md.
Eugene Underwood, Jr., ... St. Paul, Minn.
Morris S. Verner, ... Pittsburgh, Pa.
Thomas H. Walbridge, ... Toledo, O.
Frederick H. Wiggin, ... New York.
George T. Wood, ... Louisville, Ky.
Jeu-ske Yamamoto, ... Bousheu, Japan.
Giro Yamaoka, ... Tokio, Japan.
Aaron J. Zabriskie, ... Jersey City, N. J.

CLASS OF 1877.

Walter F. Baldwin, ... Columbia, S. C.
Clarence M. Barber, ... Cleveland, O.
Fred A. Belknap, ... Erie, Pa.
Arthur J. Best, ... Chatham Village.
Coddington Billings, Jr., ... Chicago, Ill.
Henry Blakely, ... St. Paul, Minn.
Augustus O. Bostrom, ... Buffalo.
George W. Bowman, Jr., ... Carlisle, Pa.
Stephen L. Breckinridge, ... Alton, Ill.
A. Scott Brown, ... Erie, Pa.
Stephen C. Bush, ... Waterford.
Joseph Bushnell, Jr., ... Titusville, Pa.
Lyman L. Carey, ... Flanders, N. J.
Frank Carryl, ... Franklin, N. J.
John Chislett, ... Indianapolis, Ind.
Richard E. Chislett, ... Indianapolis, Ind.
Daniel W. Church, ... Wegatchie.
Edward Colley, ... Washington, D. C.
Walter F. Crosby, ... New York.
Chester B. Davis, ... Troy.

WILLIAM P. DENEGRE, A. B., ... New Orleans, La.
LOUIS H. DICKERMAN, ... Troy.
ALBYN P. DIKE, ... Brooklyn.
H. BREWERTON DUANE, ... Portland, Me.
HOWARD N. ELMER, ... Bridgeton, N. J.
FRANK M. FABER, ... Pittsburgh, Pa.
EMANUEL S. GANS, ... Philadelphia, Pa.
EDWARD GIBSON, ... Yonkers.
VOLENTINE W. GRANGER, ... Toledo, O.
HENRY R. GRIFFEN, ... Phœnixville, Pa.
CHARLES G. GRIFFITH, ... Brooklyn.
JAMES R. HIRST, ... Philadelphia, Pa.
J. HOLABIRD HORTON, ... Chicago, Ill.
FRANK E. HOUSE, ... Houseville.
CARROLL HUTCHINS, ... Concord, N. H.
GEORGE E. INGERSOLL, ... St. Paul, Minn.
MERWIN S. H. JACKSON, ... Toledo, O.
OSCAR JARECKI, ... Erie, Pa.
ELIAS M. JOHNSON, ... Spuyten Duyvil.
GILBERT H. JOHNSON, ... Spuyten Duyvil.
THOMAS T. JOHNSTON, ... Washington, D. C.
WILLIAM KEMP, Jr., ... Troy.
EDWARD J. LANDOR, ... London, Canada.
ALBERTO F. LARRIEU, ... Matanzas, Cuba,
HORACE W. MANN, ... Blue Rapids, Kan.
CHRISTIAN I. MCKEE, ... Pittsburgh, Pa.
CHARLES S. MCMULLAN, ... Cohoes.
PAUL S. MERRIFIELD, ... New York.
GEORGE T. NELLES, ... Leavenworth, Kan.
BENJAMIN B. NEWTON, Jr., ... Brooklyn.
WILLIAM A. NICHOLSON, ... Beekman.
GEORGE A. NIXON, ... Covington, Ky.
JOHN J. O'HARA, ... Albany.
CHARLES C. ORMSBY, ... Waterford.
EDWARD A. PATTISON, ... Troy.
WILLIAMS PROUDFIT, ... Troy.
ADOLPHUS W. RAHT, ... Cleveland, Tenn.
FREDERICK S. RAND, ... Troy.
RICHARD D. RICKARD, ... Stamford, Conn.
GEORGE W. RIDGELY, ... Springfield, Ill.
WILLIAM B. RIDGELY, ... Springfield, Ill.
ALPHEUS T. SABIN, ... Oneonta,
A. T. SCOFIELD, ... Warren, Pa.
ALFRED P. SCULL, Jr., ... Phœnixville, Pa.
JUAN SEMINARIO, ... Piura, Peru.

MINOT M. SEYMOUR, ... Greenville, N. J.
JOHN G. SHACKLEY, ... West Brookfield, Mass.
RICHARD E. SHAW, ... Charlottesville, Va.
HENRY C. SHOCK, ... Baltimore, Md.
BENJAMIN V. SIMPSON, ... Winona, Minn.
ROBERT R. SINGER, ... Pittsburgh, Pa.
FRED P. SMITH, ... Waterford.
C. R. HERMAN SONNTAG, Jr., ... Stapleton.
A. WILTON STEIGER, ... Washington, D. C.
WILLIAM H. STORRS, ... Scranton, Pa.
CHARLES F. STOWELL, ... Rochester.
LINTON W. STUBBS, ... Monroe, La.
HERMAN STUTZER, Jr., ... Stapleton.
AUGUSTIN TOVAR, ... Puno, Peru.
SEYMOUR W. TULLOCK, ... Washington, D. C.
ALLEN UNDERWOOD, ... New York.
WILLIAM G. WALBRIDGE, ... Saratoga Springs.
ROBERT S. WALKER, ... Richmond, Ky.
JOSEPH E. WALTZ, ... Dayton, O.
GEORGE H. WARREN, ... Troy.
WILLIAM F. WATERS, ... Cambridge, Md.
JAMES C. WHITON, ... Troy.
CLIFTON G. WILLIAMS, ... Cincinnati, O.
FREDERICK A. YEAGER, ... Allegheny, Pa.
HORACE G. YOUNG, ... Honesdale, Pa.

SPECIAL STUDENTS.

JOHN A. BERKEY, ... St. Paul, Minn.
CHARLES P. BONNETT, ... New York.
ALFRED F. BRAINERD, ... St. Albans, Vt.
ROYAL CHAPIN, ... Wickford, R. I.
CLANCEY R. DEMPSETR, ... San Francisco, Cal.
ROBERT L. HOLLIDAY, ... Bell's Mills, Pa.
JOHN W. HUGHES, ... Sharon, Pa.
WILLIAM D. ISETT, ... Spruce Creek, Pa.
W. NOBLE JONES, ... Savannah, Ga.
JOSEPH R. KINGSLAND, ... Franklin, N. J.
FRANK T. L. LANE, ... New York.
J. MACNAUGHTON, Jr., A. B., ... Albany.
JOSE J. DE LOS REYES, ... Lima, Peru,
FRANCIS B. SHEPHARD, ... Jerseyville, Ill.
CHARLES M. SMITH, ... Hardwick, Mass.
LYMAN C. WILDER, ... Hoosick Falls.

INDEX TO THE
CATALOGUE OF GRADUATES.

Buxton, Clifford............ 1865
Caldwell, James N......... 1874
Campbell, Charles.......... 1873
Campbell, James........... 1843
Campbell, Joseph H........ 1868
Carnrick, George W........ 1874
Carr, Ezra S............... 1838
Casanova, José N........... 1859
Casatt, Alexander J........ 1859
Castro, Alberto de.......... 1860
Ceballos, Gaspar F. de...... 1868
*Chamberlaine, Nicholas H... 1856
*Chandler, Jonathan........ 1827
Chubb, A. Lamont......... 1848
Church, W. Lee............ 1872
Clark, Joseph E. 1845
Clarke, John M............ 1856
*Clarke, Joseph B......... 1829
Cleemann, Thomas M....... 1865
Clement, William H........ 1835
Clinch, J. Morton......... 1854
*Cobb, James C............ 1831
Coit, James C............. 1858
Collin, David.............. 1842
Collingwood, Francis........ 1855
Collins, Charles............ 1840
*Comstock, Daniel O........ 1829
Cook, Charles R............ 1837
Cook, George H............ 1839
Cook, Robert G............ 1847
Cooley, Lyman E........... 1874
Cooper, Theodore.......... 1858
*Cotes, Elihu W............ 1839
*Cotterell, Nathan......... 1841
Cottman, Joseph B......... 1835
Cox, Abraham B., Jr........ 1867
Craft, Charles C............ 1866
Crafts, Walter............. 1859
Crehore, C. Frederic....... 1848
Crocker, Edwin B.......... 1833
*Cromwell, James.......... 1861
Crosby, Horace............ 1862
*Cross, Charles E. 1855
Cross, Charles S........... 1838
Cummings, Charles A....... 1849
Curtis, Henry.............. 1854
Curtis, John H............. 1873
Dabney, Frederic Y......... 1857
Danforth, Henry W......... 1842
*Danker, Albert............ 1826
Dauchy, Edward N.......... 1840
Davis, Joseph P............ 1856
Davy, John J.............. 1827
*Decker, Theodore W....... 1830
Dennis, George R........... 1839
*Devol, Edward............ 1831
Dias, Luiz da R., Jr......... 1860
Dodge, Richard D........... 1860
Doughty, William Howard... 1858
*Drayton, Henry J.......... 1839
Drayton, James S 1836
Drew, Francis G............ 1827
Drowne, Charles............ 1847
Duane, James............. 1873
Durham, Anson............ 1840
*Eaton, Hezekiah H......... 1826
*Eaton, Timothy Dwight..... 1826
*Eddy, Jacob F............ 1835
*Edgerton, Fay............ 1828
Edwards, Richard, Jr.,....... 1847
Ells, George F.............. 1856
Ely, Theodore N............ 1866
Emerson, Rufus H.......... 1861
Emery, Albert H............ 1858
*Emmons, Ebenezer......... 1826
Emory, Thomas............ 1828
Endicott, Mordecai T........ 1868
Ensign, Milton W.......... 1871
*Escobar, José............. 1867
Escobar, Roberto........... 1857
Estabrook, John D.......... 1856
Fabian, William J.......... 1874
Farnum, Henry H., Jr....... 1865
Fay, Francis F............. 1868
Felton, Herbert C.......... 1866
Fenton, William............ 1861
*Ferrao, José Tell.......... 1850
*Field, Charles S.......... 1838
Fields, Samuel J........... 1867
Fisher, Clark.............. 1858
Fisher, Joseph S............ 1849
Fitch, Asa, Jr.............. 1827
Follin, Ormond W.......... 1859
Ford, Frank L............. 1874
Ford, John Q. A............ 1866
Forsyth, Robert............ 1869
Foster, Albert W.......... 1871
Fox, Albert R.............. 1830
Fox, Joseph G.............. 1861
Fox, Peter H............... 1864
Frith, Arthur J 1873
Frothingham, James H...... 1849
Fuertes, Estévan A........ 1861
Gale, E. Thompson......... 1837
*Gale, George A............ 1847
Garcia, Federico G......... 1872
*Garlinghouse, Leman B..... 1837
Garlinghouse, Fred. L....... 1871
Geer, Harvey M 1872
Gest, Alexander P 1874
Goicouria, Alberto V. de.... 1871
Gold, Miner............... 1829

Goldstein, Max L. 1867
Gonzalez, Juan Jr. 1870
Gould, James P. 1863
Gowing, Burdett. 1861
Grant, Edward M. 1860
Greele, Samuel S. 1846
Greene, Albert S. 1859
Greene, B. Franklin. 1842
Greene, Dascom. 1853
Greene, David M. 1851
Greene, George M. 1859
Griffen, George S. 1874
Grimes, Charles L. 1871
Grinnell, Frederic. 1855
Griswold, John W. 1865
Guerrero, Cárlos. 1867
Gurley, Lewis E. 1845
Gurley, William. 1839
Haddock, Arba R. 1862
Hall, Fitz Edward. 1842
*Hall, George M. 1849
Hall, George T. 1868
Hall, James. 1832
*Hall, William. 1846
Harley, Henry. 1858
*Harper, Albert M. 1867
Harris, Charles P. 1873
Harris, Henrique. 1860
Harris, Joel B. 1841
Harris, William P. 1866
*Haskell, Stephen E. 1845
Haskin, Abel N. 1840
Haskin, Alfred B. 1840
Haskin, Leonard W. 1841
Haskin, William L. 1861
Hawley, Fletcher J. 1837
Hearne, Frank J. 1867
Heizmann, Theodore I. 1859
Henry, William 1828
Hernandez, José. 1867
Heyl, Jacob E. 1870
Hill, Augustus G. 1831
Hinckley, Frank. 1863
Holmes, Henry. 1855
Holton, George C. 1860
*Hopkins, T. Orlando 1857
Hopkins, Theron R. 1834
Horsford, Eben N. 1838
Horton, George F. 1827
Horton, James S. 1829
*Houghton, Douglass. 1829
Houghton, J. Franklin. 1848
House, Samuel R. 1834
*Howard, Jerome B. 1838
Hulbert, Addison. 1826
Humphreys, John G. 1873
Hunt, George. 1858
Hunt, George M. 1866
Hurd, Tyrus W. 1836
Hyde, Charles B. 1841
Hyde, Douglass W. 1841
Illsley, Charles E. 1867
Ingham, William A. 1846
Jackson, Samuel C. 1827
Jenny, Joseph H. 1841
Johnson, George. 1837
Johnson, Isaac G. 1848
Keeney, John C. 1827
Kellogg, Edward R. 1841
Kellogg, Nathan. 1841
Kellogg, Norman B. 1873
Kellogg, Warren T. 1861
Kendall, David 1838
*Kingman, Lysander H. 1829
Kirby, G. Frederic. 1857
Kirtland, Alfred P. 1871
Kneass, Strickland. 1839
Knap, Joseph M. 1858
Knap, Thomas L. 1866
Lacerda, Augusto de. 1855
La Coste, Louis. 1841
Lally, James. 1861
*Lapham, William G. 1838
Lawrance, Benjamin R. 1868
Lea, George H. 1872
Lent, George B. 1838
Lesley, Alexander M. 1846
Leverich, Gabriel. 1857
*Lewis, William. 1840
Lilienthal, Benjamin N. 1866
Lindsley, Aaron L. 1842
Locke, Elmer H. 1848
Lockling, Levi L. 1837
Long, Thomas J. 1873
*Loomis, Charles L. 1851
Loomis, Horace. 1865
Lowe, Lewis G. 1848
Lowrey, Goodwin. 1845
Luaces, Ernesto L. 1867
Mabbett, Henry J. 1833
McClellan, Henry G. 1869
McCaughin, John. 1842
Macdonald, Charles. 1857
Macfarlane, Graham. 1872
MacGregor, George C. 1871
McKee, Aaron G. 1836
McKee, Robert G. 1835
McManus, P. C. W. T. 1826
McMillan, Charles. 1860
Mallory, George B. 1867
Mallory, Marshall H. 1865
Man, Albon P., Jr. 1866

Mann, Elias P.......... 1872
*Mann, George H.......... 1870
Mansfield, M. William...... 1871
*Marks, J. Harrod......... 1871
Marlett, Seneca H.......... 1841
Marling, William.......... 1872
Marshall, Thomas F......... 1867
Martin, Charles C.......... 1856
Martin, William H.......... 1856
Mason, William P.......... 1874
Masten, Cornelius S........ 1850
Matas, Ramon............. 1860
Mather, Charles R.......... 1870
May, John E............. 1846
Megear, Alter............. 1868
Menocal, Aniceto G. de 1862
*Merian, Henry W.......... 1858
*Metcalf, Jeremiah......... 1829
Metcalf, William........... 1858
Miller, Solomon V. R........ 1841
Millet, Albert H............ 1867
Mills, Hiram F............. 1856
Mills, William H........... 1868
*Moak, Joseph A........... 1854
Moore, Frank L............ 1867
Morris, Thomas O'Neil...... 1870
Morse, Henry G........... 1871
Morton, Nathaniel.......... 1850
Moss, Charles H........... 1867
Mullin, Anthony T. E....... 1861
Mullin, Joseph, Jr.,......... 1869
Murphy, John W........... 1847
Mynderse, Edward 1838
Naranjo, Francisco R........ 1863
Neal, Robert C............ 1870
Neilson, Robert........... 1861
Nichols, Edward........... 1871
Nichols, Othniel F.......... 1868
Nickel, George D........... 1870
Nickerson, J. G............ 1848
Oakey, James............ 1837
*Oatman, Orlin............ 1827
Olmstead, Aaron B......... 1837
Olmstead, Lemuel G......... 1830
Olyphant, Harwood V....... 1868
*Osborn, George K.......... 1830
Osborne, Charles M......... 1853
*Ostrom, John............. 1857
Otto, John B............ 1871
Packard, Ralph G........... 1864
Painter, Augustus E. W...... 1863
Pardee, Ario, Jr........... 1858
Pardee, Calvin.......... 1860
Park, Austin F............. 1840
Parrish, Edward Jr........ 1870
Parsons, Samuel B.......... 1840
Patterson, Stephen V. R..... 1837
Pattison, Harry D.......... 1874
Pearce, Allen.............. 1838
*Peck, Hollam L........... 1849
Peck, William A........... 1869
Peebles, Robert C.......... 1869
Pelaez, Manuel A.......... 1873
*Pelton, William S......... 1826
Pemberton, John, Jr........ 1860
Penfield, James A.......... 1846
*Percy, James R............ 1859
Perkins, Charles P.......... 1866
Peterson, B. Walker....... 1873
Pettibone, C. Vallette....... 1867
*Philip, John H............ 1832
*Philip, John Van Ness.... 1839
Pierce, George H........... 1858
Pierpont, John............. 1869
Pike, Samuel J............. 1830
Pirajá, José R. da S., Jr..... 1865
Platt, Joseph C., Jr......... 1866
*Platt, Merritt............. 1830
Plympton, George W........ 1847
Pomeroy, Henry......... 1841
*Post, James H............ 1839
Potter, Clarkson N.......... 1844
Potter, George C.......... 1839
Potts, Benjamin C.......... 1863
Powell, Ambrose V......... 1868
Powell, Jonathan R......... 1846
Powell, William J.......... 1839
Powless, William H........ 1874
*Pratt, Ira R.............. 1842
Pratt, William M.......... 1857
Prescott, Richard,.......... 1871
*Prime, Alanson J....... 1829
Putnam, George........... 1838
Quackenbush, John H....... 1856
Rae, Charles W.......... 1866
Randolph, John H......... 1870
Raymond, Thomas C....... 1865
Reed, James......... 1873
Reeves, David............ 1872
Reeves, William H....... 1873
Reynolds, James D......... 1870
*Rice, Joseph G............ 1858
Rice, L. Frederic........... 1858
Rice, Spencer V............ 1871
*Riddell, John L........... 1829
Rider, Jonathan B.......... 1844
Rider, Thomas B. 1845
Ripley, Thomas C........... 1828
Roberts, George B.......... 1849
Roberts, Percival...... 1846
*Robison, John A.......... 1838
Rockenstyne, Porter........ 1849

Roebling, Charles G........ 1871
Roebling, Washington A..... 1857
Rogers, Horace N.......... 1837
Root, Bennet F............. 1826
Ropes, Charles F........... 1871
*Rossman, Augustus......... 1847
Rothwell, Richard P........ 1858
Rowland, Henry A.......... 1870
Royce, Harrison A.......... 1859
Russell, Nathaniel E....... 1870
Sage, Russell, 2d........... 1859
Sager, Abraham............ 1831
Salisbury, James H 1846
Saltar, John, Jr............ 1867
Sanders, William S......... 1833
Sanderson, J. Gardner...... 1858
*Sanford, Edward.......... 1827
Sariol, Pompeyo............ 1867
Saulles, Arthur B. de....... 1859
Saylor, Francis H 1867
Schaeffer, John S........... 1866
Schermerhorn, Richard...... 1871
Schott, C. Ridgely......... 1868
Scott, Charles H............ 1870
Searles, William H. 1860
Sedley, Henry............... 1848
*Serrano, Aurelio........... 1860
Sherman, William B........ 1872
Sherrill, Rush.............. 1830
Silliman, Justus M......... 1870
Simpson, William S......... 1860
Skilton, George S......... 1868
Skilton, James A........... 1845
Skilton, Julius A........... 1849
Slade, Israel............... 1836
Sloan, Robert I............. 1859
*Small, Thomas B........... 1843
Smalley, D. S.............. 1835
Smith, Charles E............ 1860
Smith, David C............. 1833
Smith, Felix R. R........... 1860
Smith, Frank G............. 1859
Smith, Milo A.............. 1867
Smith, T. Guilford.......... 1861
Smith, Thaddeus S.......... 1861
Smith, Theodore S., Jr...... 1868
Snyder, Henry R........... 1837
Sosa, Pedro J.............. 1873
*Sothers, Edward.......... 1870
Squires, John 1869
Stanton, Lodowick, Jr....... 1841
Starbuck, George H......... 1840
Starr, Arthur B............. 1869
Stearns, George A.......... 1849
Stearns, Irving A........... 1868
Stebbins, Orrin............. 1839
Steinacker, Theodore....... 1873
Stevenson, Holland N........ 1866
*Stevenson, P. Eugene...... 1830
Stilson, William B.......... 1867
Stodder, George T.......... 1863
Stone, Cyrus R............. 1867
Stone, Lowell H............ 1869
Storrs, Abel............... 1831
Stowell, Ellery............. 1872
Stratton, Norman........... 1838
Strawbridge, William C...... 1870
Suffern, Edward............ 1835
Sutherland, Mosher A........ 1861
Sutherland, Samuel W....... 1846
Swift, Alexander J.......... 1872
Symington, William N...... 1861
Taylor, Gilbert T............ 1844
Thacher, Edwin............. 1863
Thomas, Joseph............ 1830
Thompson, Albert A........ 1838
*Thompson, Charles B....... 1860
Thompson, James G........ 1848
Thompson, John C.......... 1865
Thompson, William A 1869
Tibbits, George............ 1841
Tilghman, James........... 1839
Tompkins, D. Augustus..... 1873
Trafton, Gilman............ 1856
Trevor, Frank N............ 1866
*Trujillo, Francisco......... 1857
*Tuomey, Michael.......... 1835
*Turner, Benjamin.......... 1849
Tweeddale, William......... 1853
Underwood, John C......... 1862
Utley, Charles H........... 1869
Van Bergen, Robert H...... 1841
Van Buren, John D., Jr...... 1860
Van Buren, Robert......... 1864
Van Ness, Sherman......... 1836
Van Rensselaer, Alexander... 1833
Van Rensselaer, Peter....... 1839
*Van Schaick, Augustus P.... 1839
Van Sinderen, Adrian....... 1847
Varona, Ignacio M. de....... 1863
Vaughan, Frederic W........ 1863
Viscarrondo, Lorenzo J. de.. 1859
Voorhees, Herman........ 1873
Voorhees, Theodore........ 1869
*Vought, William G......... 1840
Vroom, Peter D., Jr......... 1862
Wade, James, Jr............ 1842
Waite, Christopher C........ 1864
Walbridge, Russell D....... 1871
Walbridge, T. Chester...... 1873
Walker, William W......... 1856
Wallace, Gurdon B.......... 1840

Wallace, James P. 1837
Walter, Alfred. 1872
Ware, R. Willard. 1850
Warren, Levi H. 1837
Warren, S. Edward. 1851
Watkins, Hezekiah. 1857
Watriss, George C. 1853
*Westcott, Amos. 1835
Weston, Charles L. 1827
*Whipple, Charles. 1837
Whipple, Stephen T. 1838
White, Alfred T. 1865
White, John H. 1840
Whitney, Drake. 1864
*Whittelsey, Philo D. 1834
*Wilde, Nathan R. 1836
Wiley, William H. 1866
Wilkinson, Alfred. 1849
Wilkinson, J. Forman. 1847
*Wilkinson, William. 1830
Williams, Norman A. 1859
Williams, Samuel W. 1832
Williams, Worthington B. ... 1835
Williamson, Thomas M. 1871
Wilson, Henry W. 1864
Wilson, John A. 1856
Wilson, Joseph M. 1858
Winslow, Charles W. 1858
Wood, De Volson. 1857
Woodruff, Joel R. 1847
Woodward, Francis G. 1839
Woodworth, Bleeker B. 1833
Woodworth, John, Jr. 1837
*Wotkyns, Alfred A. 1847
Yardley, Edmund. 1856
Young, Jonas F. 1872
Zegarra, Enrique C. 1874

INDEX TO THE

CATALOGUE OF NON-GRADUATES.

Bixby, Orin S. 1867
Blackington, Frank R. 1869
Blackstone, Manning C. 1852
Blackstone, Richard. 1867
Blackwell, Edward D. 1870
Blatchford, John T. 1836
Bloss, Richard D. 1843
Bloss, Richard Jr 1848
Booth, James C. 1829
Bonesteel, William 1842
Bosworth, Isaac F. 1867
Boudinot, Theodore F 1836
Bourland, Rudolphus R. 1871
Boutelle, George W. 1854
Bradford, Thomas. 1865
Bradley, Franklin 1829
Bradshaw, Milton S. 1856
Brady, Samuel. 1865
Braem, Frederick 1853
Brainard, Halsey. 1845
Brazelton, James A. 1838
Brinsmade, H. W. 1844
Brockway, Josephus C. 1836
Brockway, Nathan. 1824
Brockway, William W. 1832
Brooks, Theodore 1844
Browning, A. E 1854
Brown, Edward H. 1851
Brown, Henry E. 1866
Bryan, Elijah 2d 1841
Bryant, John Howard. 1824
Buck, Reuben 1838
Buel, Clarence 1842
Buel, David H. 1855
Buel, Hampden 1849
Buel, John G. 1832
Buel, John G. 1849
Buel, Oliver P. 1852
Buel, Samuel 1824
Buel, Samuel 1832
Bull, John 1836
Bull, William H. 1844
Burden, I. Townsend. 1855
Burden, James A. 1849
Burden, Joseph W. 1872
*Burden, Peter A. 1834
Burden, William F. 1845
Burnham, Julius R. 1871
Burns, Robert T. 1853
Burt, Aaron. 1849
Burt, John Otis. 1851
Burt, Oliver T. 1843
Burrage, Charles W. 1849
Burrall, Charles E. 1862
Burrus, Charles D. 1854
Burtis, Daniel H. 1832
Burtis, William H. 1845
Bush, Calvin 1848
Buswell, John G. 1842
Butler, James D. 1856
Cades, W. H. 1834
Cady, Daniel B. 1824
Calkins, Ripley R. 1850
Callender, Charles E 1843
Cammack, Thomas D. 1847
Camp, John, Jr. 1853
Camp, Nathan H. 1836
Campbell, Edward. 1853
Campuzano, Felix A. 1864
Canal, Justo M. del. 1863
Canfield, Edmund 1865
Cannon, LeGrand B. 1829
Cantero, Pablo B 1863
Cardona, Pedro A. 1868
Carhart, Daniel 1856
Carmichael, Gideon W. 1863
Carpenter, James 1853
Carpenter, John B. 1856
Carpenter, W. O. 1848
Carroll, John T. 1859
Carroll, William B. 1869
Cary, S. Matthews. 1866
Caryl, Alexander H., Jr. 1864
Casanova, Antonio S 1857
Cass, Samuel K. 1871
Cassidy, John. 1829
Castro, Lucas A. de 1868
Caswell, Bloomfield W. 1848
Catlin, George O. 1862
Chamberlain, Augustus P. . . . 1847
Chamberlin, James R. 1843
Chapman, Jerome M. 1853
Chapman, William B. 1856
Charlton, Thomas 1869
Chase, H. M. 1849
Chase, March. 1824
Chatfield, H. S. 1853
Cheney, Jehiel W. 1854
Chenoweth, Alexander C. 1868
Chenoweth, George B. 1868
Chisholm, Stewart F. 1868
Chism, Richard 1872
Christie, Albion M. 1858
Church, Henry S 1853
Church, Robert S. 1862
Clapp, Robert C. 1872
Clark, Matthew Dorr 1837
Clark, Theodore E. 1832
Clarkson, Frank M. 1872
Clarkson, T. Chalmers 1866
Clary, O. W. 1849
Clifford, John C. 1851

Clum, Henry 1847
Cobb, Lewis T.... 1824
Cochrane, William G.... 1863
Coe, George B 1870
Coffin, William H.... 1868
Coggeshall, Robert C. P.... 1867
Cogswell, William B.... 1849
Cole, Edmund L 1861
Cole, Hiram 1849
Cole, William H.... 1839
Coleman, Frederick W.... 1851
Coleman, James P.... 1866
Collins, Augustus 1824
Comegys, Cornelius M 1866
Comstock, Daniel O 1824
*Conkling, Edward H.... 1872
Connity, Hugh.... 1839
Constable, William B.... 1836
Cook, Charles A.... 1834
Cook, John H.... 1841
Cook, Matthias M.... 1845
Cook, Clarence L.... 1868
Cooper, Charles G.... 1865
Cooper, Hugh 1870
Copeland, Eugene M.... 1856
Corliss, John A.... 1870
Cornell, D. E.... 1854
Cornell, James T.... 1837
Cornell, William 1824
Cornish, W. F.... 1855
Cortlan, J. Wakefield.... 1864
Coryell, Elias E.... 1852
*Covell, Silas T 1849
Coughlin, William H.... 1863
Cox, Walter E.... 1863
Cozzens, Frederick S.... 1864
Cramer, Eliphalet 1829
Cramer, George H.... 1832
Cramer, James L.... 1838
Cramer, John C.... 1838
Cramer, L. Huntley.... 1863
Crandall, Martin 1829
Crane, Benjamin E.... 1854
Crane, Edward B.... 1866
Crane, Heber 1852
Crary, John S.... 1844
Crawford, Clay 1866
Crittenden, Churchill 1858
Crombie, J. Caldwell.... 1858
Crosby, Wilson 1855
Cross, Andrew B.... 1836
Cross, Luther.... 1824
Cullen, Edgar M.... 1858
Curtis, Abijah C.... 1850
Curtis, Albert W.... 1837
Curtis, Charles D.... 1852
Curtis, Frederick R.... 1853
Curtis, Melville 1868
Cueto, Honorato F. de 1866
Davis, Charlton H.... 1843
Davis, Theodore W 1861
Davis, Thomas.... 1849
Davis, Samuel D.... 1850
Davison, Charles 1862
Dauchy, Burr.... 1852
Dauchy, Charles H.... 1857
Dauchy, Harvey B.... 1848
Dauchy, Nathan.... 1848
Dater, Jacob Henry 1835
Dawson, George S.... 1855
Day, Hanford.... 1858
Delafield, Bertram.... 1862
Denny, St. Clair.... 1865
Denton, Preston.... 1837
De Peyster, Johnston L 1862
Desvernine, Antonio E.... 1864
Devlin, Michael E.... 1871
Dickerman, Mark S.... 1837
Dickson, Frank A.... 1870
Dillon, Arthur J.... 1861
Disbrow, Charles S.... 1829
Diver, Jacob A.... 1849
Douglass, Andrew A.... 1836
Douglass, George E.... 1842
*Doughty, Richard H.... 1855
Doughty, Thompson H 1860
Dolsen, Samuel L.... 1864
Dorlon, John W.... 1844
Dorr, B. Dalton.... 1863
Dorsey, Dan B.... 1854
Downing, Joseph K.... 1843
Douw, John D. P.... 1854
Drake, Garret.... 1834
Drake, Isaac.... 1838
Drake, Rutger L.... 1837
Draper, Francis C.... 1853
Drayton, Henry E.... 1871
Drowne, William L.... 1849
Du Bois, Charles L.... 1867
*Dunbar, Walter G 1859
Dungan, James B.... 1829
Durand, Fred F.... 1856
Durkee, Richard P. H.... 1855
Duval, Charles.... 1829
Dwelle, Franklin 1864
D'Wolf, James F.... 1872
Eaton, Amos B.... 1824
Eaton, Augustus H.... 1863
Eaton, D. Cady,.... 1847
Eaton, Cuvier 1834
Eaton, Daniel Cady.... 1852
Eaton, Edward O.... 1832

*Eaton, George H.......... 1843
Eaton, J. Humboldt........ 1838
Eaton, Johnson H.......... 1842
*Eaton Thomas,............ 1855
Eaton, Thomas H.......... 1824
Eaton, William B.......... 1829
Eddy, E. T............... 1858
Eddy, James A............ 1850
Eddy, Newton............. 1852
Eddy, Titus C............. 1850
Edgington, Asahel......... 1862
Edson, Chauncey C......... 1869
Edson, John............... 1848
Egerton, Lebbeus, Jr....... 1853
Egleston, Zina Pitcher...... 1834
Eigenbrodt, David S........ 1832
Elliott, Harry A 1871
Elston, Francis W.......... 1863
Ely, Jonathan............. 1824
Emery, Cyrus F............ 1856
Evans, Louis H............ 1872
Evans, Walton W.......... 1835
Everest, George H......... 1847
Ewen, Warren, Jr.......... 1871
Fellows, Charles H......... 1829
Fellows, Louis A........... 1844
Fellows, Peter............. 1834
Field, Francis K........... 1842
Field, Franklin Jr 1871
Figueredo, Fernando M.... 1864
Filley, Mark L............ 1868
Filley, Oliver B........... 1854
Fisher, A. W.............. 1832
Fisher, Charles D.......... 1857
Fisher, Charles H.......... 1851
Fisher, G. Merriam........ 1841
Fisher, Isaac D............ 1851
Fisher, Nathaniel Jr......... 1851
*Fisher, Otis............. 1858
Fitch, William H.......... 1866
Flagler, Isaac P........... 1872
Fletcher, Frank A.......... 1869
Fleury, Paul A........... 1872
Floyd, Charles R.......... 1856
Floyd, William H Jr 1871
Ford, Ira................ 1839
Foster, Asa E............. 1829
Foster, Bela.............. 1824
Fouquet, J. D............. 1849
Fouquet, John M........... 1849
Franchot, Richard H........ 1838
Franklin, Benjamin......... 1853
Freedman, Edgar........... 1872
Freeland, William H........ 1829
Freeman, William R........ 1865
Freer, S. De Puy.......... 1862
Freiot, Charles............. 1832
French, Edmund B......... 1851
French, John F............ 1829
Frisbie, Byron F........... 1853
Gale, Alfred De F......... 1863
Gamble, Francis C.......... 1872
Gardinier, John H.......... 1866
Gardner, Charles........... 1829
Gardner, Wright........... 1867
Garnsey, Nathan D......... 1834
Gary, Joseph Jr............ 1832
Gary, Joseph S............ 1834
Gates, George N........... 1838
Gatzmer, H. S............. 1853
Gay, Lusher............... 1844
Geer, Erastus.............. 1841
Gerard, Charles C.......... 1863
Gerrish, Henry P........... 1854
Gibson, Darwin............ 1824
Giddings, G. R............. 1854
Gilbert, William.......... 1855
Gillett, William H.......... 1859
Gimbernat, Teofilo......... 1864
Giro, Emilio............... 1868
Gonzalez, Guillermo P 1863
Goold, Henry 1870
Goodnough, F. A........... 1848
Goodrich, Charles R........ 1845
Goodwin, John A.......... 1846
Goodwin, Leonard.......... 1858
Gordon, Thomas 1862
Gould, David H............ 1864
Gould, Edward T........... 1870
Grant, Bryan.............. 1851
Grant, Job P.............. 1851
Gray, Alexander........... 1865
*Gray, Charles O........... 1855
Gray, James A............ 1845
Gregg, J. Leslie............ 1864
Gregory, Henry P.......... 1858
Green, Edward M.......... 1862
Greene, Henry F........... 1856
Greer, Joseph............. 1853
Gridley, Edwin R.......... 1854
Gridley, Orrin S............ 1865
Guernsey, William B....... 1847
Guest, William R.......... 1835
Guillot, Ramon 1869
Gulick, William H.......... 1858
Gunnison, George S........ 1865
Guthrie, Edward B......... 1871
Haight, William S......... 1834
Hale, Richard H............ 1824
Hall, Eugene J............ 1865
Hall, Franklin S............ 1858
Hall, George B............ 1865

Hall, George C. 1844
Hall, John K. 1872
Hall, Samuel 1870
Hall, Sewell W. 1840
Halliday, John T. 1870
Halsey, John R. 1857
Hamilton, Thomas A. 1866
Hammond, A. Park. 1852
Hammond, Edward H. 1861
Hammond, John. 1846
Haniford, William G. 1824
*Hanks, Arthur. 1834
Hanks, Oscar. 1824
Harleston, Edward. 1853
Harley, Willard. 1872
Harris, Charles. 1854
Harris, Jr., Ira. 1858
Harris, Nelson J. 1863
Harrison, James P. 1869
Harrison, William. 1869
Hart, William T. 1858
Haskins, Joseph Abel. 1834
Hastings, Marshall. 1858
Hatch, Henry S. 1844
Hauschild, Theodore W. H. . . 1871
Hawley, Gideon. 1865
Hawley, James M. 1857
Hayes, DeWitt C. 1854
Haynes, John H. 1829
Hayward, Henry F. 1852
*Heartt, Charles S. 1838
Heartt, Jonas S. 1844
Heermans, Thomas B. 1846
Heimstreet, J. W. 1854
Heller, Henry M. 1855
Henry, T. Charlton. 1846
Henry, William W. 1853
Hernandez, Pedro F. 1868
Herthel, George P. 1857
Hewitt, Henry W. 1835
Hickes, J. L. 1853
Hickman, George B. 1860
Hicks, Charles R. 1862
Hicks, Charles S. 1850
Hicks, J. Lawrence. 1855
Hidalgo, Emelio M. 1855
Higgins, Alfred W. 1863
Higman, Baron. 1855
Hill, George P. B. 1853
Hillhouse, William. 1836
Hitchcock, William A. 1824
Hoag, J. P. 1848
Hodgman, Romanus. 1852
Hodgeman, Lansing. 1834
Hodson, Eugene. 1849
Hollister, Calvin. 1829
Hollister, Thompson. 1832
Hollister, William. 1832
Holton, Albert. 1844
Holton, Charles M. 1846
Hooper, John. 1836
Horne, E. Pearce. 1854
*Horsefall, Edgar. 1857
Howard, Ezra E. 1840
Howard, Joseph H. 1849
Howell, Charles P. 1863
Hubbard, Albert W. 1864
Hubbard, Charles M. 1870
Hubbard, William P. 1850
Hubbell, Edward. 1844
Hubbell, Theodore. 1855
Huger, Eustis. 1853
Hughes, Andrew S. 1861
Hull, William T. 1865
Humphrey, Frederick H. 1864
Hunt, George B. 1851
Huntington, Calvin. 1832
Hutchinson, Amos S. 1829
Hutton, M. E. 1849
Hurley, Richard. 1854
Hyde, William B. 1858
Ingalls, H. Reeve 1863
Ingalls, S. Warren 1870
Ingraham, Charles A. 1869
Irish, Nathaniel. 1859
Irish, Samuel L. 1849
Irvine, Francis 1848
Irvine, James. 1848
Ives, Chauncy E. 1856
Ives, Stewart 1857
Jacobs, Ferris 1824
Jacobs, Ferris. 1832
Jackson, Amasa C. 1863
Jackson, J. Ross. 1863
James, Walter. 1861
Jarvis, William D 1853
Jenkins, David T. 1853
Jenkins, Josiah W. 1865
Jewett, Freeborn G. Jr. 1861
Johnson, Benjamin F. 1854
Johnson, Edward R. 1848
Johnson, George C. 1868
Johnson, George P. 1854
*Johnston, Thomas L. 1856
Jones, Charles Henry. 1854
Jones, Eugene B. 1870
Jones, Hayward. 1853
Judah, Samuel B. 1862
*Judah, Theodore D. 1837
Junco, Leopoldo del. 1868
Kaley, John R. 1870
Kaufman, Llewlyn M. 1858

Keeler, Nathan N.......... 1856
Keim, Beverly R........... 1854
Kellogg, Frank R 1868
Kellogg, William P......... 1853
Ketchum, James D.......... 1868
Kenyon, Ervin B........... 1861
Kidder, John F............. 1846
Kimball, William S.......... 1854
Kimberly, George E........ 1851
King, Charles H......... ... 1871
King, George M... 1863
*King, William A.......... 1824
Kingsbury, Benton L....... 1854
Kinsey, Carolan J.......... 1853
Kinzie, John C. Jr......... 1854
Knap, James G............ 1859
Kneisly, Charles C.......... 1869
Knickerbacker, J. H........ 1849
Knight, William 1863
Lacerda, Antonio F. de...... 1853
Ladieu, Peter A.... 1838
Laisdell, Robert C........ . 1853
Lamadriz, Ambrosio D...... 1864
Lamadriz, Domingo L....... 1868
Lane, Augustus............ 1849
Lane, Derrick............. 1842
Lane, George T........ ... 1850
Lane, George W........... 1859
Lane, Henry 1832
Landon, Gardner Jr. 1846
Landon, Henry G.......... 1844
Landon, John M......... . 1849
Langworthy, J. Hamilton.... 1863
Lansing, Gerritt G.... 1838
Lansing, William 1832
Larkin, Eugene S........... 1870
Larkin, James R.... 1849
Larrinaga, Julius J......... 1865
Lathrop, Hollister.......... 1829
La Paugh, Harry A......... 1870
Law, Archibald P.......... 1866
Law, Isaac 1836
Lawvere, A. Mayor... 1855
*Lay, Robert............. 1839
Leavenworth, Rev. Mr 1829
Leavitt, John H............ 1851
Lee, Albert L.............. 1849
Lee, William A............ 1840
Lee, William N............ 1865
LeRoy, Sherman H 1866
Lester, Henry... 1849
Lindley, Charles Henry...... 1834
Lindsay, Frank A.......... 1867
Lippman, Jacob............ 1858
Livingston, Francis R....... 1832
Livingston, Joseph B....... 1853
Lloyd, Horatio............. 1850
Lockwood, Charles Nichols.. 1834
Lockwood, Jordan W....... 1857
Lohnes, Henry............. 1852
Longnecker, Gustavus A.... 1868
Longnecker, John K........ 1868
Loomis, Abiel T............ 1849
Lomax, Joseph D........... 1857
Lord, Charles McC..... ... 1860
Lord, N. B................ 1855
Lord, T. Ellery............. 1856
Low, Alexander C.......... 1850
Luce, Robert T........... 1854
Lybrand, Joseph S......... 1870
Lyle, George W........ .. 1853
MacArthur, Arthur 1868
McChesney, Hiram......... 1845
McConihe, Isaac M......... 1843
McConihe, Samuel 1851
McConihe, William W...... 1844
McCulloch, Walter P....... 1870
MacDonald, James..... ... 1855
MacGregor, Gardner........ 1865
Macguire, Charles.......... 1853
McKean, Frederick G.... .. 1854
McKell, Thomas G......... 1865
McManus, Robert 1824
McMaster, Charles W....... 1869
McMurray, A. W........... 1849
McMurray, John C......... 1861
Macomber, G. Elliott....... 1853
Macpherson, John J........ 1853
Mactier, Henry............ 1871
Maidment, Edward T 1857
Malcher, Jose J. C.......... 1872
Malibran, Pedro........... 1864
Mallary, J. R............. 1850
Mallary, John S........... 1845
Mallory, Charles R......... 1837
Mann, Charles W..... 1853
Marble, Benjamin 1847
Marble, Daniel............. 1846
March, Leonard............ 1859
Marsh, Charles M.......... 1869
Marsh, John F............. 1862
Martinez, Jose Ygnacio..... 1870
Marquetti, Frederico J...... 1865
Mason, Frederick........... 1861
*Mason, George A......... 1852
Mason, James D............ 1867
*Massey, Henry R.......... 1868
Masten, Nathan K.......... 1837
Maurice, C. Stewart,........ 1861
Maxon, John H............ 1851
Maxon, R. L............ .. 1854
Maxwell, Horace........... 1850

May, James S.............. 1832
May, John E.............. 1824
Mendenhall, Judson 1866
Mendive, Pablo.......... 1865
Mercur, Frederick.......... 1854
Merriam, W. Henry........ 1847
Merritt, Jonathan H........ 1836
Merwin, H. Frederick....... 1864
Meyer, Robert E........... 1850
Meylert, G. W............. 1852
Middleton, Francis K....... 1852
Middleton, H. A. Jr 1849
Miller, Charles............. 1835
Miller, George W........... 1858
Miller, John N............. 1848
Miller, William T.......... 1869
Mills, Edmund S. Jr........ 1870
Mills, Samuel J............ 1836
Mills, William............. 1838
Mitchell, Thomas H........ 1865
Moffatt, John J............ 1847
Moncure, Edwin C.......... 1860
Moody, George L........... 1850
Moon, George H........... 1851
Moore, Philander 1829
Mora, Maximo E........... 1864
Morejon, Luis M........... 1864
Morrison, Edward H 1863
Morse, Franklin A.......... 1852
Morton, Edward G......... 1866
Mott, John M. Jr........... 1852
Munn, James T............ 1862
Munson, George H.......... 1862
Murdock, George A......... 1848
Murney, Edmund H......... 1853
Musgrave, Charles W....... 1863
Myers, John K.......... 1832
Myers, Matthew P.......... 1852
Myers, William G.......... 1856
Myers, William J........... 1861
Mygatt, William R......... 1870
Nadal, Alberto J........... 1866
Nadal, Jose R.............. 1864
Narvarte, Nestor J......... 1872
Navarro, Raimundo......... 1865
Neal, James................ 1847
Neff, Montague P........... 1861
Nettleton, George H........ 1849
Newton, J. Caldwell 1854
Newton, Silas C............ 1836
Nicholson, J. Henry 1850
Nickerson, Reuben......... 1851
Noble, George M........... 1829
Norton, William H 1832
Noyes, Richard B.......... 1849
Nunez, Jose A............. 1865
Oakey, James.............. 1837
Ogden, Gouverneur......... 1872
Ogden, Julien S............ 1863
Olcott, Dudley............. 1856
Oliver, G. Frederick......... 1862
Onderdonk, Andrew........ 1864
Openheimer, William P..... 1852
Osborn, John W........... 1847
Osgood, Worth............ 1864
Otis, William L............ 1870
Packer, Robert E.......... 1863
Paddock, George........... 1854
Paige, Austin B............ 1853
Painter, Christopher L. 1861
Painter, Jacob............. 1836
Palfrey, Carl F............. 1864
Palmer, Alexander S. Jr..... 1862
Palmer, Samuel L.......... 1845
Park, Sidney W............ 1842
Park, William G........... 1865
Parker, Francis H 1855
Parrish, William W........ 1861
Parsons, David B.......... 1847
Parsons, Henry C.......... 1871
Parsons, Hial Kenyon....... 1839
Patton, James G........... 1850
Paulding, Robert P......... 1867
Payrol, Francisco A........ 1857
Peacock, George........... 1845
Peckham, Merritt Jr........ 1866
Pelton, M................. 1852
Pendleton, Alexander G 1869
Perez, Juan............... 1863
Perkins, Charles E 1868
Perry, James H 1856
Peter, Robert Jr........... 1824
Peters, Joseph H........... 1867
Petrikin, Reuben W........ 1859
Philip, George............. 1824
Philip, John H............. 1824
Philip, Peter George........ 1834
Pickett, James............. 1829
Pierce, Franklin............. 1829
*Pierce, T. H.............. 1850
Pinto, G. L. M............. 1870
*Pitcher, Augustus......... 1824
Place, Frank 1865
Place, James H............ 1853
Platt, Myron 1851
Poinier, P. Porter.......... 1870
Ponce, Jose............... 1863
Pope, Charles C............ 1853
Pott, Thomas O. B......... 1864
Powell, F. W.. 1829
Powell, William D.......... 1853
Powers, Albert E........... 1832

Powers, Longworth......... 1853
Powers, Nathaniel B........ 1842
Powers, William............ 1845
Pratt, Thomas W........... 1824
Pratt, William H........... 1840
*Prescott, Charles L........ 1832
Preston, Matthew.......... 1865
Price, David............... 1835
Price, Overton............. 1871
Prindle, Franklin C......... 1859
Prindle, Solon B........... 1869
Prioleau, Charles M. B...... 1853
Pritchard, Emilio........... 1869
Prudhomme, M. S.......... 1856
Pugsley, V. A............. 1855
Putnam, A. E.............. 1849
Quereau, Frank W.......... 1866
Quesada, Gregorio C........ 1871
Quintana, Manuel 1853
Radenhurst, William........ 1853
Randall, Jedediah 1845
Randall, Robert M.......... 1845
Rathbone, J. Lawrence...... 1860
Read, William L........... 1832
*Reading, Robert B........ 1864
Redington, Robert F. E...... 1856
Redmund, Henry........... 1855
Reilay, John P............. 1841
Rice, Peter H.............. 1836
Richards, Charles H......... 1852
Richards, Benjamin......... 1824
Richards, Joseph........... 1824
Ridgway, Joseph, Jr........ 1858
Rivas, Manuel E........... 1865
Roberts, Mortimer H 1860
Roberts, William C......... 1867
Robertson, Charles 1829
*Robertson, William A...... 1853
Robinson, John E.......... 1870
Rockwell, James, Jr........ 1865
Rodefer, Thornton A........ 1871
Rodman, Thomas J......... 1869
Roff, John 1853
Rogers, Arthur A........... 1865
Rogers, Edward I........... 1869
Rogers, George B........... 1865
Rogers, Julian A........... 1865
Roosevelt, Cornelius....... 1864
Rorer, Patterson H......... 1871
Ross, John W.............. 1853
Ross, William C........... 1872
Rossiter, Charles D......... 1846
Rossiter, William H......... 1841
Rouillier, Gustave.......... 1867
Rousseau, Achilles J........ 1848
Rousseau, L. A............ 1846
Rousseau, William W....... 1856
Rowland, Charles E 1853
Rowland, Thomas 1856
Rua, Rafael J.............. 1868
Russell, Charles H.......... 1835
Rutherford, Robert W....... 1838
Sabat, Francisco R......... 1856
Sackett, Augustus.......... 1858
Sanchez, Antonio........... 1865
Sanderson, William......... 1865
Sandkuhl, Henry G......... 1867
Sanford, George H......... 1853
Sargent, James T........... 1845
Satterlee, Edward R. Jr..... 1861
Sauvalle, Carlos E.......... 1855
Sawyer, Roswell D.......... 1869
Sayles, Charles E........... 1867
Scarborough, Rev. George... 1832
Schanck, Charles W........ 1865
Scheiner, Frederick F....... 1872
Schenck, Daniel F.......... 1855
Schermerhorn, Lewis Y..... 1859
Schermerhorn, Simon P..... 1849
Schimpf, Charles H........ 1869
Schuyler, William R........ 1832
Scranton, William H........ 1857
Scribner, E. Sheldon........ 1858
Selleck, Theodore D........ 1854
Sento-Se, Justino Nunes de.. 1855
Seward, George W......... 1824
Sexton, Pliny T............ 1855
Sharp, George N........... 1840
Sharpe, Alexander H........ 1852
Shaw, John................ 1841
Shaw, William R........... 1843
Shelly, Frederick........... 1854
Shepard, George V.......... 1863
Sherrerd, Samuel........... 1835
Sherrill, James H........... 1841
Sherwood, Charles.......... 1824
Sherwood, Charles.......... 1832
Shippen, Francis............ 1869
Shirland, William H........ 1870
Shoemaker, Michael M...... 1869
Silliman, Robert F.......... 1844
Simmons, Duane........... 1851
Simmons, Ovid T........... 1852
Sinnickson, Clement H...... 1852
Sinnickson, John W........ 1868
Slataper, Daniel L.......... 1872
Slingerland, Augustus....... 1829
Smith, Adam R............ 1842
Smith, Alexander.......... 1855
Smith, Charles............. 1832
Smith, Charles H. L........ 1861
Smith, Charles M........... 1872

Smith, George............ 1824
Smith, H. Martin........... 1835
Smith, Isaac............. 1832
Smith, James G............ 1851
Smith, J. Dayton F........ 1846
Smith, Jesse M............ 1865
Smith, Joseph O........... 1835
Smith, J. Sterling.......... 1853
Smith, Orison B............ 1863
Smith, Walter M........... 1851
Smith, Warren S........... 1835
Snow, Charles L............ 1863
Snow, Frederick W......... 1870
Sollenberger, John H........ 1871
Southwick, Lewis L......... 1834
Spooner, Manning L........ 1868
Spoor, Edward E........... 1837
Spoor, Sylvester E.......... 1838
Sprague, John W.......... 1832
Stanley, Ethelbert A........ 1870
Starbuck, N. Henry......... 1863
Starr, William C........ . 1854
Stedman, William S........ 1838
Stephens, Clinton F......... 1864
Stephens, Melvin........... 1862
Stetson, Charles A. Jr....... 1854
Stevens, Francis K....... . 1855
Stevens, Plowdon.......... 1862
*Stickney, Clifford......... 1854
Stodder, James C.......... 1856
Stoney, Edgar G............ 1869
Storm, Abraham J......... 1858
Storm, William McManus.... 1839
Stowe, Frederick R......... 1850
Strader, John H............ 1857
Strawbridge, A. B.......... 1847
Suffern, James A.......... 1835
Sullivan, J. A............ 1847
Sutton, Charles T.......... 1869
Sweet, Stephen........... 1842
Swift, Henry M.......... . 1832
Swift, L. M................ 1854
Talbot, Josiah M........... 1832
Tanco, Nicholas............ 1860
Tator, Frederick D......... 1848
Taylor, George............ 1866
*Taylor, John H........... 1856
Taylor, Stoughton N........ 1836
Ten Eyck, Charles 1854
Ten Eyck, Egbert.......... 1854
Thatcher, Charles H........ 1866
Thayer, Asa P............. 1832
*Thayer, Floyd S........... 1870
Thayer, H. E.............. 1846
Theobald, W. W........... 1837
Thomas, William S......... 1847
Thompson, Alexander R..... 1866
Thompson, John I.......... 1846
Thompson, Robert H....... 1862
Thompson, William A...... 1850
Thomson, John............ 1829
*Thorn, James S........... 1852
Thornton, George M........ 1868
Thurston, Robert B......... 1853
Thurston, Thomas W....... 1854
Tibbal, William A......... 1871
Tibbits, C. E. Dudley....... 1849
Tibbits, John B............ 1840
Tilden, George H........... 1869
Tilghman, Tench F......... 1851
Tillinghast, Thomas A...... 1835
*Tinker, Frederick........ . 1866
Topp, Edward L......... 1856
Tracy, Charles C........... 1832
Tracy, James G............ 1853
Tribino, Jose M........... 1869
Trimble, James M.......... 1824
Trippe, Frederick W........ 1855
Trott, John W............. 1865
Trotter, Edward A......... 1854
Turnbull, Charles F........ 1858
Turnbull, Sinclair G........ 1860
Tuttle, Charles F........... 1829
Twing, Augustus W........ 1849
Twing, Cornelius L......... 1852
Tyler, Edmund L.......... . 1857
Tyler, James M............ 1853
*Underhill, Charles......... 1863
Underhill, James W........ 1832
Underhill, John B.......... 1872
Underwood, Warner........ 1864
Upson, Walter F........... 1868
Vail, Samuel M............ 1848
Valdes, Leopoldo........... 1864
Valentine, David H......... 1863
Van Allen, E.............. 1829
Vandercook, Wesley........ 1864
Vanderpool, Eugene........ 1863
*Vandervoort, William A.... 1863
Vanleer, Rush............. 1856
Van Meerten, Nicholas G.... 1845
Van Namee, Nicholas....... 1845
Van Rensselaer, Courtland... 1824
Van Rensselaer, Westerlo.... 1836
Van Valkenburgh, Thomas.. 1859
Vermilye, Thomas E. Jr.... 1867
*Vought, William G........ 1839
Wade, Edward............. 1848
Walsh, Braine............. 1842
Ward, H. H 1850
Warner, James D.......... 1858
Warren, Charles H......... 1849

Warren, Charles S......... 1849
Warren, Frank............ 1863
Warren, Henry B.......... 1847
Warren, John E........... 1845
Warren, John H........... 1844
Warren, Joseph M......... 1829
Waters, William........... 1863
Watson, Leslie J.......... 1870
Wead, Charles K........... 1864
Weaver, G. Norman........ 1869
Weaver Louis H........... 1848
Webb, Albertus............ 1854
Webb, J. Watson Jr........ 1852
Webb, J. Watson 2d....... 1852
Welch, E. H............... 1853
Welling, Edward B......... 1869
Wellington, Charles........ 1849
Wells, William D.......... 1854
West, J. Beckwith......... 1852
West, Preston C. F......... 1851
Westermann, Edwin L 1869
Westinghouse, Jay......... 1855
Weston, George W......... 1824
Wheatley, William Jr....... 1871
Wheelwright, William...... 1861
White, Joseph L........... 1832
White, P.................. 1849
Whipple, Herman.......... 1839
Whitlock, Frank W........ 1871
Whittaker, John George... 1837
Wickham, Charles H....... 1870
Wickes, Graham R......... 1841
Wickes, Stephen........... 1832
Wicks, George T. 1861
Wikidal, Edward A......... 1870
Wilkens, H. Glyde 1872
Willard, John H........... 1832
Willard, John P........... 1844
Williams, Addison G....... 1836
Williams, Daniel........... 1829
Williams, Eugene L........ 1851
Williams, George.......... 1824
Williams, Malcolm E 1854
Williams, Richard H 1824
Williams, William S 1850
Willis, Hiram F............ 1865
Wilmarth, Edwin.......... 1829
Wilson, Albert M.......... 1871
Wintermute, P. P.......... 1849
Winslow, George E 1870
Winslow, Howard S........ 1868
Witherbee, Thomas F....... 1861
Wodell, Isaac P 1856
Wood, Artemas............ 1853
Wood, Thomas G.......... 1855
Woodford, B. Franklin...... 1851
Woodrow, Harry E......... 1867
Woods, Charles C.......... 1868
Woollett, William M........ 1867
Worcester, George W...... 1866
Wotkyns, Thomas S........ 1870
Wright, Charles D......... 1867
Wright, John.............. 1824
Wylie, John............... 1856
Yates, John D............. 1839
Yeager, J. Clifford.......... 1848
Yorke, Lewis E........... 1848
Young, William E.......... 1849
Yturbide, Sabas J.......... 1866
*Yvonnett, Charles M...... 1836
Yznaga, Marin F........... 1857
Zambrano, Teofilo......... 1865
Zimmermann, William...... 1858

SUMMARY.

Whole number of Trustees,	102
Number Elected,	72
Number *Ex-Officio*,	30
Number of Trustees, 1874,	23
Whole number of Faculty and Instructors,	81
Number 1874,	13
Whole number of Students for fifty years,	1632
Number of Graduates,	573
Number of Graduates deceased,	85
Number of Non-Graduates, a large number of whom entered only for Special Courses,	1059
Number deceased so far as known,	38
Number of Students, 1874,	209

NOTE.

The Records of the Institute were destroyed by the great fire of 1862, and the list of Annual Catalogues is incomplete. Therefore it has been found very difficult to obtain the correct names and dates for the earlier years of the Institute. Without doubt, many errors will be found, and even some names may have been entirely omitted. All information concerning graduates and former students of the Institute, and also corrections of any errors in this Catalogue, are earnestly desired, and will be carefully preserved for future editions.

It is proposed to publish as soon as possible the "Records of the Graduates," and the Editor requests all those who have not yet responded to the circulars sent out a year ago, to do so as soon as possible.

H. B. N.

www.ingramcontent.com/pod-product-compliance
Lightning Source LLC
LaVergne TN
LVHW050530100826
845148LV00002B/507